WRITING RESEARCH PAPERS

A Guide
to the Process
Third Edition

STEPHEN WEIDENBORNER
DOMENICK CARUSO

topic : Joan of Arc

St. Martin's Press   New York

Senior editor: Mark Gallaher
Project editor: Elise Bauman
Production supervisor: Chris Pearson
Cover design: Judy Forster

For information, write:
St. Martin's Press, Inc.
175 Fifth Avenue
New York, N.Y. 10010

ISBN: 0-312-01701-4

Acknowledgments

"Mather, Cotton" reprinted with permission of *The Encyclopedia Americana*, 1987 edition, © Grolier Inc.

"Goldman, Emma" from *Notable American Women*, Volume II, edited by Edward T. James: The Belknap Press of Harvard University Press. Copyright © 1971 by Radcliffe College. Reprinted by permission of Harvard University Press.

The Readers' Guide to Periodical Literature, 1984–1985 Copyright © 1985 by The H. W. Wilson Company. Material reproduced by permission of the publisher.

Excerpt from *The New York Times Index* for 1985. Copyright © 1985 by The New York Times Company. Reprinted by permission.

Helmut A. Abt, paragraph from "The Companions of Sunlike Stars." Reprinted with permission from *Scientific American*, April 1977.

Malcolm W. Browne, "Arguing the Existence of ESP." Copyright © 1980 by The New York Times Company. Reprinted by permission.

Roger D. McGrath, "The Myth of Frontier Violence," based on chapter 13 of his book, *Gunfighters, Highwaymen, and Vigilantes: Violence on the Frontier* (University of California Press, 1984). Reprinted by permission of the author. The material appearing on pp. 114–116 was excerpted from a lecture given November 1984 at California State University, Long Beach.

Annalyn Swan, "The End of Eden." Reprinted with permission from *Newsweek*, February 18, 1985. All rights reserved.

"Cassatt, Mary" reprinted with permission from *The New Columbia Encyclopedia*. Copyright © 1975 by The Columbia University Press.

Emily Dickinson, "Poem 1475," reprinted by permission of the publishers and the Trustees of Amherst College from *The Poems of Emily Dickinson*, edited by Thomas H. Johnson, Cambridge, Mass.: The Belknap Press of Harvard University Press, Copyright © 1951, 1955, 1979, 1983 by the President and Fellows of Harvard College.

Emily Dickinson, "Poem 406." Copyright 1929 by Martha Dickinson Bianchi. Copyright © 1957 by Mary L. Hampson.

Preface

The third edition of *Writing Research Papers: A Guide to the Process*, like the first two editions, is concerned with explaining the process of producing a research paper, with particular attention to the steps that give students the most trouble. Although writing a research paper can be a college student's most exciting and liberating assignment, we have found that students need considerable help in choosing a research topic, gathering and evaluating sources, and drafting and revising a paper.

The first such steps involve planning. Every experienced researcher knows that the success or failure of a research project often depends on the first choice made: that of a topic. The risk of a mistake is especially great when the researcher is a beginner, with only a sketchy knowledge of the field in which he or she is working. Consequently, *Writing Research Papers* begins with suggestions and problem-solving strategies that show students how to inform themselves about a particular subject so that they can choose practical, worthwhile topics. We also demonstrate how a tentative thesis, or hypothesis, can be a powerful tool for evaluating the potential usefulness of sources and for guiding the actual research. The earlier a student can determine what he or she is looking for, the more focused and efficient the process becomes; and even if the hypothesis or topic is subsequently changed, the student still benefits from preliminary researching and reading of sources.

Another complex stage in the research process involves getting from a stack of note cards to a rough draft. We continue to devote two chapters to explaining strategies for developing a paper. Chapter 6 provides clear-cut directions for moving from hypothesis to thesis, and also for composing an introductory paragraph and developing a preliminary outline. Chapter 7 is a guide to drafting and rewriting, and includes detailed advice about revising paragraphs, sentences, and individual terms.

Finally, Chapter 8 presents a fully updated discussion of documenting sources, beginning with a thorough explanation of when documentation is required. The bulk of this chapter now offers a complete description of the new MLA style of parenthetical notation, incorporating a wide range of sample notes and works cited entries as well as guidelines for inserting references effectively. We also illustrate the traditional footnote/endnote system and the author/year format of the American Psychological Association (APA), and we show students which among the various styles of documentation to use for specific disciplines across the college curriculum.

As in the previous two editions, chapters 2 through 8—the core of the book—include questions and exercises to help students review and apply research strategies. We also illustrate each step in the research process by following the work of several student writers as they choose topics, formulate (and reformulate) hypotheses, gather and evaluate sources, read and take notes, organize and revise their drafts, and prepare their final manuscripts. In response to requests for a sample student paper that analyzes as well as summarizes sources, we offer a new research paper in history. This new paper, along with one in literary criticism and one in science, provides guides to writing research papers that show students how they can both agree with and challenge the sources they use. Reproduced in full in chapter 9, these three papers exemplify the three primary modes of documentation: the new MLA system, the traditional endnote system, and the APA system.

In addition to the changes already described, we have completely updated our list of basic reference sources in chapter 2. In chapter 3, more information has been included about library computers, particularly on-line catalogs of holdings. The inside cover of the book now features a comprehensive checklist for students to use as they make their way through the research process.

In making these revisions, we have benefited greatly from the thoughtful, constructive advice we received from composition instructors across the country. In particular, we wish to thank Louise Ackley (Boise State University), William Askins (Community College of Philadelphia), Ken Cooney (Shasta State College), Kate Mele Feldstein (Roger Williams College), Roland S. Jones (Bucks County Community College), Irma Luna (San Antonio College), Patricia Murray (De Paul University), Thomas Recchio (Rutgers University), Frank Roehl (St. Cloud State University), Brenda Williams (University of Hartford), and Bruce Young (Brigham Young University). We also want to express our appreciation to the editorial staff at St. Martin's Press.

Steven Weidenborner
Domenick Caruso

Contents

9   PREPARING THE FINAL MANUSCRIPT   184

Index   260

1
An Introduction to the Process

As you think about writing a research paper, you may wonder how this assignment differs from other kinds of papers you have written. The fundamental difference is that most of the information that goes into a research paper comes from materials found in a library. Research papers do not grow out of your personal experiences and opinions to the same extent that other compositions do.

Sometimes virtually all the information and ideas will have been drawn from books, magazines, newspapers, and even nonprint sources. In these cases, your work will consist mainly of finding the information and organizing it into a coherent report. More often, however, you will be encouraged to make judgments about the information you discover in the sources. For example, if you had chosen to investigate the controversy over the effect of acid rain on forests and lakes, you would be expected to evaluate (as an intelligent citizen, not as an expert, of course) the arguments put forth by both sides. You might conclude that the environmentalists have made the better arguments, or you might believe the experts working for the smokestack industries have given good reasons for doubting the accuracy of their opponents' charges. Or you might feel there is little to choose between the two positions, but that would also amount to a judgment on your part.

Producing a good research paper is no easy task. But completing this work has its rewards, not only in the beneficial effect a good paper will have on your course average, but also in the satisfaction you will get from having met this formidable challenge. Furthermore, as you increase your knowledge of a topic and begin making judgments as to which sources are most believable, you rapidly become an "expert" on the topic—someone who knows the subject well and whose opinions other people will listen to.

Before you examine the research process step by step, it is important to cut through the numerous details and discover the basic kinds of work you must be ready to perform. The research process boils down to three essential operations—searching, reading, and writing.

- **Searching**—You must search harder than most people realize for a good topic; rarely can you find a topic merely by thinking about the matter. Then, you must learn how to find information within a library, going far beyond the card catalog.

- **Reading**—This operation involves more than understanding the materials you are reading; you must learn how to recognize what information is likely to be truly useful to your research goals.

- **Writing**—Since you will be dealing with a great many ideas and pieces of information, most of which will have come from your sources, the ability to organize intelligently may count as much if not more than a fine writing style. But that does not mean that style doesn't count, as you well know.

All three of these operations demand constant exercise of good judgment as well as competence in dealing with language. And neatness counts! Not just from the instructor's point of view, but from your own, for carelessness can prove very costly when you are working with large amounts of information.

Mastering these skills and developing your judgment will take time and experience; so you should plan to spend several weeks, more likely a month, completing your first research assignment.

Some Essential Definitions

By now, you should be ready to look at an outline of the full research process. Before we do that, however, it is necessary to present some basic definitions. Be careful to note the specific ways these terms are used here, for they are often tossed around much more loosely in daily conversation. You will need to understand their precise meanings if you are to benefit fully from the discussions that follow.

- **Subject**—an area of interest that can be narrowed down to a suitable topic; subjects are either too broad or too loosely defined to serve as topics for research papers.

Too broad: adolescent behavior; Italy's political troubles; Shakespeare's tragedies; prehistoric animals. Entire books have been written on these subjects.

Too loosely defined: acid rain; cancer cures; computer assisted education; illegal immigration. What would you be looking for in your readings? What questions would you be answering?

* **Topic**—a reasonably narrow, clearly defined area of interest that could be thoroughly investigated within the limits set for a given research assignment. Here are some topics that might work quite well for a paper of seven to ten pages.

1. the effect of parental attitudes on teenage alcoholism
2. the effects of terrorism on the social policies of the Italian government over the last ten years
3. the relationship between young women and their fathers in several Shakespearian tragedies
4. the role of humans in the extinction of large prehistoric mammals
5. acid rain's effect on the recent deterioration of forests and lakes in the Northeast
6. the role of emotions in the cure of certain cancers
7. the effectiveness of computer programs in the remediation of writing problems
8. the effect of illegal immigration on unemployment in the Southwest

* **Thesis**—a general statement that announces the major conclusions you reached through a thoughtful analysis of all your sources. This statement appears at the beginning of your paper; the main body will then explain, illustrate, argue for, or in some sense ''prove'' the thesis.

* **Hypothesis**—your prediction, made sometime before reading the sources, as to what your research will reveal about the topic; that is, what answers you expect to find for the major questions raised by the topic. As you will see, this ''educated guess'' helps you to find exactly the information you need, as quickly and efficiently as possible, by keeping your attention focused on a limited number of specific aspects of the topic.

A More Detailed Look at the Research Process

Now that you have these definitions clearly in mind, we can examine the process more closely.

PHASE ONE: SEARCHING FOR A TOPIC AND FOR SOURCES

STEP ONE: preliminary research

Choose an interesting subject, if the choice is left to you. Then read up on that subject in your textbook, encyclopedias, and other general reference works, looking for a topic that can be easily covered within the assigned limits for your paper. This background reading will help you form a hypothesis that will guide the rest of your research.

STEP TWO: finding sources

In the library, search for any and all sources that seem likely to provide information relevant to your hypothesis. (Broaden the topic if you cannot find enough potential sources; limit the topic further if you find far too many.) Then skim through the sources, weeding out those that turn out to be irrelevant. Finally, check to see if your hypothesis still sounds reasonable. Be ready to revise the hypothesis to conform to whatever information the skimming reveals.

PHASE TWO: READING SOURCES AND REACHING CONCLUSIONS

STEP THREE: reading and taking notes

Only after you feel that you have a reasonable hypothesis and a sufficient number of sources should you begin reading the sources closely and taking detailed notes. Be sure to take notes on all information that has a direct bearing on your hypothesis.

STEP FOUR: arriving at the thesis

Analyze the information contained in your notes to determine whether your hypothesis was correct. If it was, it becomes your thesis. If the hypothesis was not fully supported by the evidence you gathered, write a thesis statement that reflects the full picture discovered through your research. Here is the point at which your judgment plays its most important role.

PHASE THREE: WRITING THE PAPER

STEP FIVE: preparing to write

Sketch out a full introductory paragraph that includes a precise statement of your thesis. Then arrange your notes into a sensible order that can serve as an outline for the paper. Write that outline.

STEP SIX: writing the paper

Write the paper in three drafts: (1) a rough version, concentrating on the flow of thought; (2) a first revision, reorganizing the paper, if necessary, and improving the style; (3) a second revision, eliminating all mechanical errors.

PHASE FOUR: ADDING NOTES AND PREPARING THE FINAL DRAFT

STEP SEVEN: noting the sources

Prepare the list of Works Cited (bibliography), showing all the sources that contributed information to the paper. Also insert parenthetical citations (or note numbers) that identify each source as it is used in the paper.

STEP EIGHT: preparing the final draft

Type the final draft (manuscript), following the format in this book or whatever format your instructor recommends. Make at least one copy for yourself to insure against accidental loss. Submit the original to the instructor.

A glance at this outline might lead you to believe that a research paper can be produced by following a simple, step-by-step prescription—moving from subject to topic to hypothesis to thesis. In actual practice, however, you must be ready at every step to revise your earlier decisions in light of the additional information you are continually discovering. This advice applies in particular to the hypothesis, which is, after all, only an educated guess as to what your research might disclose.

Much of the discussion so far has been rather abstract. To get a good idea of what an actual research paper consists of, read a couple of the sample student papers in chapter 9. Note how each writer states, in the first or second paragraph, the thesis that he/she intends to "prove." As you go through the main body of a paper, think about the way the writer presents the ideas and information that led to that thesis. Finally, notice the parenthetical (or numbered) notes that indicate where the various pieces of information were found. After you finish looking over the sample papers, return to chapter 2, where we begin discussing each step of the process in detail.

360
300
+
3,300

2
Laying the
Groundwork

At the heart of a successful research paper lies a clearly defined *thesis*, which states in a sentence or two the major conclusions reached after a thorough investigation of a topic. The main purpose of the paper itself is to explain, illustrate, argue for, or in some sense ''prove'' that thesis. The proof, or defense, of the thesis consists of evidence gathered from a fair number of sources, expressing various points of view toward the topic. The task of finding such sources can be very difficult if you have nothing more than a topic as a guide. That is why we recommend that you proceed one step further and form a hypothesis, or prediction of your eventual thesis. A hypothesis, if it is carefully worded, can greatly reduce the problems of searching for sources and extracting from them the most useful information.

An effective hypothesis focuses your attention on the essential questions that the research is intended to answer, and thereby helps you to select the most valuable sources from the large number of possibilities you are likely to come across. And when reading a particular source, you need a sharply defined objective to keep you from taking too many notes. A good hypothesis provides you with such guidance.

The more you know about your topic, the easier it is to form a good hypothesis. In many courses, however, you will be required to deal with relatively unfamiliar topics. At such times, it will be important to have an orderly procedure for coming up with an effective hypothesis. This chapter describes several ways to accomplish this first crucial objective in the research process.

Choosing a Subject

Step One of the research assignment consists of deciding just what question the research will answer—what problem will be worthwhile exploring. Your first thoughts, however, are likely to be very general, only indicating the direction of your immediate interests. "I want to write about the trouble in the Middle East." "I want to know more about dinosaurs." "I am interested in some problems faced by the Catholic church today." "I've always been fascinated by the Salem witchcraft trials." You don't yet know what to say about the subject, or even whether it will lead to a satisfactory topic, but you are moving in the right direction. The question now becomes, "How do I know the subject is any good?"

First of all, you must like the subject well enough to spend a good many days and nights working on it. More important, however, the subject must lead to a good topic—one that raises some questions which have not been answered to the satisfaction of all the authorities in the field. Such uncertainty among the experts gives you the opportunity to examine the different points of view and arrive at those conclusions which will become your paper's thesis. We have found that the best subjects are those that suggest a good many interesting topics to choose from, for then, if the first one you pick does not work out well, you have several alternatives ready at hand.

One last point about the subject: Start thinking about it as soon as you know a research paper is required. Don't wait for the instructor to push you into action.

Finding a Topic

Never choose a topic hastily. Many students make the mistake of picking the first attractive topic that comes along, then rushing to the library, getting a stack of books off the shelves, and taking piles of notes, all before they have defined a problem to be solved. After days or even weeks of work, they suddenly realize that they have no control over the project, no clear sense of direction, and worst of all, no time to go back and begin again.

A good topic raises questions that have no simple answers. When there is no single, accepted answer, the experts (your sources) will disagree to some extent, which is just what you want. This means you should avoid topics that can be fully covered by reading just one, or two, brief sources. For example, the question "Why is the sky blue?" has been answered to everyone's satisfaction. Any general science book or encyclopedia contains the explanation. And all such "sources" say much the same thing, although they may use different examples as well as different words to express the idea. In order to complete your research, you would need just one of these sources, for they all present you with the same idea. There would be no challenge in such a project. The same holds true for many seemingly more complex questions, such as "How does vitamin C help the body fight disease?"; "Why did the popes leave Rome for southern France in the 1300s?"; or even "Why did Guiteau shoot President Garfield?" (Perhaps no one really knows, but historians—the experts—agree on one view of the event.)

As you are searching for a topic, then, remember that research should take you beyond mere reporting, beyond just finding information. Be prepared to demonstrate your ability to evaluate the information and ideas that you discover, to arrive at a clear, well-thought-through conclusion, which gives the reader something to think about. Therefore, in your quest for a topic, look for significant points on which the experts disagree.

Such disagreements tend to fall into two categories:

1. highly controversial issues, such as *the value of a new, expensive weapon; the causes of alcoholism; the long-range benefits of a particular vitamin, such as C or E.*

2. less well-known questions, such as *the reasons behind Cotton Mather's involvement in the Salem witch trials; Emily Dickinson's reasons for not publishing her poems; the possibility of extending the human life span.*

Warning: you should probably avoid topics in which the controversy derives solely from opinion. For example, these questions would *not* lead to the kind of research you are expected to perform: "Is football too violent?" "Was Ali the greatest boxer ever?" "Should public schools be allowed to mandate that pupils pray?" "Should selling marijuana be legalized?" "Should abortion be banned?" We are not saying that these issues are not important. Some of them may be more important to more people than any topic you will write about. But such questions can only be resolved by each individual in light of his/her personal values.

Similarly, you must beware of topics involving the paranormal (UFOs and ESP, for example) because almost all the "sources" consist of personal accounts of occult phenomena or weird sightings. This is not to say that good topics cannot be found in these subjects; however, you must take great care to avoid simply reporting mere opinion and unusual tales. The subject *UFOs* could lead to a reasonable topic such as *the Air Force's response to reports of UFO sightings*. (Questions: "Are they hiding something? out of fear of public panic? or to keep new weapons secret?") And the subject *ESP* could lead to the topic *scientific techniques for investigating ESP*. (Question: "Have scientists found any reason to consider parapsychology a valid field of study?")

Some excellent topics do not concern issues as such; they pose the general question, "What is being done in this area?" Your research in such a case does not move toward a judgment as to who is right. Instead, the research consists of assembling information from various sources in order to present your readers with a composite picture. This kind of topic almost always deals with very current events, such as the use of genetic engineering to detect and cure disease, or the use of computers in banking or education. When the topic is so current, you are unlikely to find a single source that describes all the work being done, much less all the possibilities currently being investigated. Therefore, you will need to locate a fairly large number of articles in magazines and journals if you are to cover the topic thoroughly.

BACKGROUND READING, OR PRELIMINARY RESEARCH

Once you believe you have a good topic, take time to do some background reading in the subject area. Background reading consists of looking up your subject or topic in general reference works—encyclopedias, biographical dictionaries, or books that survey wide areas such as the Middle Ages, Eastern religions, native Americans, English literature, and the history of psychology. Textbooks may also serve as general references if they cover broad areas such as business administration, vertebrate biology, and United States history 1900–74.

For example, if your subject were *astronomy* and your idea for a topic *the beginning of the Universe*, you could (1) look up "the Universe" in the *Encyclopedia Americana* or an encyclopedia of science; (2) read the section on astronomy in an atlas such as *Earth and Man*. And, (3) if writing the paper for a science course, you could read ahead, or reread, the section on astronomy in your textbook.

Unfortunately, you will sometimes be required to work with a subject about which you are not very well informed. In that case, you can start your search for a topic by reading one or more background studies in the assigned subject area. If you begin your search in a textbook, do not stop there. Go to the reference room of the library and look up other background sources which might offer different points of view. (A list of such reference materials can be found at the end of this chapter. And you can always ask the reference librarian for others if you need them.)

The purpose behind preliminary research, or background reading, is twofold. First, you want to feel certain that you have chosen the best available topic. Other possibilities may appear during your background reading, and one of them might be even better than your first one. One of the students whose papers appear in chapter 9 found his topic in the *Encyclopedia Americana*, as we shall see on pages 11–14. Second, even if your original idea for a topic was a fine one, you will benefit from refreshing your knowledge of the subject, thereby giving yourself a better handle on the many new facts and ideas your research will uncover.

Do not read entire books during preliminary research. For instance, if your subject is *Martin Luther King, Jr.*, do not begin by reading a full-length biography. Since you have not yet settled on a topic, most of the book will not be directly relevant to whatever topic you eventually select. Even if you have a definite topic in mind, such as *King's relationship with militant black leaders*, you should first review King's career as a civil rights activist in an encyclopedia or a biographical dictionary, where you would find a concise account of the major events of his life.

When reading background studies, take notes you can refer to later if you need to revise your topic and/or hypothesis. In taking these notes, avoid recording detailed factual information. Concentrate instead on major ideas and possible topics. You want to prevent the general outlines of the subject area from becoming lost in a flood of facts.

BRAINSTORMING

Another useful approach to finding the best topic is an exercise called "brainstorming." If you are already fairly familiar with your subject area, a little brainstorming may turn up a number of good possibilities for research. Brainstorming consists of wide-open, no-holds-barred thinking about some subject, in which your mind is free to produce any and all ideas that come along. Since you are looking for a problem to investigate, these ideas will probably come to you as questions. Note: Do not reject any idea during the brainstorming session. Record every thought, large or small, either in shorthand notes or, better yet, on a tape recorder. The important point is to collect every idea, even if it sounds irrelevant or silly or otherwise useless. Stop after about fifteen minutes (a little longer if writing rather than taping) and review your notes. Check off the ideas that seem best. Then put all the notes aside overnight and review them again in a fresh light the next day.

Let's look at what one student's mind produced when unleashed on what was for her a fairly familiar subject, *dinosaurs.*

What exactly was a dinosaur? How do we know what it was, aside from the bones? When did people first find dinosaur bones? Where did they live? What did they eat? Did any other creatures prey on them? What caused dinosaurs to die out? How long were they around? Did they evolve from earlier life forms? from sharks? from little lizards? Are crocodiles really modern dinosaurs? Are there any other dinosaurs around now, possibly in some unexplored jungle or on a deserted island? Someone said birds evolved from dinosaurs—are they right? What caused the extinction of dinosaurs? Did they just become too big? But what about the smaller ones? Did they run out of food? If so, how could that happen? Did they become unfit for survival? How? Were other creatures smarter than they were? How could we know how smart they were? Their brains were probably larger than ours. How do we know about these long-gone beasts? Or don't we know? Is it all guesswork? Do we find each skeleton all in one spot, or do we assemble possible skeletons from a mixed heap of bones? How come no animals are that big today (except whales)? Why are today's lizards and other reptiles no larger than alligators?

Obviously, this student had to know something about this subject or she couldn't have produced so much specific material. Notice that she returned to some points and that some ideas lead to dead ends.

Did you sense several themes recurring throughout the notes?

Why did dinosaurs become extinct? Topic: *cause of extinction.*

What exactly was (or is) a dinosaur? Topic: *their place in evolution.*

How do we *know* what we say we know? Topic: *the basis of our knowledge of prehistoric creatures.*

Any of the three topics would do just fine, for these questions have no simple, uncontroversial answers.

THREE STUDENTS FIND THEIR TOPICS

We asked the writers of the papers in chapter 9 to describe how they went about getting started. Their approaches were not identical, but all three used effective procedures for coming up with topics that lent themselves to worthwhile research. The student who wrote the paper on Cotton Mather, for example, decided upon his topic while reading background sources.

While in high school, Fred Hutchins had seen a television program dealing with the Salem witch-hunt of 1692. The half-hour program was, of necessity, superficial, and it managed to provide little more than an overview of the witchcraft hysteria and trials. Nonetheless, the program sparked Fred's interest in Cotton Mather, a Puritan minister involved in the witch trials.

Several years later, Fred enrolled in an elective history course called "Witchcraft in America" that included a unit on the Salem witch-hunts. Throughout the course, Fred mulled over the possibility of doing specific research on Cotton Mather. When his instructor asked for possible topics for research papers, Fred responded immediately, for he saw an opportunity to learn more about Mather.

In an after-class discussion, the instructor asked Fred if he had a more specific idea of what he wanted to find out about Cotton Mather. Fred realized that *Cotton Mather* was far too broad to be considered a workable topic, so he narrowed that down to *Cotton Mather and the Salem witchcraft trials*. The instructor said that although this topic still seemed too broad, it did provide Fred with a starting point for his background reading.

The instructor then offered Fred some advice: "I think you need to do some reading about Mather that uncovers a controversy or angle that you can dig into—maybe a specific question about Mather's character that you'd like to answer for yourself." The instructor suggested that Fred begin his background reading with the *Encyclopedia Americana*. Here is the Cotton Mather entry, reproduced in its entirety. Marginal notes point out how Fred used the article to help him focus on a more specific topic.

Fred notes that Mather was a theologian as well as a minister. He wonders about the connections between Mather's religious beliefs and his involvement in the witchcraft hysteria.

MATHER, math'ər, Cotton (1663–1728), American clergyman, theologian, and author. The eldest son of Increase Mather and the grandson of Richard Mather, he was born in Boston, Mass., on Feb. 12, 1663. He graduated from Harvard in 1678, received his M.A. in 1681, and in 1685 joined his father at the Second Church in Boston, where he served until his death.

Fred realizes this paragraph deals with matters about which he knows little. He doesn't expect this paragraph will be useful.

Fred reads carefully here because the material refers to the subject of his interest. He also jots down "spectral evidence" because he wants to learn what it means.

Mather was active in the rebellion in 1689 against Sir Edmund Andros, royal governor of Massachusetts, and wrote the manifesto of the insurgents. He vigorously defended the new Massachusetts charter of 1691 and supported Sir William Phipps, appointed governor by King William III at the request of Increase Mather.

During the witchcraft excitement of 1692, Cotton Mather wrote the ministers' statement exhorting the judges to be cautious in their use of "spectral evidence" against the accused, and he believed that "witches" might better be treated by prayer and fasting than by punitive legal action. In spite of this, Mather's popular reputation is that of a fomenter of the witchcraft hysteria who rejoiced in the trials and the executions. He was ardently interested in what he believed to be witchcraft, and his writing and preaching may have stimulated the

Fred notes Mather's humane attitude toward accused witches, and considers exploring the reasons why Mather took this position. After reading about Mather's "popular reputation," Fred notes how this seems to contradict evidence of Mather's humane attitude.

hysterical fear of "witches" revealed at Salem, Mass., in 1692. In writing about the trials he defended the judges and their procedure more than seems consistent with his earlier warnings against "spectral evidence." He was no doubt unwise in helping to keep the witchcraft excitement alive, but the idea that he was a ruthless tormentor of the innocent is not justified by the evidence. If the court had paid more attention to his advice some lives might have been saved. The witchcraft trials ended before he was 30; most of the achievements that made him the most famous of American Puritans came later.

Fred notes Mather's defense of the witchcraft judges: Was Mather confused about how he regarded witches?

Fred is impressed by Mather's accomplishments. Was it unusual for a person of such learning to believe in witches?

Renowned as a preacher, man of letters, scientist, and scholar in many fields, he read widely and wrote more than 450 books. The most celebrated is the *Magnalia Christi Americana* (1702), an "ecclesiastical" history of New England and the most important literary and scholarly work produced in the American colonies during their first century. It shows an amazing range of erudition and great stylistic skill.

Mather's interest in sciene is revealed principally in other books, notably *The Christian Philosopher* (1721). He admired Sir Isaac Newton, advocated inoculation for smallpox when it was generally regarded as a dangerous and godless practice, and wrote one of the earliest known descriptions of plant hybridization. He was one of the few American colonists elected to the Royal Society of London and probably was better known abroad than any of his countrymen before Jonathan Edwards and Benjamin Franklin.

From the mixture of characteristics given in this paragraph, Fred concludes that Mather was a complicated person. Is it possible that his fascination with witches had something to do with his erratic personality?

Mather was vain, ambitious, hot tempered, and sometimes a pedant, but had genuine piety and worked tirelessly for moral reform. His tolerance increased with age, and his later thinking moved somewhat away from the strict Puritan orthodoxy of the 17th century toward the rationalistic and deistic ideas of the 18th. He died in Boston on Feb. 13, 1728.

KENNETH B. MURDOCK
Author of "Literature and Theology in Colonial New England"

Fred now turned to the Bibliography that followed the article to give him a head start in his search for sources.

Bibliography

Breitweiser, Mitchell R., *Cotton Mather and Benjamin Franklin* (Cambridge 1985).

Holmes, Thomas J., *Cotton Mather: A Bibliography of His Works,* 3 vols. (1940; reprint, Crofton Pub. 1974).

Levin, David, *Cotton Mather: The Young Life of the Lord's Remembrancer* (Harvard Univ. Press 1978).

Middlekauf, Robert, *The Mathers: Three Generations of Puritan Intellectuals, 1596–1728* (Oxford 1971).

Silverman, Kenneth, *The Life and Time of Cotton Mather* (Harper 1984).

Wendell, Barrett, *Cotton Mather: The Puritan Priest* (1981; reprint, Arden Library 1978).

Wood, James P., *The Admirable Cotton Mather* (Seabury 1971).

After Fred finished the article, he reviewed the possible topics he had noted about Mather and his involvement in the Salem witchcraft outbreak: a possible connection between his religious beliefs and his attitude toward witches; his humane stance toward accused witches; the origin of his popular reputation as a bloodthirsty witch-hunter; his intense interest in witchcraft and the possibility that this interest may have flamed the hysteria; his possibly confused attitude toward witches; his erratic personality as a source of his fascination with witches; his view of the outbreak in later life. In the end, Fred decided that the question he had asked himself several times: "What did the witches mean to Mather?" was the question he wanted to research. The question seemed to be at the heart of most of the possible topics he had extracted from his reading and, more importantly, it was the question about Mather that most interested him. Thus, looking ahead to further reading, Fred framed his question in the form of a statement to guide his research, and *What the Salem witches meant to Cotton Mather* became his preliminary topic.

Finding a topic consumed less time in Susanna Andrews's case. While taking a course in American literature, she had been excited by Emily Dickinson's rather mystical poetry. While thinking about a possible topic, Susanna remembered reading in the introduction to her textbook that Dickinson "did not write for publication and was easily discouraged from it." Only 8 of her nearly 1,800 poems appeared in print during her lifetime. This point had also been made (changing 8 to 6) in *The Oxford Companion to American Literature*, a standard background resource which Susanna had consulted.

In lectures, her instructor had painted a fascinating picture of this remarkable woman, and Susanna had no trouble finding an account of Dickinson's life in the biographical dictionary *Notable American Women*. Once Susanna felt she knew a fair amount about her subject, she reviewed her notes and discovered that one idea for a topic persisted in her thoughts about the poet and her work: *her failure to publish her poetry.*

Susanna naturally wondered why such a great poet had published so few of her works. Consulting her instructor, she learned that the question had not been decisively resolved, so Susanna confidently chose as her topic, *Emily Dickinson's reluctance to publish her poems.*

Our third student, Anita Barrone, became interested in the subject of increasing human life expectancy after reading an article in a 1983 issue of *U. S. News and World Report,* which she picked up in her dentist's waiting room. The article consisted of an interview with Roy Walford, a scientist dedicated to slowing down the aging process. The reporter's questions focused on the chances for extending healthy human life beyond the limits nature seems to have imposed on us, and Walford's responses were decidedly optimistic. The interview was so brief that Walford could mention but a few of the life extension theories now being investigated. But Anita's curiosity was aroused. Her instructor encouraged her to look into the subject as a possible research project, and she was on her way.

Because most of the work in this field had been performed so recently, Anita's background reading in a handbook of biological science gave her little more than an overview of the biology of aging. But after looking up "Walford" in the card catalog and reading the introduction to his book, *Maximum Lifespans,* she felt certain her topic was an excellent one: *extending human life: a dream or a real possibility?*

Forming a Hypothesis

We have been discussing the choice of a topic as though you had to make this decision before moving on to the next step: forming a hypothesis. In practice, however, you should begin to form a hypothesis while you are choosing your topic. This is only natural when you consider that the topic involves unanswered questions, and the hypothesis predicts possible answers.

The key to successful research lies in forming a reasonable hypothesis as early as possible, for you cannot rely entirely on the topic to guide you through this complex process. The problem is that the topic by itself offers very little help when you are trying to decide whether a potential source is useful or not. Although your research may uncover a great deal of information that touches on your topic in some way or other, unless you have a clear idea of where you are going, all these ideas and facts will seem only loosely related to each other. Any notes you take would look like a "grocery list." If you tried to write a paper based on such materials, the result would be lacking in focus and direction. Your readers would become confused and feel no sense of having learned something valuable. Such a paper would do little more than show you had spent a lot of time in the library.

To avoid getting lost, look ahead to the writing stage, when you will need a thesis, just as you do for most other kinds of writing. It would be nice to know the thesis from the beginning so that you could limit your reading in each source to just those passages that relate directly to it. Of course, this is not possible, but you can give some direction to your investigation by thinking about your topic in terms of a possible thesis, or hypothesis.

There are two good reasons for starting out with a hypothesis, even if it may prove to be somewhat inaccurate. First, a hypothesis points you in the right direction by indicating the specific questions you need answers for. As you look for information that either agrees or disagrees with your hypothesis, you move closer to the ''truth''—and that will be your thesis.

Second, the hypothesis can test the thoroughness of your research. If your conclusions are to be considered valid, you must consult a variety of sources representing different viewpoints. You should not try to defend your hypothesis by using only those sources that support it. Your mission is to present readers with the full picture so they will have enough information to evaluate your conclusions.

Let's look at an example. If you are investigating the theory that intelligence is inherited, you cannot restrict your search to the work of Arthur Jensen, E. O. Wilson, and other advocates of this theory. You need to find additional experts, such as Steven Rose and Stephen Jay Gould, who are less than enthusiastic, if not downright opposed to this theory. Of course, your thesis might eventually state either that Jensen and his supporters seem to be right, or that Rose and other critics have proved them wrong, or even that the issue has not yet been satisfactorily resolved. But the paper would have to show that you weighed all sides of the question before reaching your conclusion. For some topics, you will find that expert opinion is divided into several camps, in which case, you must fairly represent them all in your paper.

In short, you have a limited amount of time to spend finding sources and then reading and taking notes. A carefully limited topic will ensure that you will be working with a manageable number of sources; but you will need a hypothesis to help you decide what ideas and facts in each source will be most useful in your effort to cover the topic thoroughly, intelligently, and efficiently.

FORMING A HYPOTHESIS BY BRAINSTORMING

Here are two examples of writers moving from subject to topic and then to a hypothesis by combining brainstorming with background reading. In the first example, the student who had brainstormed about dinosaurs was able, after a little background reading, to reject several potential topics. (She discarded *the basis of our knowledge* and *what dinosaurs really were* because she was not very interested in either one, and the extinction problem seemed likely to lead to some exciting ideas, some of which had been mentioned in her background reading.)

After this student had settled on *causes for their extinction* as her topic, another brainstorming session helped her form a hypothesis. Here are her notes.

> Did the evolution of smaller, smarter animals somehow lead to the extinction of the slow-witted dinosaurs? Were these new creatures mammals? Or did major climatic changes bring about the extinction by eliminating the tropical swamplands in which the dinosaurs thrived? How fast might such changes take place? Could a meteor striking the Earth cause such a change? Or did deadly radiation from an exploding nearby star do them in? In that case, wouldn't some have survived? Or did dinosaurs become so large they could not find enough food in their environment?

All these ideas made sense—her background reference materials did not take a stand on the question, and she had not yet read her sources closely enough to be able to judge the relative merits of the theories. She decided, therefore, to go with the newest idea—''radiation from an exploded star caused the Great Extinction.'' This became her hypothesis. (Her thesis, however, took another turn. After reading all her sources, she believed equal support had to be given to the theory that a meteor hit the Earth 65 million years ago, drastically cooling the atmosphere and killing off the dinosaurs. Thus, she left resolution of the puzzle up to future research paper writers who would probably have more evidence to go on.)

After some background reading, another student narrowed the subject *alcoholism* to the topic: *treatment of alcohol addiction*. A bit of brainstorming at that point produced the following notes:

> How well do support therapies, such as Alcoholics Anonymous, work in their efforts to treat alcoholism? Does the addict have to be religiously inclined for such therapies to work? How successful are aversion therapies that use chemicals to make liquor repellent? Doesn't the effect wear off? How effective are cognitive therapies that try to get alcoholics to stop drinking by showing them films of their own drunken behavior? Is psychotherapy able to treat alcoholism by helping the patients understand the unconscious reasons for their drinking? How would knowing why you drink help you stop?

Again, we find someone faced with several possible answers to his research question. However, this student could see no grounds for choosing any one of them while still in the preliminary research stage. Also, he had personal reasons for doubting whether any method offered successful treatment. So, he took a neutral position that expressed his intuition: "Of the four most common alcoholism therapies, none seems to have convinced its critics that it offers a strong likelihood of success."

The student did not feel committed to this pessimistic view; he hoped that his sources would show him good reason to believe that one of the approaches was definitely on the right track. Considerable research into this problem, however, did not fulfill this hope. His thesis read: "The success of a particular alcoholism therapy depends almost entirely upon the personality of the individual addict."

THE THREE STUDENTS FORM THEIR
HYPOTHESES

What about the writers of our sample research papers? Fred came up with a preliminary topic after reading the "Cotton Mather" entry in an encyclopedia. The entry indicated to Fred that Cotton Mather had shown mixed reactions to the Salem witchcraft outbreak. On the one hand, Mather had tried to influence the judges against accepting doubtful evidence against accused witches. But on the other hand, he harbored great suspicions about witchcraft and may have prolonged the Salem community's fear of witches. These somewhat contradictory pieces of information led Fred to his preliminary topic: *What the Salem Witches Meant to Cotton Mather.*

Fred then began to gather and read through sources; he wanted to establish a hypothesis—a controlling idea—to guide his thoughts as he continued his research. The first few sources Fred consulted tended to agree that Mather's belief in witches was not at all unusual, considering the times in which he lived. In late seventeenth-century America, almost everyone, intellectuals included, believed in witches. True, Mather's interest in witches was particularly intense, but that was because he liked to delve into subjects that challenged his intellect and imagination. In fact, Mather was noted for publishing numerous tracts on diverse subjects that had caught his interest. Thus, based upon his early research, Fred wrote down the following hypothesis: "Cotton Mather accepted the existence of witches because such a belief was deeply imbedded in the culture of his time."

Fred felt that Mather's interest in witches was something more than intellectual curiosity about the Devil, and he was eager to gather additional sources against which to test his hypo .1esis. In the end, Fred's final pa-per was based upon a different topic and a different thesis than the topic and hypothesis with which he began his research. However, the impor-tant point here is that Fred's initial hypothesis was useful. It helped Fred to focus his research efforts on sources and passages supporting or dis-puting his initial hypothesis: "Cotton Mather accepted the existence of witches without question because he was a person of his times."

Susanna thought she had a good topic, *Emily Dickinson's reluctance to publish*, but her background reading offered only a vague suggestion that the poet's not publishing her poems grew out of her eccentric character. If that was the only answer to the question, then Susanna's topic was too weak to pursue. So, she brainstormed a bit to see whether she had good reason to continue. Finding a hypothesis would indicate that the topic was worth the effort. Here are a few notes from her brainstorming.

Why didn't she publish most of her poems? Why would any poet do that? Did she think they weren't good enough? Didn't she know how great her po-ems were? Or did she write them for her own pleasure only? Was she too shy to let other people see her thoughts? Who did she let read them? her family, her friends, or other writers? What did these readers say? Did she ever *try* to have the poems published? Why did she write poetry anyway? What did writ-ing mean to her? What might publication have done for her, or her poems? How did the poems get published eventually?

These notes did not immediately yield a hypothesis, but as Susanna looked them over, she sensed that the answer might be found in Dickin-son's idealistic attitude toward the art of poetry and toward herself as an artist. Upon reviewing her lecture notes, Susanna recalled the instruc-tor's saying that these themes run through many of the poems. Susanna then reread some of the poems in the textbook and read some others in a collection of Dickinson's poems she had borrowed from the library. These lines caught her eye: "The Soul selects her own Society / Then—shuts the Door—. . . ." Remembering her background reading notes, which said the poet was extremely shy, Susanna decided upon the hy-pothesis: "Emily Dickinson chose not to publish her poems because she was a shy, reclusive person, not interested in public praise." This hy-pothesis seemed good because it would force Susanna to focus her read-ing of sources on those comments and facts which shed light on the poet's character and her motivation regarding the poems and their publi-cation.

Anita, having been influenced by the optimism expressed in a maga-zine interview with a leading gerontologist, Roy Walford, quickly formed this hypothesis: "Science will soon make it possible for us to live for 100 years or more.'' Anita fully expected to find a wealth of articles, and perhaps even a book or two, that would support her rosy hypothesis. A trip to the reference room added to her knowledge of the aging process but gave little indication of the exciting work presently under way in this field. So, leaving her hypothesis intact, Anita compiled a solid working bibliography and started skimming the potential sources. She had not gone very far into this step before she began to suspect that Walford had been too enthusiastic about the prospects for lengthening the human life span. To be sure, a variety of approaches to the problem were being pursued with interesting results, but none seemed to have the answer firmly in hand. Furthermore, a number of informed observers said it was not presently within the power of science to extend life expectancy by more than several years.

As Anita prepared for a close reading of those sources that survived skimming, she became noticeably more cautious. Her revised hypothesis read: ''The varied experiments performed in the last decade have yielded such promising results that a number of scientists believe people may soon be living considerably longer and healthier lives.''

As you have seen, none of these students' hypotheses proved to be entirely accurate. In each case, the student's research into specific sources disclosed additional information and persuasive reasons for coming to a somewhat different conclusion (thesis). Nevertheless, their hypotheses served them well as guides through the difficult steps of finding sources and extracting useful information from them.

Some General Reference Sources

Here are some reference books which you will find in many college libraries and which you can use for background reading in your subject.

GENERAL ENCYCLOPEDIAS

Academic American Encyclopedia. 21 vols. with annual revisions. Danbury, CT: Grolier, 1988.

Collier's Encyclopedia. 24 vols. with annual supplements. New York: Macmillan Educational, 1981.

The Concise Columbia Encyclopedia. 5th ed. 32 vols. with annual supplements. New York: Columbia UP, 1983.

Encyclopedia Americana. 30 vols. with annual supplements. New York: Encyclopedia Americana, 1978. Emphasizes subjects related to the United States.

McGraw-Hill Encyclopedia of Science and Technology. 4th ed. New York: McGraw, 1977.

The New Encyclopedia Britannica. 15th ed. 32 vols. with annual supplements. Chicago: Encyclopedia Britannica, 1985. Editions prior to the current edition emphasized subjects related to Great Britain and Europe.

Van Nostrand's Scientific Encyclopedia. Ed. Douglas M. Considine. Princeton: Van Nostrand, 1988.

ART AND ARCHITECTURE

De La Croix, Horst, and Richard G. Tansey. *Art through the Ages.* 7th ed. 2 vols. New York: Harcourt, 1980.

Encyclopedia of American Art. New York: Dutton, 1981.

Encyclopedia of World Art. 15 vols. with annual supplements. New York: McGraw, 1959–68.

McGraw-Hill Dictionary of Art. Eds. Bernard S. Myers and Shirley D. Myers. 5 vols. New York: McGraw, 1969.

McGraw-Hill Encyclopedia of Architects. 4 vols. New York: McGraw, 1982.

Oxford Companion to Art. New York: Oxford UP, 1970.

ASTRONOMY

Cambridge Encyclopedia of Astronomy. The Institute of Astronomy, University of Cambridge. New York: Crown, 1977.

Encyclopedia of Astronomy. Ed. Gilbert E. Satterthwaite. New York: St. Martin's, 1971.

International Encyclopedia of Astronomy. New York: Orion, 1987.

BIOGRAPHY

Chambers's Biographical Dictionary. Ed. J. O. Thorne. Rev. ed. T. C. Collocott. 2 vols. New York: Two Continents, 1974.

Current Biography. New York: Wilson, 1940–present. Published monthly with annual and ten-year cumulations into volumes.

Dictionary of American Biography. 16 vols. plus supplements. New York: Scribner's, 1927–81.

Dictionary of American Negro Biography. New York: Norton, 1982.

Dictionary of Canadian Biography. With supplements. Toronto: U of Toronto, 1966.

Dictionary of Literary Biography. 38 vols. with annual supplements. Detroit: Gale, 1978.

Dictionary of National Biography. Eds. Leslie Stephen and Sidney Lee. 22 vols., 1882–1953; rpt. New York: Oxford UP, 1981. Including supplements through 1970. Ed. George Smith. Detailed biographies of deceased Britons.

Dictionary of Scientific Biography. 16 vols. New York: Scribner's, 1970.

Great Lives from History: American Series. 5 vols. Englewood Cliffs: Salem, 1987.

Great Lives from History: British and Commonwealth Series. 5 vols. Englewood Cliffs: Salem, 1987.
Great Lives from History: Ancient and Medieval Series. 5 vols. Englewood Cliffs: Salem, 1988.

BIOLOGICAL SCIENCES

Cambridge Encyclopedia of Life Sciences. New York: Cambridge UP, 1985.
Encyclopedia of Biological Sciences. Ed. Peter Gray. 2nd ed. New York: Van Nostrand, 1970.
Grzimek's Animal Life Encyclopedia. 13 vols. New York: Van Nostrand, 1971–75.
McGraw-Hill Dictionary of the Life Sciences. Ed. D. N. Lapedes. New York: McGraw, 1976.
Oxford Companion to Animal Behavior. New York: Oxford UP, 1982.

BUSINESS

Dictionary of Business and Economics. Eds. Christine and Dean S. Ammer. New York: Free, 1977.
VNR Dictionary of Business and Finance. New York: Van Nostrand, 1980.

CHEMISTRY

Encyclopedia of Chemistry. 4th ed. New York: Van Nostrand, 1984.
Lang's Handbook of Chemistry. 12th ed. New York: McGraw, 1979.

COMPUTER SCIENCES

Belzer, Jack. *Encyclopedia of Computer Science and Technology.* 14 vols. New York: Dekker, 1980.
Spencer, Donald. *Computer Dictionary for Everyone.* New York: Scribner's, 1981.

DANCE

Concise Oxford Dictionary of Ballet. Ed. Hurst Koegler. New York: Oxford UP, 1977.
Encyclopedia of Dance and Ballet. Eds. Mary Clarke and David Vaughn. New York: Putnam's, 1977.

DRAMA

Major Modern Dramatists: A Library of Literary Criticism. New York: Unger, 1984.
Matlaw, Myron. *Modern World Drama: An Encyclopedia.* New York: Dutton, 1972.
McGraw-Hill Encyclopedia of World Drama. 5 vols. New York: McGraw, 1984.
The Oxford Companion to the American Theater. New York: Oxford UP, 1984.
The Oxford Companion to the Theater. 4th ed. New York: Oxford UP, 1983.

EARTH SCIENCES

Cambridge Encyclopedia of Earth Sciences. New York: Cambridge UP, 1981.
McGraw-Hill Encyclopedia of Geological Sciences. New York: McGraw, 1980.
McGraw-Hill Encyclopedia of Ocean and Atmospheric Sciences. New York: McGraw,
    1980.

ECONOMICS

Dictionary of Economics and Business. Ed. Erwin E. Nemmers. 4th enl. ed. Totowa,
    NJ: Littlefield, 1978.
Greenwald, Douglas, et al. *McGraw-Hill Dictionary of Modern Economics: A Hand-
    book of Terms and Organizations.* 3rd ed. New York: McGraw, 1983.

EDUCATION

Dictionary of Education. Ed. Carter Victor Good. 3rd ed. New York: McGraw,
    1973.
Encyclopedia of Education. Eds. Lee C. Deighton et al. 10 vols. New York: Macmil-
    lan, 1971.
Page, G. Terry, and J. B. Thomas. *International Dictionary of Education.* Cam-
    bridge, MA: MIT P, 1980.

ENGINEERING

Jones, Franklin D., and Paul B. Schubert. *Engineering Encyclopedia.* 3rd ed. New
    York: Industrial, 1963.
Perry, Robert H. *Engineering Manual: A Practical Reference of Design.* 3rd ed. New
    York: McGraw, 1976.
Schenck, Hilbert. *Introduction to the Engineering Research Project.* New York: Mc-
    Graw, 1969.

ENVIRONMENTAL SCIENCE

Encyclopedia of Ecology. Ed. Bernhard Grzimek. New York: Van Nostrand, 1976.
Encyclopedia of Environmental Science. Ed. Daniel N. Lapedes. New York: McGraw,
    1974.

FILM

Bawden, Liz Anne. *The Oxford Companion to Film.* New York: Oxford UP, 1977.
The New York Times Film Reviews. With supplements. New York: The *New York
    Times* and Arno, 1977.

GEOGRAPHY

Brewer, J. Gordon. *The Literature of Geography: A Guide to its Organization and Use.* Hamden, CT: Shoe String, 1978.
Monkhouse, F. J. *A Dictionary of the Natural Environment.* Ed. John Small. Rev. ed. New York: Halsted, 1977.

HEALTH

Foundations of Physical Education. 8th ed. St. Louis: Mosby, 1981.
Menke, Frank G. *Encyclopedia of Sports.* 6th ed. New York: Barnes, 1978.
Tver, David F., and Percy Russell. *The Nutrition and Health Encyclopedia.* New York: Van Nostrand, 1981.

HISTORY

An Encyclopedia of World History: Ancient, Medieval, and Modern Chronologically Arranged. Comp. and ed. William Leonard Langer. 5th ed. Boston: Houghton, 1972.
Cambridge Ancient History. Eds. J. B. Bury, et al. 2nd ed. 12 vols. New York: Cambridge UP, 1923–39. (Third edition in progress.)
Cambridge Medieval History. Eds. H. M. Gwathin, et al. 8 vols. New York: Cambridge UP, 1911–36. (Second edition in progress.)
Martin, Michael, and Leonard Gelber. *Dictionary of American History.* Rev. ed. Totowa, NJ: Littlefield, 1978.
New Cambridge Modern History. Ed. G. R. Potter. 14 vols. New York: Cambridge UP, 1970.
See also Political Science.

LANGUAGE (ENGLISH) AND LINGUISTICS

Hayes, Curtis W., Jacob Ornstein, and William W. Gage. *The ABC's of Languages and Linguistics.* Rev. ed. Silver Spring, MD: Inst. of Mod. Lang., 1977.
Pyles, Thomas. *The Origins and Development of the English Language.* 2nd ed. New York: Harcourt, 1971.

LITERATURE

Black American Literature, A Critical History. Totowa, NJ: Littlefield, 1974.
Cassell's Encyclopedia of World Literature. Ed. J. Buchanan-Brown. Rev. ed. New York: Morrow, 1973.
Columbia Dictionary of Modern European Literature. Eds. Jean-Albert Bede and William Edgerton. 2nd ed. New York: Columbia UP, 1980.
Crowell's Handbook of Classical Literature. Ed. Lillian Feder. New York: Crowell, 1964.

The Oxford Companion to American Literature. Ed. James David Hart. 4th ed. New York: Oxford UP, 1965.
The Oxford Companion to Canadian History and Literature. New York: Oxford UP, 1967. Supplemented, 1973.
The Oxford Companion to English Literature. Ed. Paul Harvey. Rev. ed. Dorothy Eagle. New York: Oxford UP, 1967.
The Oxford History of English Literature. 12 vols. New York: Oxford UP, 1947–78. Other volumes in preparation.
The Penguin Companion to World Literature. 4 vols. New York: McGraw, 1971. Includes European, American, Oriental, and African literature.
Rush, Theresa G., et al. *Black American Writers, Past and Present: A Biographical and Bibliographical Dictionary.* Metuchen, NJ: Scarecrow, 1975.
The Literary History of the United States. Eds. Robert E. Spiller et al. 4th ed. 3 vols. New York: Macmillan, 1974.

MATHEMATICS

VNR Concise Encyclopedia of Mathematics. Eds. W. Gellert et al. Florence, KY: Van Nostrand, 1977.

MEDIA

Educational Media Year Book 1980. 6th ed. Eds. James W. Brown and Shirley N. Brown. New York: 1980. Annual review of developments in educational media.
Rivers, William L., et al. *The Mass Media and Modern Society.* 2nd ed. New York: Holt, 1971.

MUSIC

Baker's Biographical Dictionary of Musicians. 7th ed. New York: Scribner's, 1984.
International Cyclopedia of Music and Musicians. New York: Dodd, 1985.
New Grove Dictionary of American Music. 4 vols. New York: Macmillan, 1986.
New Grove Dictionary of Music and Musicians. Ed. Stanley Sadie. 20 vols. Washington, D.C.: Grove's Dictionaries of Music, 1980.
The Oxford Companion to Music. Ed. Percy A. Scholes. 10th ed. Rev. ed. John Owen Ward. New York: Oxford UP, 1970.
Westrup, J. A., and F. L. Harrison. *New College Encyclopedia of Music.* Rev. ed. Conrad Wilson. New York: Norton, 1976.

PHILOSOPHY

Angeles, Peter A. *Dictionary of Philosophy.* New York: Harper, 1981.
Copleston, Frederick. *A History of Philosophy.* 9 vols. New York: Paulist, 1976.
Encyclopedia of Philosophy. Ed. Paul Edwards. 4 vols. New York: Macmillan, 1973.
Reese, William. *See* Religion.
Russell, Bertrand. *History of Western Philosophy.* New York: Simon, 1945.

PHYSICS

Encyclopedia of Physics. Ed. Robert M. Besancon. 2nd ed. New York: Van Nostrand, 1974.

Encyclopedia of Physics. Ed. E. Fluegge. 54 vols. New York: Springer, 1956–present.

POLITICAL SCIENCE

Plano, Jack C., and Milton Greenberg. *American Political Dictionary*. 5th ed. New York: Holt, 1979.

Encyclopedia of Crime and Justice. 4 vols. New York: Macmillan, 1983.

Worldmark Encyclopedia of the Nations. 5th ed. 5 vols. New York: Worldmark, 1976.

Yearbook of World Affairs. Published annually under auspices of London Institute of World Affairs. Boulder, CO: Praeger, 1947–present.

PSYCHOLOGY

Baker's Encyclopedia of Psychology. Grand Rapids, MI: Baker, 1985.

Encyclopedia of Occultism and Parapsychology. 2nd ed. 3 vols. Detroit: Gale, 1984.

Encyclopedia of Psychology. New York: Wiley, 1984.

Encyclopedia of Psychology. Ed. H. J. Eysenck. 3rd ed. 4 vols. New York: Continuum, 1984.

Encyclopedia of Social Work. Ed. John Turner. New York: National Association of Social Workers, 1977.

The Oxford Companion to the Mind. New York: Oxford UP, 1987.

RELIGION

Adams, Charles J. *A Reader's Guide to Religions*. 2nd ed. Riverside, NJ: Free, 1977.

Concise Encyclopedia of Living Faiths. Ed. Robert C. Zaehner. New York: Hawthorn, 1959.

Encyclopedia of Religion. Ed. Mircea Eliade. 16 vols. New York: Macmillan, 1987.

Encyclopedia of Religion and Ethics. Ed. James Hastings. 12 vols. New York: Scribner's, 1961.

Reese, William. *Dictionary of Philosophy and Religion, Eastern and Western*. Atlanta: Humanics, 1981.

SOCIAL SCIENCES

Cambridge Encyclopedia of Africa. New York: Cambridge UP, 1981.

Cambridge Encyclopedia of China. New York: Cambridge UP, 1981.

Cambridge Encyclopedia of Latin America and the Caribbean. New York: Cambridge UP, 1985.

Cambridge Encyclopedia of Russia and the Soviet Union. New York: Cambridge UP, 1982.

Dictionary of Sociology and Related Sciences. Ed. Henry Pratt Fairchild. Totowa, NJ: Littlefield, 1977.
International Encyclopedia of the Social Sciences. Ed. David L. Sills. 8 vols. New York: Free, 1977.
Reader's Guide to the Social Sciences. Ed. Bert F. Hoselitz. Rev. ed. New York: Free, 1972.

SOCIOLOGY

Bart, Pauline B., and Linda Frankel. *Student's Sociologist's Handbook.* 3rd ed. Glenview, IL: Scott, 1981.
Dictionary of Sociology and Related Sciences. Totowa, NJ: Littlefield, 1977.
Encyclopedia of Sociology. Ed. Gayle Johnson. Guilford, CT: Dushkin, 1974.

WOMEN'S STUDIES

Baker, M. A., et al. *Women Today: A Multidisciplinary Approach to Women's Studies.* Monterey, CA: Brooks, 1979.
Index to Women of the World from Ancient to Modern Times: Biographies and Portraits.
Lerner, Gerda. *Black Women in White America.* New York: Pantheon, 1972.
Notable American Women 1607–1950: A Biographical Dictionary.
Oakes, Elizabeth H., and Kathleen E. Sheldon. *Guide to Social Science Resources in Women's Studies.* Santa Barbara, CA: ABC-Clio, 1978.
Who's Who of American Women. Chicago: Marquis, 1958–present.

Review Questions

1. Explain the difference between a subject and a topic, as the terms are used in this book.

   - What is your primary concern when choosing a subject?
   - What must be your first concern when looking for a topic?

2. Which of the following items seem likely to work out well as topics for research papers? Explain why you reject each item that seems to have poor potential. (Some are too broad for a paper seven-to-ten pages long; others would lead no further than an encyclopedia for a full investigation; yet others are too deeply involved with personal values or deal with areas in which there is no hard knowledge.)

   - working women in America today
   - the way FM radio signals are sent and received

- the CIA's role in Nicaragua
- the invention of gunpowder
- the cause of measles
- the cause of cancer
- the British colonization of Africa in the nineteenth century
- programs for prevention of child abuse
- the *real* author of Shakespeare's plays
- the cause of teenage alcoholism
- the generation gap
- the role of computers in business today
- automation in heavy industry
- the effectiveness of capital punishment in reducing the crime rate
- the arms race as a threat to peace
- the effect of illegal immigration on the economy of the Southwest
- the effect of high salaries on the quality of baseball being played today
- the ability of some people to see the future in their dreams

3. What is the value of brainstorming? At what point(s) in the research process is this activity likely to help you?
4. What is the purpose of background reading? If you know your topic from the start, should you skip this step?
5. Why is it a good idea to look for a controversy of some sort when trying to come up with a topic?
6. Why do you need to form a hypothesis if you have an excellent topic? How does a hypothesis help at various stages of research?

Exercises

1. Read this article on Emma Goldman, which comes from *Notable American Women*, an excellent background resource for topics in women's studies. Take notes, much like those that accompany the Cotton Mather article on pages 12–14, identifying several potential topics suitable for a seven-to-ten-page research paper. For each topic, think of a reasonable hypothesis.

> **GOLDMAN, Emma** (June 27, 1869–May 14, 1940), anarchist rebel, lecturer, and publicist, agitator for free speech and popularizer of the arts, feminist and pioneer advocate

of birth control, was born in Kovno, Russia (Kaunas in modern Lithuania). Born to ride whirlwinds, as someone once said, she appropriately came from the Baltic, a region notorious for its political and social tensions, and from a ghetto Jewish family in which all these tensions were intensified. She was the first child of the marriage of Abraham and Taube (Bienowitch) Goldman. Taube Goldman, who had two girls from a previous marriage, responded coldly to her new husband and looked upon her infant daughter as an additional burden. Abraham Goldman, a lower-middle-class shopkeeper, was embittered by his wife's attitude, by an initial business failure, and then by the birth of a daughter instead of a son. Even after he subsequently had two sons, he could not forgive his daughter her sex. His choleric disapproval and her mother's unsympathetic brusqueness clouded Emma's earliest experiences in Kovno and later in the small village of Popelan, where her father kept the inn and managed the government stagecoach.

After her family, dogged by failure, moved to Königsberg, Prussia, Emma Goldman attended *Realschule* for a few years. Her teachers successfully instilled in her a distaste for their own cruel pedantry. Only a teacher of German took an interest in her, helped develop her taste for literature and music, and guided her preparations for the Gymnasium examinations. Her justifiable pride in passing these was cut short by the refusal of her religious instructor to give her the requisite certificate of good character. In St. Petersburg, where the Goldmans moved in 1881, her formal schooling lasted only six months more. But even her work in a cousin's glove factory did not keep her from meeting nihilist and populist university students and reading widely in the new radical literature which had the capital in a ferment. The free-spirited Vera Pavlovna, heroine of Nicolai Chernyshevsky's *What Is to Be Done?* (1863), became the model for her own life.

In 1885, gladly escaping her father's demands that she submit to an arranged marriage, she emigrated to America with her half sister Helena Zodokoff. She settled in Rochester, N.Y., with another half sister and found work in a "model" clothing factory at $2.50 a week. She soon became a critic of the capitalism which prompted German Jews, like her employer, to welcome their Eastern brethren to Rochester only to exploit them in their factories and shops. In early 1887 she was married to Jacob Kersner (also Kershner), a fellow factory worker and naturalized citizen, and was shocked to discover that he was impotent. Each passing month made more obvious the hopelessness of their relationship, which, after a divorce and a reconciliation, ended finally in a permanent divorce.

In later years she always said that her life really began in August 1889 when she moved to New York City, met Johann Most, editor of the inflammatory paper *Freiheit*, and Alexander Berkman, a young émigré Russian revolutionist, and joined them in the anarchist movement. Her experiences had indeed prepared her for this moment: the harsh parental authority of her home; the rich ethical demands of the prophetic strain in Judaism; brutal Russian anti-Semitism and her vantage point on the margins of two cultures; her contacts with radical literature and students in St. Petersburg; the gap between the ideality and the reality in America; the judicial murders in 1887 of the so-called Haymarket rioters in Chicago; her own native intelligence, which led her to seek intellectual solutions to her problems—all readied her for her role as one of America's outstanding rebels. The anarchism of Peter Kropotkin, the brilliant Russian scientist and social philosopher, had an appeal which she could hardly resist, for it promised to replace authoritarian social hierarchies, the coercive political state, and supernaturalistic religion by a society of equals, a polity of small organic organizations in free cooperation with each other, and a warm humanism rooted in a concern for decency and justice in this world. Never a seminal social or political thinker, she made only one serious attempt to contribute to anarchist theory: at the Amsterdam Anarchist Congress of 1907 she presented a paper wherein she maintained that true anarchism meant both Kropotkin's emphasis on the community and Henrik Ibsen's emphasis on the strong, independent individual.

Her most serious mistake was an early acceptance of the tactic of individual acts of violence. During the Homestead conflict of 1892 she helped Berkman prepare to kill Henry Clay Frick and regretted that a lack of funds prevented her from being at her comrade's side when the attempt was made. Though Frick survived, Berkman disappeared for fourteen years behind the heavy gates of Pennsylvania's Western Penitentiary. In 1893 Emma herself began a one-year term on Blackwell's Island in New York, convicted of advising a Union Square audience of unemployed men that "it was their sacred right" to take bread if they were starving and their demands for food were not answered. Her prison work as a practical nurse led her to study midwifery and nursing at the Allgemeines Krankenhaus in Vienna in 1895–96. Meanwhile her ideas on individual violence were gradually changing as she came to reject the fallacy that great ends justify any means. By 1901, when President McKinley was shot by Leon Czolgosz, a demented young man possessed by the delusion that he was an anarchist with this particular personal mission, she could sympathize with both the pathetic assassin and the stricken president. Notwithstanding the most energetic efforts of the authorities, no evidence was ever unearthed to establish her complicity. Aside from a few chance remarks on another occasion, Czolgosz had heard her talk only once, and then she had vigorously maintained that anarchism and violence had no necessary connection.

In the opening decades of the new century, Emma Goldman involved herself in a wide range of activities. Perhaps the most accomplished, magnetic woman speaker in American history, she crisscrossed the country lecturing on anarchism, the new drama, the revolt of women. Subject to stubborn and sometimes brutal police and vigilante attempts to censor her remarks or to silence her completely, she joyfully waged countless fights for free speech. As the editor, along with Berkman, of the radical monthly *Mother Earth* (1906–17) and the publisher of numerous pamphlets, her own book *Anarchism and Other Essays* (1911), and Berkman's important *Prison Memoirs of an Anarchist* (1912), she aroused the concern of radicals and liberals over threats to freedom of expression and such cause célèbres as the Tom Mooney case. Roger Baldwin, whose professional interest in civil liberties dated from the influence of her lectures, hardly overstated the case when he said: "For the cause of free speech in the United States Emma Goldman fought battles unmatched by the labors of any organization."

As an integral part of her libertarian message she discussed the works of Ibsen, Shaw, Strindberg, and other playwrights. Her lectures, begun as early as 1897, were published in 1914 under the title *The Social Significance of the Modern Drama*. Though she was not primarily responsible for making Shaw known in the United States, as Rebecca West has suggested, nor a "distinguished critic of the drama," as the *New York Times* once observed, she was a great popularizer of new literary currents.

Her concept of the New Woman owed something to Ibsen's influence, as seen in her attacks on the "conventional lie" of marriage and her advocacy of "free love." By the latter she did not mean a promiscuous "wild love," as some of her critics seemed to think, but the uncoerced mutual regard and affection of two mature persons for one another. She agreed with such feminists as Charlotte Perkins Gilman in rejecting for women the role of a mere "sex commodity," but criticized their "narrow, Puritanical vision" which sought to banish "man, as a disturber and doubtful character, out of their emotional life." The suffrage demand she dismissed as a mere fetish. For over two decades a public advocate of voluntary motherhood and family limitation, in 1915 she was moved by Margaret Sanger's arrest to lecture on preventive methods; one such lecture the following year brought her fifteen days in jail. Her efforts influenced Mrs. Sanger and prepared the way for a systematic birth control campaign. With some reason, then, the *Nation* insisted in 1922 that the name of Emma Goldman should be on any list of "the twelve greatest living women."

Government officials had long had a quite different view. In 1908 they deprived her of her citizenship by denaturalizing the missing Jacob Kersner. It was decided not to make her a party to the court proceedings against Kersner, for that, as Secretary of Commerce and Labor Oscar S.

Straus confidentially wrote the Attorney General, "would too obviously indicate that the ultimate design . . . is not to vindicate the naturalization law, but to reach an individual . . ." (Feb. 11, 1909, National Archives). In June 1917 she and Berkman were arrested for their leadership of the opposition to conscription and sentenced to two years in prison. After her release from Jefferson City Penitentiary in September 1919, immigration officials, with the energetic aid of J. Edgar Hoover, took advantage of wartime legislation to order her deported to Russia. Three days before Christmas 1919 Emma Goldman and Alexander Berkman, along with 247 other victims of the postwar Red Scare, sailed back past the Statue of Liberty aboard the transport *Buford*.

Two years later she expatriated herself from Russia. An early supporter of the Bolsheviki, she had soon discovered their suppression of all political dissent. From Sweden and later Germany she lashed out at the emergent totalitarianism in newspaper articles and in her book *My Disillusionment in Russia* (1923). The egregious myopia of the liberals and radicals who cried out against the suppression of civil rights in the West and remained silent about much worse in Russia was the target of her sharpest attacks. In 1925 she married James Colton, a Welsh collier, to obtain British citizenship. Fearful of economic dependence, she sought to establish herself through her lectures and royalties from her autobiography, *Living My Life* (1931). When she was not touring England or Canada, she lived in Saint-Tropez, France, where friends had helped her buy a small cottage. In 1934 she was granted a ninety-day stay in the United States, but her visit made her return to exile more a torment than ever. In 1936 Berkman, seriously ill and despondent over his forced inactivity, committed suicide. Emma Goldman was saved from utter despair over his death by an urgent request from Barcelona that she come help combat Franco and help advance the social revolution. Apart from three visits to Catalonia during the Spanish Civil War, she stayed in London to enlist understanding and support for her Latin comrades. In 1939 she went to Canada to raise some money for the lost cause. As she had wished, she went out fighting: in February 1940 she suffered a stroke, and three months later she died in Toronto. Since she was now merely a dead "undesirable alien," United States officials allowed her body to be returned for burial in Chicago's Waldheim Cemetery, near the graves of the Haymarket martyrs.

When "Red Emma" was in her twenties, reporter Nellie Bly (Elizabeth Cochrane Seaman) was surprised to discover that she was attractive, "with a saucy turned-up nose and very expressive blue-gray eyes . . . [brown hair] falling loosely over her forehead, full lips, strong white teeth, a mild, pleasant voice, with a fetching accent." Four decades later the English novelist Ethel Mannin saw her as "a short thickset scowling elderly woman with grey hair and thick glasses.'' Throughout her life, Emma Goldman had an extraordinary capacity for close, lasting friendships, though she could be imperious and, on occasion, insensitive to the feelings of others. Offering an invaluable counterstatement to the pragmatic faith of progressives and socialists in the omnicompetent state, she fought for the spiritual freedom of the individual at a time when the organizational walls were closing in. When she died, radicals had almost unanimously rejected her message, but hers was, in the words of the novelist Evelyn Scott, ''the future they will, paradoxically, hark back to in time.''

[The principal holdings of Emma Goldman's papers are in the Labadie Collection, Univ. of Mich. Library; the N.Y. Public Library; and the Internat. Institute for Social Hist., Amsterdam. There is important material also in the files of the Dept. of Justice, Dept. of State, and Post Office Dept. in the Nat. Archives, Washington. For a fuller description and bibliography, including a list of her own writings, see Richard Drinnon, *Rebel in Paradise: A Biog. of Emma Goldman* (1961). See also Frank Harris, *Contemporary Portraits, Fourth Series* (1923); Eunice M. Schuster, *Native Am. Anarchism* (1932); Margaret Goldsmith, *Seven Women against the World* (1935); Ethel Mannin, *Women and the Revolution* (1939) and *Red Rose: A Novel Based on the Life of Emma Goldman* (n.d.); Van Wyck Brooks, *The Confident Years* (1952).]

2. Using the list of subject areas below, choose one subject area, and then do sufficient background reading to find two or three potential topics for a seven-to-ten-page research paper.

   - Asian or Italian or Irish immigration to the United States
   - the banking industry and the Great Depression
   - endangered species
   - European colonization of Africa (or Asia)
   - environmental controls on large industries
   - safety and the automobile industry
   - group therapy for emotional problems
   - the US judicial system's problems
   - the welfare system
   - causes of urban decay
   - religious cults of the 1960s and 1970s
   - organized crime in America
   - genetic experimentation
   - government's role in medical care
   - pre-Columbian American peoples
   - Ethel and Julius Rosenberg, spies executed in the 1950s

- Theodore Roosevelt, conservationist, imperialist
- Marcus Garvey, black nationalist of the 1920s
- Martin Luther King, Jr., civil rights leader of the 1960s
- Malcolm X, militant black leader of the 1960s
- Huey Long, powerful populist senator of the 1930s
- James Hoffa, union leader accused of being involved with organized crime
- Theodor Herzl, Zionist of early twentieth century
- Mother Jones, union organizer of early twentieth century
- Susan B. Anthony, women's rights activist of early twentieth century
- Elizabeth I, queen of England in a crucial era
- Catherine the Great, empress of Russia
- Eleanor Roosevelt, humanitarian
- V. I. Lenin, leader of Russian Revolution of 1917
- Mao Tse-Tung, leader of Chinese Revolution of 1949
- Mohandas Gandhi, leader of Indian independence movement
- Winston Churchill, leader of England during World War II
- Japanese businesspeople: their customs, their ethics, their relations with labor and government
- South Africa's system of racial segregation, apartheid
- Brazil's economy, growing pains of a Third World nation of enormous potential
- OPEC, the troubles that come with instant wealth
- Harry Truman, controversial president in critical postwar period, 1945–52
- Pope John XXIII and the New Catholicism

3. Start your own research paper now, following these steps:

   1. Choose a subject—one of the above or any other that meets the requirements of this course (also see the list in Review Question 2);
   2. go to three or more background sources and find two to five potentially workable topics (record the titles of the sources, and take some notes as you read through them);
   3. select the topic that seems most interesting and/or most workable.

3
Using the Library

After you have chosen a research topic and formed a hypothesis, you are ready to take the next step: finishing your list of sources dealing with your topic. You began your list by noting possible items you found listed in bibliographies of general reference works you read when choosing your topic. To add to the list, you must search for sources on a wider scale, and this means becoming familiar with the resources and services of your library. Find out what materials your library has on hand. Investigate whether you can use the services of your library to locate sources in other libraries.

Working with Librarians

One of the most valuable sources of information in a library is the reference librarian. It is a good idea to introduce yourself early to the reference librarian and to describe your project briefly. Librarians are professionals. They are trained not only to manage libraries but also to keep abreast of existing sources. Their job is to help people with research projects on any subject. This expert can tell you about any special resources your library offers and can often help you to solve problems quickly that might take hours to solve on your own. The research librarian might even have helped someone else working on a topic related to yours and could give you tips and suggestions leading you to valuable sources you might otherwise miss.

Nevertheless, you must remember that although most librarians are quite willing to assist you with your research, they are not obliged to do your research paper for you. Do not go to the librarian and announce, ''I have a paper to do for my American history course, but I don't know what to write about. Can you help me to get some books?'' The librarian has not attended your classes or read your textbooks and cannot invent a topic for you. If you are at a loss for a topic, see your instructor, not your librarian.

Kinds of Sources

In your research you will be working mainly with books and periodicals. (A periodical is a publication that appears regularly under the same title: *Washington Post, Newsweek, Science News, Publications of the Modern Language Association [PMLA]*, and so on.) Books are cataloged and shelved in one way, periodicals in another, and most of this chapter describes how to find sources of each kind.

Although many students think of library research as being limited only to books, periodical articles offer several important advantages. Periodicals can be more current. A book takes many months or even years to write, and months more to be published, so that it may be at least partly out of date by the time it first appears, and still more so by the time you read it. Articles can be published much more quickly, so in some fields where information and interpretations change rapidly, such as science and technology, articles have replaced books as the primary way professionals exchange information and ideas. Even in fields such as history and literature you need to check the periodical indexes to make sure your research is up to date. And subjects in current affairs, such as *government energy policy* and the *Equal Rights Amendment*, will have to be heavily researched in such periodicals as newspapers, newsmagazines, and journals of political commentary.

Another frequent advantage of periodical articles is their depth. They usually focus on a specific topic in a narrower but more detailed way than a book. For example, a book about the world's food supply might include a chapter on innovative proposals for increasing agricultural production, and only a paragraph or two might be about ''farming'' the ocean floor. But in your library you can probably read several recent articles on ocean farming which cover the topic in much greater detail and depth. Furthermore, since a periodical article usually focuses on a specific topic, its title can often tell you exactly what that topic is, and you save time in your search for relevant sources. If you were planning a paper on ocean farming, titles like these would immediately catch your eye:

"A Proposal for Implementing Ocean Farming Off the Southeastern Coast of the United States"

"Ocean Farming: The Crop Will Not Cover the Cost"

In addition to books and periodicals, your library probably has materials available on microfilm—film on which books, periodicals, indexes, and other sources are reproduced in miniature. To read microfilm, you use a special machine that expands the tiny print and projects it onto a screen for easy viewing. In some libraries, an aide is in charge of setting up the microfilm reader. In other libraries, you can load the reader yourself, following instructions posted nearby. Using such readers is simple, and you should get the hang of how to operate one after a couple of attempts.

Your library may also contain unpublished sources such as manuscripts, letters, and business and personal diaries that can prove valuable in certain kinds of research projects.

In addition, most libraries carry nonprint sources such as sound recordings and pictorial material. The reference librarian knows what special sources the library holds and whether or not these sources will help you in your research.

Library Systems—Traditional and Computerized

In all fields where the storage and retrieval of information play important roles, computers are becoming increasingly valuable tools. So it is with libraries. Take time to find out just what computer-assisted services your library offers to make your search for sources easier and more efficient.

Because technological change occurs at different rates across the country, libraries today are in different stages of computerization. Your school library may be one of those in the process of transferring traditional systems to computerized ones, leaving you to discover—in cooperation with your instructors and librarians—how computers can help your research. We expect that most large libraries will eventually carry out their main information storage and search procedures electronically, but for now, most libraries maintain traditional systems while integrating computerized systems for special purposes.

We write on the assumption that, for the most part, the basic concepts and tools of the traditional system—card catalogs and periodical indexes, for example—will form the essentials of computerized systems, and that a working knowledge of these tools prepares you to use present and future computer systems.

The Library Card Catalog

You are probably already familiar with the card catalog. This catalog is an alphabetical index, usually made up of three-by-five-inch file cards, but sometimes published in book form, that contains information about all the books in the library. Actually the card catalog has more cards than the library has books because at least two cards, and often more, are filed, each with a different way of presenting information about a book:

1. an *author* card
2. a *title* card
3. one or more *subject* cards (optional)
4. *cross-reference* cards (optional)

In some libraries the author and title cards are in one set of cabinet drawers and the subject cards in another. In other libraries all the cards are interfiled.

All books are listed under more than one heading. For example, in one library, you will find cards for Kenneth Silverman's *The Life and Times of Cotton Mather* under these headings:

1. (author) SILVERMAN, Kenneth
2. (title) *The Life and Times of Cotton Mather*
3. (subject) Mather, Cotton (1663–1728)
4. (subject) Massachusetts—History—Colonial period, ca. 1600–1775

FINDING A CARD

When you are compiling a list of sources, which card should you consult first? You will often begin looking for subject cards whose subjects are related to your topic. For example, if you are looking for sources about Cotton Mather, you might first look under "Mather, Cotton." Looking under the letter *M* in the subject cards, you will find a number of cards like the one in Figure 3–1.

If you know the name of an author who has written a book or books about your subject, you can look up the author card in the catalog under the first letter of the author's name; then, if necessary, use his or her

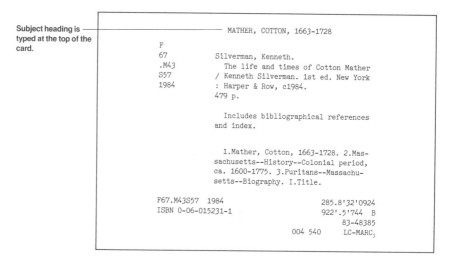

Subject heading is typed at the top of the card.

```
                                        MATHER, COTTON, 1663-1728
        F
        67
        .M43        Silverman, Kenneth.
        S57             The life and times of Cotton Mather
        1984        / Kenneth Silverman. 1st ed. New York
                    : Harper & Row, c1984.
                    479 p.

                        Includes bibliographical references
                    and index.

                        1.Mather, Cotton, 1663-1728. 2.Mas-
                    sachusetts--History--Colonial period,
                    ca. 1600-1775. 3.Puritans--Massachu-
                    setts--Biography. I.Title.

        F67.M43S57  1984                       285.8'32'0924
        ISBN 0-06-015231-1                     922'.5'744  B
                                                       83-48385
                                    004 540       LC-MARC₃
```

Figure 3–1. A subject card

other names. The author card for *The Life and Times of Cotton Mather* is shown in Figure 3–2.

The author card looks virtually the same as the subject card, except that it lacks the subject heading typed across the top. It is filed under *Silverman*.

To locate a title card, look for the first word in the title of the book, omitting the words *A, An,* or *The.*

```
        F
        67          Silverman, Kenneth.
        .M43            The life and times of Cotton Mather
        S57         / Kenneth Silverman. 1st ed. New York
        1984        : Harper & Row, c1984.
                    479 p.

                        Includes bibliographical references
                    and index.

                        1.Mather, Cotton, 1663-1728. 2.Mas-
                    sachusetts--History--Colonial period,
                    ca. 1600-1775. 3.Puritans--Massachu-
                    setts--Biography. I.Title.

        F67.M43S57  1984                       285.8'32'0924
        ISBN 0-06-015231-1                     922'.5'744  B
                                                       83-48385
                                    004 540       LC-MARC₃
```

Except for the heading, the author card is identical to the subject card. It is filed under the heading, the author's name.

Figure 3–2. An author card

The title card is
identical to subject and
author cards except for
the title typed at its top.

```
                            The life and times of Cotton Mather

                F
                67        Silverman, Kenneth.
                .M43          The life and times of Cotton Mather
                S57        / Kenneth Silverman. 1st ed. New York
                1984       : Harper & Row, c1984.
                           479 p.

                           Includes bibliographical references
                           and index.

                           1.Mather, Cotton, 1663-1728. 2.Mas-
                           sachusetts--History--Colonial period,
                           ca. 1600-1775. 3.Puritans--Massachu-
                           setts--Biography. I.Title.

            F67.M43S57  1984                    285.8'32'0924
            ISBN 0-06-015231-1                  922'.5'744  B
                                                       83-48385
                              B  004 540        LC-MARC₃
```

Figure 3–3. A title card

The title card looks the same as the author card except that the title is typed across the top. It is filed under *Life and Times of Cotton Mather*—not under *The*. See Figure 3–3.

Here are two alphabetical rules that might save you some time.

1. Abbreviations are alphabetized as if they were spelled out. For example, *St. John* is filed under *Saint John*.

2. *Mc*, as in *McAllister*, is alphabetized as if it were spelled *Mac*.

The card catalog most likely also includes cross-reference cards that list subject headings under which you can find related materials. Look for a cross-reference or "see also" card, such as that in Figure 3–4, at the end of a set of subject cards.

A cross-reference card can lead you to sources that you might otherwise miss or to sources that lead you more directly to your area of interest. For example, Fred went to the subject card catalog to look for sources under the heading "Witchcraft—New England." That cross-reference card directed him to look also under "Witchcraft—Salem, Massachusetts," where he found more specific sources.

UNDERSTANDING A CATALOG CARD

The organization of information on a catalog card is standardized, so if you understand the format and the significance of the various pieces of information, the card can help you. On the author card shown in Figure 3–5, ten key pieces of information are identified.

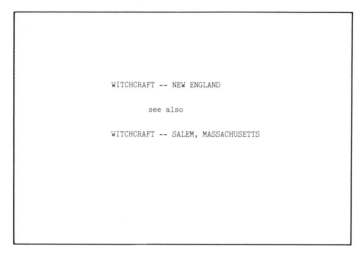

Figure 3–4. A cross-reference or "see also" card

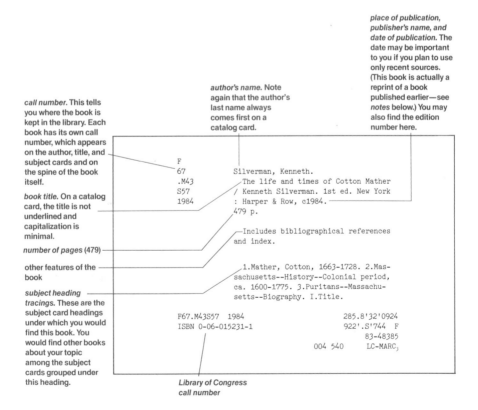

Figure 3–5. An annotated author card

Three items—*call number, author's name,* and *book title*—are essential to your search for sources. The remaining seven items may also be useful to you when you evaluate sources for possible use in your research paper.

COMPUTERIZED CATALOGS

A knowledge of the traditional card catalog system should make it easy for you to use catalogs that are arranged and maintained by computers. If your library owns a Computer Output Microfilm Catalog (COMCAT), then printed catalog cards may no longer be used in your library. Instead, card catalog information has been put on microfilm and you will have to use a microfilm reader to search for sources. The COMCAT terminals may be in a special room, or they may be placed in strategic spots throughout the library. Instructions about how to use the microfilm catalog will be posted on or near each reader.

For the most part, the information you see on a microfilm catalog reader will be similar to that found on a traditional file card in a card catalog. If you bring *Writing Research Papers* with you when you use the microfilm catalog the first time, you should be able to identify the various pieces of information that the microfilm reader provides about a source. The placement of information may differ a bit from the traditional format of a card catalog file card, but you should have no trouble in spotting the call number and the other information you need to find the source you want.

However, not all libraries that have COMCAT have transferred their complete catalog to microfilm. Thus, you may find yourself using both COMCAT and the traditional card catalog in the course of your research. Your librarian will be able to tell you which will be most helpful to you, given your particular topic. And even if your library has gone completely to COMCAT, there may be a gap of several months before new library acquisitions are listed in the microfilm system. If you do not locate the information about a recent source, check with the librarian. The information you need may be filed in a special place, awaiting the update period to be incorporated into the microfilm catalog.

As with a card catalog, using a computerized catalog presents no problems when you know either an author or a title; just type in the name or title. The challenge lies in locating books and articles starting with only a topic. Let's look at a typical computerized search procedure, ignoring the special command buttons that any particular college's system might be using.

Step one. Type in "AIDS," and you get a message saying there are 3,200 items. That's too many even if you were willing to look at the list hoping to find useful titles.

Step two. Type in "New York City," and you see a message saying there are 12,000 items. If you think this means you are going nowhere fast, think again. Of course, a great deal more is written about New York City than about AIDS. What you want now is to connect "AIDS" and "New York City" for a list of articles about AIDS in New York City.

Step three. Type "Print," and the machine will print this list. Note: Some machines are not connected to printers. With them, you must work with the list on the computer monitor's screen and copy down the information that seems valuable. The computer will respond to your typed-in subject by telling you the total number of entries (in this case 19), and by showing you these entries in alphabetical order. You can "scroll down" and all the titles will appear, about 25 at a time. If the total number seems too high, you would not bother "scrolling down" and going through the list.

After looking over the 19 titles and finding too little of value, you might want to expand your topic by typing in "1988." This would yield perhaps 48,000 entries; next you would type in "AIDS" and "1988" and find 300 titles. If this list seems overwhelming, it indicates how essential sufficient background reading is to give you a strong fix on a workable topic. You might, however, be able to treat a 300-item list as an extensive "brainstorming" exercise and search for interrelated items. (Be alert, by the way, to alternative terms when asking the computer about a topic. For instance, typing in "Acquired Immune Deficiency Syndrome" instead of "AIDS" would result in a different list of items because the computer does not know that these two terms refer to the same thing.)

Early in your college research paper experience, you are unlikely to need to go beyond your own library's materials, but if you should ever want to locate items in other libraries, you can employ specialized services such as DIALOG, BRS, and INFOTRAC, which operate via the telephone system. (The computers are connected to the telephone system via modems, devices you can purchase and use in your own home.) As you might well imagine, these services can be expensive, and if you intend to use your library's modem, you must expect to be charged a fee, since the library has to pay for every minute its computer is receiving information from an outside database.

Locating Books

Once you have decided which books you should read, locating those books within the library is relatively easy.

STACKS

Some libraries allow you to enter the *stacks*—the shelves where the books are kept; others do not. In order to get books in libraries where stacks are closed to you, you must fill out a *call slip* and give it to a library employee, who will find the book and give it to you. On the call slip, you supply basic information which you copy from the catalog card for the book.

CALL NUMBERS

In the stacks, books are shelved according to the call numbers you found given with each book's name. Call numbers are of two major classification systems: the *Library of Congress* or the *Dewey Decimal*.

The Library of Congress system uses a combination of letters and numbers to arrange books by subject area and within the subject area. The Dewey Decimal system uses numbers to designate major subject areas, and then a combination of letters and numbers to designate subdivisions under the major classifications. You do not have to memorize the codes for the system your library uses, and you need no specialized knowledge to use it yourself. However, if you have access to the stacks, familiarizing yourself with the call numbers for your particular field will enable you not only to locate the books you have found listed in the card catalog, but also to browse in appropriate sections for other books that may prove valuable. As always, your librarian is the professional to turn to if you have any problems understanding the organization and location of materials in the library.

BOOKS ON RESERVE

Most college libraries have a *reserve reading room* or a *reserve shelf*. In this area you find books that instructors have asked a librarian to pull out of the stacks and set aside for particular classes. However, the books remain available for anyone to use, with certain restrictions. A book placed on reserve must be checked out only for use in the library, or, at best, can be taken out overnight.

When a book is put on reserve, a librarian usually notes that on the catalog cards that list the book. Should you discover that a book you need for your research has been put on reserve, plan to read it and take notes on it in the library. Try to use reserve books as early in the term as possible, for you can be sure that other students will soon be competing with you to consult the same books.

Periodical Indexes

Titles of specific articles published in periodicals are not listed in the library's card catalog but in guides known as *periodical indexes*. Recent articles are cataloged at intervals throughout the year in paperbound supplements to the past year's index. At the end of the year complete annual indexes appear as one or two hardbound volumes. These volumes, as well as the periodical supplements, are usually kept available on shelves or tables in the reference room of the library and must be used there.

In a periodical index, you will find subject entries and, sometimes, author entries, condensed into abbreviations to save space. The indexes are not standardized. Different indexes use different formats and abbreviations and include somewhat different amounts and kinds of information. At the beginning of each volume each abbreviation is explained; you should consult these explanations before using the index. In this chapter you will have a chance to examine typical entries.

Once you have found an index entry for an article that promises to be a good source for your paper, you need to find out whether your library has a copy of the periodical in which that article appeared. In some libraries, periodicals the library subscribes to are listed, alphabetically by title, in the card catalog or in a separate periodicals card catalog. In others, you might consult pamphlets, loose pages at the main desk, or computer printouts. Whatever system your library uses, find out from the librarian how it operates.

The library's periodical list normally tells you how long the library has been accumulating issues of each periodical, so you will need to see if the dates you want are covered. The list also gives the location in the library of each periodical and will usually indicate if some or all issues are available only on microfilm.

Types of Periodicals

Periodicals fall into two broad categories—popular and professional—according to their intended audiences. Within each category you may have to use several indexes, most of which you will find in the reference room of your library.

Some of the most frequently used indexes to periodicals are the following:

popular periodicals (magazines and newspapers)	*Readers' Guide to Periodical Literature* *New York Times Index* *Book Review Digest*
professional periodicals (often called journals)	*Humanities Index* *Social Sciences Index*

In addition, many indexes have been published for periodicals in specific fields, such as art, medicine, and psychology. (A list for your convenience is provided at the end of this chapter.)

Indexes to Popular Periodicals

THE *READERS' GUIDE TO PERIODICAL LITERATURE*

The *Readers' Guide to Periodical Literature*, or *Readers' Guide*, is an index to articles on a wide variety of subjects published in periodicals aimed at a cross section of American readers. Some periodicals, such as *Newsweek, Reader's Digest,* and *National Geographic,* appeal to general interests; others, such as *Aviation Week, Business Week,* and *Art in America,* appeal to special interests. Here is a sampling of the 175 magazines indexed by *Readers' Guide* and the subjects they cover:

The American City—architecture, city planning, urban problems

Atlantic Monthly—current affairs, short fiction

Consumer Reports—evaluations of the performances of commercial products for the general consumer

Cosmopolitan—features, fashions, primarily for career women

Ebony—features, fashions, of particular interest to African-American readers

Foreign Affairs—political topics, aimed at readers up on current events

HG (House and Garden)—architecture, interior decoration, landscaping

National Review—political issues, aimed at politically conservative audience

New Republic—political issues, aimed at politically liberal or moderate audience

Psychology Today—reports on recent research in all branches of psychology, designed for the general reader

Scientific American—reports of recent scientific research, aimed at scientifically informed readers

Sports Illustrated—sports and excellent photographs for the general public

Time—news items from the current week for the general public

United Nations Monthly Chronicle—issues pertaining to the work of the United Nations

Vital Speeches of the Day—transcripts for those who want to know *exactly* what was said

The *Readers' Guide* has been published, since 1900, as a series, each volume covering one or more years (the *Guide* year currently runs from

March through February). (If you need material from the nineteenth century, go to *Poole's Index to Periodical Literature*, which covers 1802 to 1906.) Consult the *Readers' Guide* for social science subjects—modern history, economics, political science, and sociology. It is especially valuable for topics that concern public reaction to an event at the time it was happening, such as Franklin Roosevelt's attempt to alter the composition of the Supreme Court, and for the latest articles on current events not yet included in books, such as changing attitudes toward old age in the United States from 1980 to the present.

For scientific topics the *Readers' Guide* offers relatively few useful sources. Scientific subjects were not even included in this index until 1953. Because magazines for the general public must avoid highly technical discussions, their science writers may oversimplify and occasionally distort some of the ideas they present. (Remember Anita's experience with the longevity article.) If you begin your investigation of a scientific topic with a popular magazine, be sure to turn to books and scholarly journals that deal with the same topic in more depth and detail.

The *Readers' Guide* lists both authors and subjects alphabetically. Regardless of whether you are looking for a subject or an author, use this index as you would a dictionary.

For example, if you were looking for articles on witchcraft published in the last ten years, you would look at several volumes of the *Guide*, checking listings under "Witchcraft." In the March 1984–February 1985 volume of the *Guide*, you would find the information shown in Figure 3–6.

To find an author's work in the *Readers' Guide*, look alphabetically for

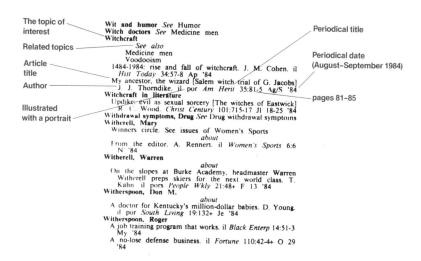

Figure 3–6. From the *Readers' Guide*

author's last name. Under the author's name you will find all articles by the author arranged alphabetically according to title, disregarding *A*, *An*, and *The*. (The word *about* above an author's name indicates that the author is the subject of an article written by someone else.)

THE *MAGAZINE INDEX*

This index covers articles from more than 400 magazines. It is available in some libraries as part of the computer system and in other libraries as a microform system. The microform system consists of a console with a large viewing screen and an operating knob. You need only turn the knob to move the microform swiftly in search of subjects or authors, both indexed alphabetically. The *Magazine Index* is most useful for locating articles that have appeared in magazines during the past five or six years. However, because the index provides information from so many magazines, it includes publications that your instructor may think inappropriate for serious research. Check with your instructor or your librarian if you have any doubts about the research value of a magazine with which you are unfamiliar. In addition, your library will almost certainly subscribe to only a relatively small percentage of the 400 magazines.

THE *NEW YORK TIMES INDEX*

The *New York Times* is generally agreed by professionals in all fields to be the most important newspaper in the United States. You can find listed, in annual volumes of the *New York Times Index*, all major news accounts and feature articles that have appeared in the *Times* since 1913, arranged alphabetically according to subject. To locate articles on a specific topic or event, select the volumes that cover the relevant time period and then look alphabetically in the volumes for the subject. To check the *Index* for very recent events, use the supplements published every two weeks. At the year's end, these supplements are republished as the new annual volume of the *Index*.

Newspaper articles are particularly useful for topics that require you to know precisely what facts and impressions were reported at the time an event occurred or to sample public opinion over a particular period of time. Here are some examples of such topics:

attitudes toward Prohibition at the time the Eighteenth Amendment was being ratified (1917–19)

reactions throughout the South to the Supreme Court decision of 1954 outlawing segregation in public schools

the extent to which the American public was misinformed about the testing of atomic bombs in Nevada after World War II

While researching public opinion preceding an event, such as an election or the ratification of a constitutional amendment, be sure to check the *Index* volume that covers not only the calendar year of the event but also the previous year, especially if the event took place early in its year. Similarly, when investigating the reactions to an event, check the *Index* volume for the year of the event and the following year.

Even if your library does not subscribe to the *Times* on microfilm, consult the *New York Times Index* for the year the event occurred; then you can find the exact days on which important events were reported. Use those dates to locate information in newspapers that your library does have, since most newspapers usually publish important stories at the same time.

Every daily issue of the *New York Times* (beginning with the very first issue in 1851), has been reproduced in microfilm, and many libraries have a complete set. Find the date, section, and page number of a particular news item in the *Index*, then request the filmstrip of the *Times* for that date, and run it through a microfilm viewer.

The *New York Times Index* offers another convenient feature: its brief summaries of many articles may help you decide whether to spend time searching for and reading a particular story.

Figure 3–7 shows a sample from the *New York Times Index*. The entry, "Witchcraft," in the bound volume of the *Index* for 1985 indicates several articles about the subject, with one referring directly to the Salem witchcraft trials.

The *New York Times Index* is most useful for social science subjects, such as modern history, economics, and political science. The *Times* also reports extensively on literature and the arts.

THE *NEWSPAPER INDEX*

A valuable addition to periodical guides is the *Newspaper Index*, which began publication in 1972. This index provides information on articles that have appeared in four of the nation's largest newspapers: the *Chicago Tribune*, the *Los Angeles Times*, the *New Orleans Times-Picayune*, and the *Washington Post*. As you might gather from the titles of the newspapers included, this index can be especially useful for looking up regional news and opinion, as well as national and international news.

THE *BOOK REVIEW DIGEST*

The *Book Review Digest* publishes excerpts from book reviews that appeared within a year after a book was first published. The *Book Review Digest* does not cite every published review, but only a sample of critical responses, both favorable and unfavorable.

An article dealing with the filming of a television mini-series based on the Salem witchcraft trials appeared in section II, page 29, column 1 of the October 28 issue of the *Times:*
(M) indicates a medium-length article, (S) a short article, and (L) a long article.

WISTAR Institute. See also Cancer, Jl 12
WIT. Use Humor and Wit
WITCHCRAFT
Article on increase in fatal lightning strikes in Khureng, South Africa, during current rainy season, which has resulted in burning to death of six local people, who were charged by witch doctors with sorcery; notes that while lightning can be explained scientifically, supernatural provides natural form of elucidation; illustration; map (M). Ja 21,I,2:3
Fox Butterfield article on filming of 'Three Sovereigns for Sarah,' about witchcraft trials in Salem (Mass) in 1692; three-hour production is public-TV mini-series being filmed outside Boston and is scheduled to be shown under 'American Playhouse' banner next May; photo (M), O 28, II,29:1
Dozens of cats, dogs and chickens have been mutilated in what police in Marysville, Ohio, think may be work of satanic cult (S). D 31,I,6:6
WITCO Chemical Corp. See also Continental Carbon Co, S 11 Oil, Ja 10
Witco Chemical Corp names Denis Andreuzzi executive vice president of commercial services, Ja 23,IV,2:6
Witco Chemical Corp elects Thomas J Bickett executive vice president (S). F 7,IV,2.2
Witco Chemical Corp promotes Dr Lawrence B Nelson to group vice president, petroleum. Jl 23,IV,2.6
WITEK, Joan. See also Art, Je 15
WITHERS, William. See also NYC - Govt Employees, Ag 11
WITHERSPOON, Roger. See also Biology, S 6,15
WITHERSPOON, Tim. See also Boxing, Mr 9,10, Ag 31, S 1,2
WITHERSPOON-Jackson Development Corp. See also Housing, Jl 1
WITKIN, Isaac. See also Art, Je 15
WITKIN-Lanoil, Georgia (Dr). See also Mental Health, Ap 8
WITKOWSKI, John. See also Football, Ag 20
WITT, Arthur P. See also Lily-Tulip Inc, Jl 31
WITT, Edna Mae. See also Nursing Homes, N 10
WITT, Jon. See also Alpha Software Corp, Ja 24
WITT, Katarina. See also Ice Skating, Ja 13, Mr 22, Olympic Games (1984), F 17,18,19

Figure 3–7. From the *New York Times Index*

Each annual volume of this digest (beginning in 1905) indexes reviews of several thousand books, according to both title and author. To use the *Book Review Digest,* you need to know the year in which a book was first published. Then you should look up the title or the author in the volumes both for that year and for the next year because some books are not reviewed during the calendar year in which they are published: a book published in November 1966, for example, might not have been reviewed until January 1967.

The *Book Review Digest* presents the initial critical reactions to a book, helpful especially if you wish to compare immediate responses with later judgments made by critics and scholars after the work has had a chance to influence other writers or after public tastes have changed. Examples of research assignments requiring you to use the *Digest* would be ''Initial Critical Reactions to Ernest Hemingway's *The Sun Also Rises*,'' and ''Changing Critical Evaluations of Willa Cather's *My Antonia*.''

The *Book Review Digest*'s value is not limited to literary topics. For example, you might want to know how reviewers reacted to a book that presented a new view of a well-known person or event or that unveiled a new social or scientific theory, such as evolution, relativity, or psychoanalysis.

Finally, check a book you want to use as a source in the *Book Review Digest*; you can find out very easily whether the reviewers thought that book informative and reliable.

Indexes to Scholarly and Professional Journals

THE *HUMANITIES INDEX* AND THE *SOCIAL SCIENCES INDEX*

These two indexes may well provide you with all the sources needed for research papers in the social sciences or the humanities. These indexes are more specialized than those discussed so far, for each indexes not general magazines but scholarly journals in a variety of fields.

Since 1974 the *Humanities Index* and *Social Sciences Index* have appeared as separate volumes. From 1965 to 1974 the two indexes were combined in the *Social Sciences and Humanities Index*, and from 1920 to 1965 its title was the *International Index to Periodicals*. From 1907 through 1919 the single index was titled *Readers' Guide Supplement and International Index*.

Together, the *Humanities Index* and the *Social Sciences Index* cover articles published in more than 500 scholarly and professional journals. (Many of these journals, however, are not available in small libraries.) The *Humanities Index* lists articles according to subject in the following academic disciplines:

archaeology	literary and political criticism
classical studies	performing arts
area studies	philosophy
folklore	religion
history (not included until 1974)	theology
language and literature	

The *Social Sciences Index* lists articles according to subject in the following academic disciplines:

anthropology	medical science
area studies	political sciences
economics	psychology (not included between
environmental science	1945 and 1974)
education	public administration
law and criminology	sociology

SPECIALIZED INDEXES

The *Humanities Index* and the *Social Sciences Index*, though highly valuable resources, cover only a small fraction of all the scholarly and professional journals published in the humanities and the social sciences. Because the number of specialized scholarly articles published each year is enormous, each field has its own annual index to specialized periodicals. Even so, areas such as English literature cannot be contained within a single annual index, so there are still more specialized indexes.

All of the indexes to scholarly and professional journals will lead you to very difficult materials. Most authors of scholarly articles are writing for fellow experts and therefore assume that their readers have a strong background in the field; many articles focus on very narrow topics and employ a highly specialized terminology. You may find much scholarly writing hard to understand, but you should become acquainted with such materials and perhaps work through an article with your instructor so you can incorporate some specialized scholarly sources into your research paper if such sources strengthen your thesis. Later in college, especially in your major field, the information in scholarly journals will become increasingly accessible and valuable to you.

At the end of this chapter is a selective list of indexes to scholarly and professional journals in many major fields. If you need to find additional sources, consult the *Bibliographic Index: A Cumulative Bibliography of Bibliographies*. This work briefly describes all the periodical indexes you will probably ever need.

Locating Periodicals

Most libraries have a periodical room where you can find the current issue of each magazine and newspaper to which the library subscribes. Most of your research, however, will involve back (previous) issues, and these may be kept elsewhere.

Libraries usually have back issues of periodical magazines and journals gathered by year—or, if the periodical is published very often or is bulky, into shorter periods—and permanently rebound in hard covers. These bound volumes are then shelved chronologically, either in the periodical room or in the stacks. Back issues that are not in the periodical room may be in the library offices awaiting rebinding or actually at the bindery; ask a librarian for any issues you cannot find.

Back issues of daily and weekly newspapers are kept unbound for one or more years. Then, in many libraries, they are thrown away. However, the Sunday magazine and book review sections may be kept much longer and may be bound for permanent storage. A librarian at your library can tell you what its policy is.

Additional Resources

Although you can produce a fine research paper based entirely on books and periodicals found through the card catalog and the major periodical indexes, there are other resources both in the library and outside it where you may find still more information and ideas.

IN THE LIBRARY

Specialized Collections. Some libraries maintain separate special collections of materials such as books, periodicals, personal letters, and manuscripts. A special collection sometimes relates to special areas of interest: a particular author's works, the history of a particular place, or a fairly narrow field (cave exploration, Broadway musicals, or aviation engineering). Other special collections are kept separate from the main collection because their holdings are fragile, rare, or otherwise unusual. The catalog for each special collection is usually separate and kept in a special section of the library.

Microforms. To save space, save wear and tear on delicate holdings, and increase usefulness, many source materials have been preserved on microforms, mainly microfilm or microfiche. The most common resources on microforms are periodicals; others include old and rare books and even facsimiles of manuscripts. Some sources, such as graduate dissertations, may be published only on microforms.

Vertical File Index. Some printed sources may not be classified either as books or as periodicals, and so will not appear in either the card catalog or the periodical indexes. Such materials include pamphlets, brochures, and clippings from hard-to-get periodicals on specialized topics. You can find these resources by using the Vertical File Index. A librarian can explain how to use this index.

Audiovisual Materials. Many libraries now contain media sections which house films, videotapes, pictures, slides, and sound recordings. If your topic concerns the performing or visual arts, architecture, or the social or natural sciences, you will often find materials useful to your research in the audiovisual collection. In addition to materials on the arts, you can find valuable documentaries, especially in those fields having to do with human and animal behavior and society.

Interlibrary Loan. If you discover a source which you believe to be crucial to your research, and your library does not have a copy of it, you may be able to borrow the source through an interlibrary loan arranged by a librarian. (*Warning*: It normally takes several weeks for the source to arrive at your library, and it may take longer. Allow sufficient time for the loan to be arranged.)

OUTSIDE THE LIBRARY

Other Libraries. Large colleges and universities may have separate, specialized libraries attached to particular graduate schools or departments, such as law, medicine, engineering, music, and art. Off campus, museums and professional societies devoted to such fields often operate their own small but excellent libraries. You may have to apply formally to use such facilities; often simply verifying your school affiliation will be enough. The public library in your city may also be a useful resource. Some, like the New York Public Library, are among the greatest research facilities in the world, but even the most modest public library may have the particular periodical or book you need.

Special Printed Materials. Private businesses, nonprofit organizations, special interest groups, and various levels of government publish reports and pamphlets in great numbers. Usually these materials can be obtained free of charge by writing to the organizations. In most cases there will be no catalog to which you can refer, so you may be able only to describe what you are looking for and hope the answer meets your needs. The United States Government Printing Office (GPO) *Monthly Catalog* lists all publications by the federal government that are available to the public, their prices, and the addresses from which they may be ordered. Your library should have a copy, and you can ask your librarian where it is kept. Be warned, however, that delivery is not overnight: one GPO distribution center in Pueblo, Colorado, alone handles some 80,000 requests every week, and you may wait a month or more for materials ordered.

Television and Radio Programs. The Public Broadcasting System (PBS) regularly presents documentaries about the performing and graphic arts and also the natural and social sciences. These programs are often repeated several times, so you may be able to watch broadcasts originally shown before you started your research project. If your topic has to do with a current issue, be alert for interviews and documentaries scheduled on any station. Transcripts of regularly scheduled news interviews are often available from the stations or networks that produce or broadcast them. Because transcripts usually require four to six weeks' delivery time, you will in most cases have to make your own transcription. If possible, record the program and later transcribe those portions of it you want to use word by word, rather than trying to take notes during the program.

Interviews. You may want to set up an interview with a person whose knowledge and opinions would be useful to your research project. Perhaps a faculty member is an authority on your topic, or a local public official administers a program relevant to your research. Depending upon your topic, you may well find that interviews with people who possess special knowledge or who have undergone unusual experiences will yield valuable information.

When you request a personal interview with someone who lives by a busy schedule, prepare the groundwork well. Always write or telephone ahead, informing the authority just why you want the meeting. Specify your field of inquiry as precisely as you can and explain why you think this interview can help you get a better grasp of the topic you are researching. Let the person know that you will limit the interview to a few pertinent questions that will not take up too much valuable time. It is a good idea to review your questions with your instructor. Forming brief questions that will bring out the kind of information you need is a kind of art, and you may need help the first time you plan for an interview. You might even offer to send the questions in advance for consideration before the actual interview. If you would like to bring a tape recorder to the interview, ask whether the potential interviewee minds. If there are objections, don't persist. Diplomatically state that taking notes will serve your recording purposes just as well. And be flexible in arranging the date and time of the interview. If you can arrange a mutually agreeable time, fine. If not, you will have to go out of your way to suit the authority's schedule.

The attitude you assume will be important to the success of your interview. Keep in mind that the authority is a research source, and that your main concern is to find out what the person knows or believes about some aspect of your topic. At the time of an interview you are gathering sources to test the hypothesis you have chosen to guide your research. This means that you have not yet arrived at a particular conclusion regarding your topic. Thus, your job is to listen carefully to the person's responses to your questions and to summarize major points in your notes. If you enter into an interview with a biased point of view, your ''source'' might catch the tone of your remarks and give you very little—if anything—in the way of useful information or opinion.

Finally, be sure to write a note thanking the person for the interview.

Questionnaires and Surveys. If your topic involves public opinion, particularly the opinions of a particular group such as college students or faculty, the parents of schoolchildren, or senior citizens, you may find that no published poll serves your purposes. Conduct a poll of your own. Whether you conduct your survey in person or by mail through questionnaires, your questions must be carefully stated to make sure that the answers are relevant and meaningful. You should probably ask your instructor to review your list of questions before you begin your poll.

Some General Bibliographies, Periodical Indexes, and Representative Journals

Here are some guides to sources which you will find in many college libraries and which you can use to develop your working bibliography. Also you know to consult the bibliographies that accompany articles in the general reference books you use for background reading.

ART AND ARCHITECTURE

The Art Index: A Cumulative Author and Subject Index to a Selected List of Fine Art Periodicals. New York: Wilson, 1933–present. (Quarterly, with biennial cumulations.) In addition to fine arts, index includes architecture, design, and decorating journals.

ASTRONOMY

Sky and Telescope. Cambridge, MA: Sky, 1941–present. (Monthly.) Publication for nonspecialists in astronomy: articles, observations, data, equipment guides, etc.

BIOGRAPHY

The Biography Index: A Cumulative Index to Biographical Material in Books and Magazines. New York: Wilson, 1946–present. (Quarterly, with annual and triennial cumulations.)

BIOLOGICAL SCIENCES

Biological Abstracts. Philadelphia: Biosciences Information Service, 1926–present. (Bimonthly.) Abstracts and index of international publications, excludes clinical medicine.

The Biological and Agricultural Index. New York: Wilson, 1964–present. (Monthly, except August.) Subject index to periodicals about agriculture and biology.

BUSINESS

Business Periodicals Index. New York: Wilson, 1958–present. (Monthly, except July.)

CHEMISTRY

Chemical Abstracts: Key to the World's Chemical Literature. Washington, D.C.: Am. Chem. Soc., 1907–present. (Weekly.)

DRAMA

Breed, Paul F., and Florence M. Sniderman. *Dramatic Criticism Index. A Bibliography of Commentaries on Playwrights from Ibsen to the Avant-Garde.* Detroit: Gale, 1972.
Cumulated Dramatic Index, 1909–1949. A Cumulation of the F. W. Faxon Company's Dramatic Index. Ed. Frederick W. Faxon et al. 2 vols. Boston: Hall, 1965.
Play Index. 5 vols. New York: Wilson, 1953–78.

ECONOMICS

American Journal of Economics and Sociology. New York: American Journal of Economics and Sociology, 1941–present. (Quarterly.)
Hughes, Catherine, ed. *Economic Education: A Guide to Information Sources.* Detroit: Gale, 1977.
International Bibliography of Economics. Ed. UNESCO International Committee for Social Science Documentation. Chicago: Aldine, 1952–present. (Annual.)

EDUCATION

Current Index to Journals in Education. New York: Macmillan, 1969–present. (Monthly, with annual and semiannual cumulations.)
The Education Index. New York: Wilson, 1929–present. (Monthly, except July and August, with annual cumulations.)

ENGINEERING

Applied Science and Technology Index. New York: Wilson, 1958–present. (Monthly.)
The Engineering Index. Ed. American Society of Mechanical Engineers. New York: Engineering Index, 1934–present. (Monthly.)
Malinowsky, Harold R., et al. *Science and Engineering Literature: A Guide to Reference Sources.* 2nd ed. Littleton, CO: Libraries Unlimited, 1976.

ENVIRONMENTAL SCIENCE

Pollution Abstracts. Ed. Oceanic Library and Information Center. Louisville, KY: Data Courier, 1970–present.

ETHNIC STUDIES

Index to Literature on the American Indian. San Francisco: Indian Historian Press, 1970–present. (Annual.)

Index to Periodical Articles by and about Negroes. Ed. Hallie Q. Brown Memorial Library. Boston: Hall, 1950–present. (Annual.)

Welsch, Ervin K. *The Negro in the United States: A Research Guide*. Bloomington: Indiana UP, 1965. Discusses books and periodicals.

Woods, Richard D. *Reference Materials on Mexican Americans*. Metuchen, NJ: Scarecrow, 1976.

HEALTH AND PHYSICAL EDUCATION

American Alliance for Health, Physical Education and Recreation. *Abstracts of Research Papers*. Washington, D.C.: AAHPER, 1971–75.

HISTORY

America: History and Life. A Guide to Periodical Literature. Santa Barbara, CA: American Bibliographical Center, Clio Press, 1964–present. (Annual.)

American Historical Association. *Guide to Historical Literature*. Ed. George F. Howe et al. New York: Macmillan, 1961.

Guide to the Study of the United States of America, A: Representative Books Reflecting the Development of American Thought. Washington: US Government Printing Office, 1960. Supplements 1956–65, 1976.

Historical Abstracts: Bibliography of the World's Periodical Literature, 1775–. Santa Barbara, CA: American Bibliographical Center, Clio Press, 1955–present. (Annual.)

International Bibliography of Historical Sciences. New York: International Publications Service, 1930–present. (Annual.)

LANGUAGE AND LITERATURE

Bond, Donald F. *Reference Guide to English Studies*. 2nd ed. Chicago: U of Chicago P, 1971.

Essay and General Literature Index 1900–1933: An Index to about 40,000 Essays and Articles in 2,144 Volumes of Collections of Essays and Miscellaneous Works. New York: Wilson, 1934–present. (Biennial supplements.)

Kennedy, Arthur G., and Donald B. Sands. *A Concise Bibliography for Students of English*. 5th ed. Rev. William E. Coburn. Stanford: Stanford UP, 1972.

Modern Humanities Research Association. *Annual Bibliography of English Language and Literature*. Cambridge: Cambridge UP, 1921–present.

Modern Language Association of America. *MLA International Bibliography of Books and Articles on the Modern Languages and Literature*. New York: MLA, 1969–present. 1922–68 as June issue of PMLA. (Formerly *American Bibliography*.)

The New Cambridge Bibliography of English Literature. 5 vols. New York: Cambridge UP, 1969–77.

Spiller, Robert E., et al. *The Literary History of the United States*. 4th ed. 2 vols. New York: Macmillan, 1974.

LAW

Index to Legal Periodicals. New York: Wilson for the Am. Assn. of Law Libraries, 1908–present. (Monthly.)

MUSIC

Duckles, Vincent. *Music Reference and Research Materials: An Annotated Bibliography*. 2nd ed. New York: Macmillan, 1974.

Music Index: The Key to Current Music Periodical Literature. Detroit: Information Service, 1949–present. (Monthly, with annual cumulations.)

RILM Abstracts. New York: International Association of Music Libraries. 1967–present. (Quarterly.)

PHILOSOPHY

The Philosopher's Index: An International Index to Philosophical Periodicals. Bowling Green, OH: Bowling Green U, 1967–present. (Quarterly.)

PHYSICS

Science Abstracts. London: Institution of Electrical Engineers, 1898–present. (Monthly.) Includes abstracts of articles about physics.

POLITICAL SCIENCE

Brock, Clifton. *The Literature of Political Science: A Guide for Students, Librarians, and Teachers*. New York: Bowker, 1969.

Harmon, Robert B. *Political Science: A Bibliographic Guide to the Literature*. Metuchen, NJ: Scarecrow, 1965. Third Supplement, 1974.

PSYCHOLOGY

The Harvard List of Books in Psychology. 4th ed. Cambridge, MA: Harvard UP, 1971.

Psychological Abstracts. Lancaster, PA: Am. Psych. Assn., 1927–present. (Monthly.)

RELIGION

American Theological Library Association. *Index to Religious Periodical Literature, 1949/1952–.* Chicago: Am. Theo. Lib. Assn., 1953–present. (Annual.)
Religious and Theological Abstracts. Youngstown, OH: Theological, 1958–present. (Quarterly.)

SCIENCE AND TECHNOLOGY

Applied Science and Technology Index. New York: Wilson, 1958–present.
General Science Index. New York: Wilson, 1978–present.

SOCIOLOGY

Social Sciences Index. New York: Wilson, 1974–present. (Quarterly.) See page 51 of this book for a complete description.
Sociological Abstracts. New York: Sociological Abstracts, 1953–present.
White, Carl M., et al. *Sources of Information in the Social Sciences: A Guide to the Literature.* 3rd ed. Chicago: Am. Lib. Assn., 1973.

WOMEN

Backscheider, Paula R., and Felicity A. Nussbaum. *An Annotated Bibliography of Twentieth Century Critical Studies of Women and Literature, 1660–1800.* New York: Garland, 1977.
Krichman, Albert. *The Women's Rights Movement in the United States, 1848–1970: A Bibliography and Sourcebook.* Metuchen, NJ: Scarecrow, 1972.

Review Questions

1. Suppose you are looking for a particular biography of Queen Elizabeth I of England, *Elizabeth the First* by Paul Johnson. How many entries in the card catalog can you find for this book? How can the card catalog help you locate other books about Queen Elizabeth?

2. How is each of these pieces of information, found on cards in the card catalog, useful to researchers?

author	date of publication
title	number of pages
subject	notation about a
call number	bibliography

3. What kinds of materials are listed in periodical indexes? Why might a researcher need to use several different indexes?

4. For each of the following topics, what additional resources (besides books from the card catalog and periodical articles from indexes) might you look for?

   - the latest government recommendations about energy conservation
   - a seventeenth-century book (all known copies are owned by British libraries)
   - the inauguration address of President Kennedy
   - the jobs located by recent graduates of your school
   - the history of the town in which your library is located
   - your city's model program for rat control
   - the major paintings of a particular artist
   - the position on a controversial issue, taken last week by the governor

Exercises

1. Just to feel more at home in your school library, pay a visit there and locate the following:

   - the reference room or reference area
   - the periodical room or area
   - the reserve reading room or reserve desk
   - the card catalog

   If your library provides a diagram or floor plan of its physical layout, obtain a copy and use it to locate these resources. If no diagram is available, draw a rough floor plan of your own, showing the locations of the main sections of the library.

2. Use the card catalog to look up a fairly recent work of fiction by a well-known author, perhaps one you have studied in high school or college. Consult your library's classification guide to find the shelf where the book should be located. Use the *Book Review Digest* to find out if the book was reviewed during the year it was published or the following year. Report your findings.

3. Using microfilms of the *New York Times,* find the most important story reported on the day and year you were born (the "lead" story

is in the upper right-hand corner of the front page). Then go to the *New York Times Index*, find a listing for this article and the next *Times* article on the same subject. Copy out both listings and convert all abbreviations to the full forms of the words that they represent.

4. Use the *Readers' Guide to Periodical Literature* to locate in your library an article published during the past year about your favorite hobby, pastime, or field of interest. Read it, determine the author's topic and thesis, and explain briefly why you agree or disagree with this thesis.

5. Choose one of the topics listed on pages 33–34 of this book. Use the subject card catalog to try to find the titles of three books related to the topic. Write out these titles and their call numbers and describe briefly where in the library each is located.

6. Think of a topic in psychology or medical science that interests you. Use the *Social Science Index* to discover how many articles have been written on that topic during the past three years. Record appropriate article and journal titles and any other information provided in the index description. Convert all abbreviations to the full forms of the words that they represent.

4
Searching for Sources

Now that you have a good idea of the research aids available in your library, you can begin the process of searching for sources by developing a *working bibliography*—a list of the books and periodical articles that may become sources of information for your research paper. Once you have collected a substantial list of possible sources, you must locate as many of them as you can and examine each one *briefly* to see whether it contains information and ideas that will further the investigation of your specific topic. Ultimately, you will use some of the information you find in these sources to support your paper's thesis. Those sources that provide specific ideas and information for the paper will be listed in your *final bibliography*.

Compiling the Working Bibliography

To begin putting together a working bibliography, get a supply of three-by-five-inch note cards for *bibliography cards*. Then, whenever you come across the title of a book or article that seems worth checking into, make out a bibliography card for it. Use a separate card for each item and keep the cards in alphabetical order. Cards are handier for this purpose than a simple list because they can more easily be kept in order as you add and drop items from your working bibliography.

THE INFORMATION ON BIBLIOGRAPHY CARDS

For a bibliography card to be useful, it must contain all the information you will need when you prepare the footnotes or endnotes and the bibliography for your paper. In addition, the card should give you whatever information is needed to find the book or article in the library.

BOOKS

To make out a card for a *book*, record the following information (see Figure 4–1):

- name of the author, last name first
- title of the book, underlined
- place of publication
- publisher's name
- date of publication
- library call number (in top right corner)

PERIODICALS

For a *periodical article*, follow this guide (see Figure 4–2):

- name of the author
- title of the article (in quotation marks)
- title of the periodical (underlined)

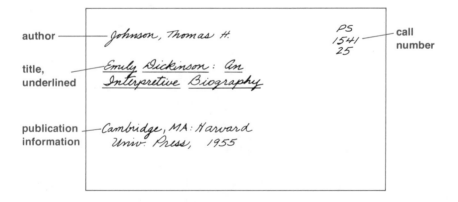

Figure 4–1. Bibliography card for a book

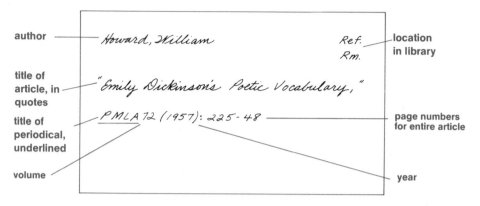

author — Howard, William   Ref. location in library
                                  Rm.

title of article, in quotes — "Emily Dickinson's Poetic Vocabulary,"

title of periodical, underlined — PMLA 72 (1957): 225-48 — page numbers for entire article

volume — year

Figure 4–2. Bibliography card for a periodical article

* volume number and date of publication
* numbers of the pages on which the article appears

Be sure to place in the upper right corner of every bibliography card the library call number or other "locator" information from the card catalog or catalog-on-line.* Take extra care to copy all bibliographical information accurately onto your cards. Misspellings, incorrect punctuation, careless omissions, and other mistakes in copying can force you to waste time in return trips to the library.

Gathering Sources

You will almost always collect more titles for your working bibliography than will appear in your final list of Works Cited because many potential sources will, upon a close reading, prove to be no help in the investigation of your hypothesis. The problem is that when you are looking through the card catalog or a periodical index, you must try to judge the value of a book or article by its title alone or by the heading under which you found it. Because you do not want to miss a potentially useful source, you must add to your working bibliography every title that sounds even slightly promising. Of course, quite a few of these potential sources will turn out to be worthless for your purposes, so your working bibliography will shrink accordingly. However, while you are dropping disappointing items from your list, you may be adding titles that are

---

*Throughout our discussion, please keep in mind that we mean to include "catalog-on-line system" anytime we refer to the "card catalog." (More and more colleges are moving into this use of computers to replace the cumbersome card catalog kept in drawers.)

mentioned in the useful sources. You should, therefore, expect to be adding and dropping potential sources from your working bibliography throughout your research.

THE THREE STUDENTS GATHER THEIR SOURCES

Fred Hutchins began assembling a working bibliography while reading background sources about Cotton Mather. First, he came across several potentially useful titles at the end of the encyclopedia article on Cotton Mather. He then went to the card catalog to learn whether those titles were available in his library. Three books were available, two of which yielded information that helped support his eventual thesis. Furthermore, all three books contained bibliographies that led to other useful sources. From these sources, Fred was able to acquire a sizable working bibliography before he began a methodical search through the card catalog and periodical indexes.

Once he had followed up these early leads, Fred went back to the card catalog. He looked under subject headings that were related to his topic, such as "Mather, Cotton, 1663–1728" and "Puritans—Massachusetts—Biography." Next, he used several cross-reference cards to find other headings that were not so obvious, such as "Witchcraft" and "Witchcraft—New England." (This procedure differs slightly from the one used for catalog-on-line systems. Your instructor or librarian can explain how to go about this work.)

Fred rejected a number of items, such as Christina Larner's *Enemies of God: The Witch-hunt in Scotland*, because their titles indicated nothing that applied to the Salem witch trials. However, he made out bibliography cards for any title that seemed likely to prove useful. Later, when he examined each of these books closely, he eliminated most of them from his working bibliography because they turned out to be general overviews or surveys, much like those in textbooks, which repeated the same information about Mather and his relationship to the Salem witch trials.

Finally, Fred searched through several periodical indexes, looking under "Cotton Mather" and other relevant headings. Some titles clearly indicated little or no relationship to the witch trials, so Fred left them off his working bibliography. Others sounded vaguely useful, but these, too, Fred later rejected—either because they did not relate directly to his topic or because the information they provided had already been recorded in his notes. In the end, Fred used two periodical articles as sources. One was extremely valuable for its brief discussions and analyses of several theories attempting to explain the Salem witchcraft outbreak; the other provided information about an important subtopic in Fred's final paper.

Do not be misled by Fred's using just two periodical articles in his paper. His case is fairly unusual. Many papers, especially those dealing with topics in the sciences and the social sciences, list more articles than books as sources. For example, Anita Barrone's paper on the human life span incorporated information from seventeen popular and specialized periodicals.

The student who researched Emily Dickinson used the same basic strategies for gathering sources but with somewhat different results. Susanna's final bibliography lists several books about Dickinson's life and works, two periodical articles, an essay from a collection of literary criticism, two volumes of the poet's works, and a collection of the poet's letters. Along the way, she found and skimmed numerous other books and articles, but most of these contained analyses of Dickinson's poems, with no useful references to the poet's life.

The search for sources is a journey into the unknown that tests your imagination, perseverance, and ability to plan. Sometimes this search can be frustrating because many clues lead nowhere and seem to waste your time. But do not try to save time by hastily rejecting items whose titles do not indicate a clear and immediate relation to your topic. Ambiguous clues must always be followed up. The possible source that is discarded unseen may be the one that could have helped you the most.

REASSESSING YOUR TOPIC

While searching for sources, you may reach a point where you doubt the topic is workable, either because you are finding far too many potential sources or because you have found too few. If after several hours of intensive searching through various indexes as well as the card catalog, you have discovered only two or three *possible* sources, your topic needs to be broadened. On the other hand, if you quickly find dozens of potential sources, you need to reduce the scope of the topic and/or sharpen the focus of your hypothesis.

We hesitate to talk in terms of specific numbers because the number of sources does not directly indicate how much information you have collected. You might take a couple of pieces of information from just one or two paragraphs in one source, and then take more than a dozen lengthy notes from an entire chapter in another source. The crucial question is whether you have enough sources, for your research cannot be considered complete unless you provide a full range of points of view. For instance, Anita Barrone gave her readers an extensive survey of the current scientific attempts to extend human longevity as well as a fair sampling of those who, for various reasons, question the value of such research.

NARROWING A TOPIC THAT IS TOO BROAD

We saw how one student limited his subject—*Cotton Mather*—to a reasonable topic—*Mather's complicated role in the witch trials*—after a conference with his instructor and a background reading session in the library. Fred had some familiarity with his subject, which made it easy for him to take full advantage of the advice he received. However, another student, who knew relatively little about her subject—*abnormal psychology*—ran into trouble with her topic at a somewhat later step in the research.

Being curious about the many strange paths human behavior often takes, this student decided to concentrate on just one disorder, schizophrenia. It seemed reasonable to plan to discuss its cause and some of the therapies presently practiced in the effort to conquer this puzzling, distressing problem. During her preliminary research, she formed this hypothesis: "Since the exact cause of schizophrenia is not yet known, treatment is often difficult."

Her psychology textbook contained fewer than three pages on the topic, and an encyclopedia covered it in just one column. So the topic did not seem too broad. Only after the student had gotten fairly well into her search for sources did she realize that there were far more books and articles on schizophrenia than she could hope to read. The college library held more than a dozen books and hundreds of articles dealing directly with the causes and treatment of schizophrenia. What she believed to be a topic was actually a subject area, and a broad one at that. What should she do? Go back to the background sources, which had not clearly indicated the trouble she ran into? She checked with her instructor, who recommended that she look through her working bibliography to see if the titles might suggest some direction in which she could reasonably move. After all, why waste the time that had gone into the search for those sources?

The student noticed that several of the titles mentioned the *nature of schizophrenia*, others its *causes*, others its *effect on those living with schizophrenics*, and still others its *treatment*. She remembered from her background reading that doctors use several different methods of treatment because of uncertainty regarding the causes of the disorder. Although she was interested in the treatment of schizophrenia, she realized from looking at her working bibliography that this, too, was likely to prove too broad for her paper. So she reviewed her background reading notes and class lecture notes once more and decided to narrow her topic still further, to one kind of treatment. Her new topic became *treatment of schizophrenia in a community setting*. She also needed to form a new hypothesis and decided on "Treating schizophrenia in a community setting is a new idea that works."

In assembling a new working bibliography, the student began with titles from the old one. But something seemed wrong. She could not eliminate very many of the thirty titles in her working bibliography because any book on schizophrenia might refer to the type of treatment she was investigating. Clearly, her hypothesis needed to be revised again, this time to give it sharper focus. Reviewing those background notes that mentioned the new method of treatment, she realized that it was applied only to severe cases. And its proponents did not claim success in all cases, only better results than treatment in institutions. This led her to recast her hypothesis again: "Treating severe schizophrenia in a community setting has in some cases proven more successful than treatment in traditional institutions."

The sharper focus provided by the revised hypothesis saved the student from reading and taking notes on matters that were not directly related to her purposes, such as treatment outside of mental institutions (but not in community settings), the history of treating schizophrenia, or the treatment of mild forms of schizophrenia.

Let's compare the way the two hypotheses are worded. The first contains only two terms, other than "community setting," that give any focus to the topic—*new idea* and *works*. *New idea* refers to a minor point that can be made simply by giving the date of the first use of this method. *Works* gives some focus, but it is rather vague, lacking the sense of scientific validity carried by "has proven more successful." In contrast, the second hypothesis has four key terms—*severe, proven, successful,* and *traditional institutions*—that helped the student to search for sources and read them far more efficiently. The word *severe* warned her to skip over passages about milder forms of the disorder which do not force sufferers to be committed to mental hospitals. *Proven* kept her attention focused on the need to find specific evidence for or against her hypothesis. The term *successful* made her think about finding a valid basis for judging success—a difficult problem in this situation because schizophrenia is rarely, if ever, cured; the sufferer's symptoms only become less distressing. The student had to look closely to find the criteria used by her various sources in order to determine how much improvement could reasonably be considered "success." *Traditional institutions* reminded her that if she wanted to show that this method is successful, she had to compare it with well-established treatments, rather than with other experimental approaches.

REVISING A TOPIC THAT IS TOO NARROW

You may never find yourself in this position, for most newcomers to research tend to come up with topics that are too broad. And, if you remember the warning about topics that can be completely researched by reading just one source—*how bees communicate*, for example—then you are even less likely to err in the direction of "too narrow."

A student who had read an article on lions in *Natural History* found himself with no sources beyond that article except for two brief summaries of that article, one in the magazine *Newsweek* and another in the

New York Times. His topic was *the effect of the severe drought of 1973 on the rearing of lion cubs in the Serengeti Plains of East Africa*. The *Natural History* article provided all the necessary information; *Newsweek* and the *Times* merely reported the story by summarizing the original article, so they could NOT be considered "different" sources, for they did not present any new information or a different point of view.

Stuck, after a long but futile search, the student went back to the step he had previously cut short—background reading. He had done nothing more than read about lions in an encyclopedia article on African wildlife.

As the student read additional background studies, he thought about ways to expand his topic. These ideas passed through his mind: "The lions had trouble due to a drought; are there other more common problems they face as parents? Is there a *mild* drought every year? (The article had dealt with a particularly severe one.) Do they normally have trouble feeding themselves as well as their cubs? Who gets fed first, the parents or the cubs?" His new readings revealed that lions face famine every year in the Serengeti Plains because they do not follow the herds of antelope who migrate each winter to greener pastures.

The student now realized that he should broaden the problem from *the drought of 1973* to the *regular shortages of food* due to droughts and the disappearance of the antelopes. He also broadened his focus to include the adult lions as well as the cubs. Thus, he arrived at the topic, *the ways in which lions manage to survive periodic food shortages*. At this point the writer still could not see how to frame a hypothesis, so he deferred that step until he had gathered some sources. He had to hope to find some difference of opinion or at least different sets of data in the sources, or else he would once more be left with a topic that could be handled entirely through one source. After collecting more than a dozen titles of potential sources, he skimmed through them to see what they had to offer. (The next section of this chapter explains how to go about this important step.) Sure enough, other observers of lions clearly had not seen the same thing or had drawn different conclusions about what they saw, especially about the roles played in the hunt by males and females. A quick glance at the sources enabled the student to form a reasonable hypothesis: "In their effort to survive under sometimes difficult circumstances, the female lion plays a more aggressive and critical role than the so-called king of beasts."

Skimming Potential Sources

Once you have compiled what seems to be an adequate working bibliography, you are almost ready to begin reading the sources and taking notes. Before you undertake this challenging work, however, check to see if the sources provide enough ideas and information to allow you to do a thorough job of research. This is best done by skimming each source to gain a rough idea of what it says about your topic.

The purpose of skimming is to find out quickly whether a source is useful or not, and if it is, how much relevant information it contains. Skimming not only allows you to avoid a close reading of unhelpful sources, but it also gives you a chance to evaluate your hypothesis. A skimming of his sources told Fred Hutchins that his initial hypothesis needed expansion to include an account of Mather's complicated personality.

If skimming leads you to reduce your list of potential sources to fewer than five, go back and look for more sources. If you cannot find any, check with your instructor to see whether you should try to broaden your topic or continue with what you have. Your instructor's advice will depend largely upon how much information the remaining sources offer and how adequately they cover the variety of views that experts have expressed on your topic.

If skimming leaves you with a great many substantial sources, you may want to limit the topic or sharpen the focus of the hypothesis. Of course, several sources may offer much the same information and arrive at the same general judgment; in that case, you need read and take notes on only one of them, thereby reducing the overload of sources. It is not easy, especially when first undertaking research, to judge whether two or more sources duplicate themselves. The main points to keep in mind are that you do not want to miss any valuable information, and you do not want to leave out any of the various viewpoints on your topic.

SKIMMING BOOKS

Skimming a book begins with the table of contents and the index. The table of contents usually presents a broad outline of the book's organization. If the author discusses your particular topic, you may be able to find out from the chapter titles the extent of the discussion and the major points it raises. Briefer discussions within chapters can be found by using the index, which gives page numbers for all references to a topic, however brief they may be.

When you are using an index, take the time to check all the headings that might be relevant to your topic, not just the obvious ones. For example, if your topic were *reading problems of grade-school boys as opposed to those of grade-school girls* (in this age group boys with reading trouble outnumber girls by a ratio of four to one), you would naturally look in a book's index under *reading, grade-school,* and *boys.* Some references would probably be listed under *reading,* but the other two terms might not appear in the index. In that case, you could look under synonyms such as *elementary school* and *male*. Do not stop at synonyms, however. Think of different ways to approach the topic which might lead you to other, possibly more fruitful headings, such as *learning disabilities* or *disabilities, learning* and *sex as a factor in learning*.

Finally, if you have reason to believe that a particular book is important to your research, but you have trouble finding what you want, do not give up. Instead, skim through the index, searching for significant headings that may not have occurred to you.

When you locate pages that deal with your topic, skim the first line or two of each paragraph. In this way, you are likely to discover the author's main points, which are often stated in topic sentences. In addition, if the book has chapter summaries, read those that pertain to your topic.

SKIMMING PERIODICAL ARTICLES

Articles rarely come with outlines that might serve as tables of contents, but some of them include abstracts that summarize their theses and major supporting points. If a summary indicates that an article may be worth a close reading, you do not need to skim it. If, on the other hand, the summary does not mention material that is likely to help you, do not discard the source; skim it by reading the first line of every paragraph to pick up the main ideas. You should not abandon the source unless such a skimming uncovers nothing useful. Even then, do not throw away the bibliography card, for if you have to revise your topic, the source might become useful.

TAKING NOTES WHILE SKIMMING

When skimming a potential source, take brief notes that tell you how the source might prove useful, or why it is not useful. Place these notes on the backs of the bibliography cards.

In order to determine how useful a source may be, keep these questions in mind:

- Is this information relevant to my topic?
- How much useful information does it seem to offer?
- Does this source support or contradict my hypothesis?

You do not have to take detailed notes at this time. Simply indicate the possible value of the source.

Keep all the bibliography cards. Do not discard them even if the sources look unpromising. If you are later forced to change your topic slightly, these items may become quite valuable. You will not want to waste time looking up a source you had previously skimmed.

Evaluating Potential Sources

As you skim through potential sources, try to evaluate each one in terms of its possible usefulness to your research. Here are some important points to keep in mind.

DEPTH OF COVERAGE

Not every book or article that deals with your topic will contribute to your investigation. In general, any source that treats your topic in depth will be more valuable than one that treats it superficially. You are looking for sources that give you a clearer, fuller understanding of some aspect of your topic and thereby provide grounds for accepting, rejecting, or in some way modifying your hypothesis.

For example, most books covering the history of New England mention Cotton Mather, and a good number of them summarize his involvement in the Salem witch trials. The information and conclusions they provide are probably boiled down from other sources that pursued the topic in greater detail. It is these detailed studies that you want to read. Most of the more recent general histories can state with some justification that Mather was not a cruel, bloodthirsty persecutor of suspected witches; rather, his attitude toward the Salem witchcraft outbreak must be studied in the context of the times in which he lived, the traditions of his religion, and the somewhat erratic nature of his personality. Such a sweeping generalization may not necessarily be wrong. In a research paper, however, you are expected to go beyond mere generalization to find specific evidence, in this case, primary accounts and well-founded interpretations of what the Salem "witches" meant to Cotton Mather. Otherwise, neither you nor your readers will have a sound basis for deciding whether or not your judgment is well supported.

Variety of Viewpoints. While putting together your working bibliography, remember to include works that express various points of view. A paper that depends mainly on the opinions and interpretations of one writer might well be criticized for being one-sided. For example, look at this list of books dealing with the strategies of the two major military commanders who faced each other during the American Civil War. The topic of the paper is *Lee and Grant: the old vs. the new style of warfare.*

> **Hypothesis:** "The South's initial military success was due in large part to Robert E. Lee's mastery of the traditional theories of warfare, but the tide of battle turned when Lee was unable to cope with Ulysses S. Grant's new strategy of Total War."

Sources: 1. *Glory Road*, Bruce Catton
               2. *Grant Moves South*, Bruce Catton
               3. *Grant Takes Command*, Bruce Catton
               4. *Mr. Lincoln's Army*, Bruce Catton
               5. *The Civil War*, Bruce Catton
               6. *Robert E. Lee*, Douglas Freeman
               7. *Lincoln Finds a General*, K. P. Williams

This bibliography is so heavily weighted with Catton's works that his views are almost certain to dominate the paper. An experienced researcher would notice this imbalance and take steps to remedy the situation. Maybe some of Catton's books could be dropped if they largely repeated each other in regard to this topic. In any event, other historians' works must be found in order to support or oppose Catton's views.

One further question about "balance" comes to mind when looking over this list of titles. Isn't something wrong when four of the sources deal with Grant while just one focuses on Lee? After all, the topic suggests equal treatment of the two men.

The Problem of Obsolescence. Another important factor to keep in mind when evaluating sources is that some may be out-of-date. Especially in the natural and social sciences, knowledge is expanding so rapidly that theories, and even facts, are often revised or discarded within a year or two. Even history may be rewritten when new evidence comes to light or when a historian examines an old event from a new angle.

Therefore, if you investigate topics that involve current issues or the developments in a scientific field such as astronomy, you *absolutely must* find the latest possible sources. A book on astronomy, for instance, is partially out-of-date before it is published. This does not mean that most of what it says is inaccurate, but some of the facts and theories concern phenomena about which new, more powerful telescopes are yielding fresh information daily. Current social problems such as child abuse and issues such as nuclear deterrence also demand that you work with the most recently published sources. Since the information in books can never be totally up-to-date, you need to rely heavily upon periodical articles when researching these kinds of topics.

PRIMARY VERSUS SECONDARY SOURCES

Another kind of topic may send you back in time for many of your sources. For example, if you picked a topic involving the constitutional amendment that granted women the right to vote, you would probably want to find out what the general public as well as the leading social commentators thought about the issue in the years immediately before its passage in 1920. A recently written historical account of those years would get you started, but you might feel that the account missed something or even slightly distorted the picture of that historic crusade. Fortunately, you could check for yourself by reading some newspaper and periodical articles of that time which have been preserved in libraries, usually on microfilm.

The two sources we just mentioned are referred to as primary and secondary sources. *Primary sources* are those that *secondary sources* write about. The newspapers and magazines published at the time of the event are the sources used by later historians, whose writings then become secondary sources for your research. In literature, the term *primary* refers to the literary works themselves, while *secondary* refers to biographies and critical studies of the author's work.

If this kind of research sounds interesting, you should be aware that some very good topics focus on the way the literary works of now-famous authors were received when they were first published. For such research, you would use the *Book Review Digest* and a newspaper index. See pages 49–51 in chapter 3.

GUIDELINES FOR WORKING WITH PERIODICALS

In chapter 3, you learned that periodicals fall into two main classes—magazines, which are designed to be read by the general public, and journals, which are written for experts in particular fields. Each class poses distinct problems for research paper writers. The journals, because they are written for experts, are often very difficult to read unless you are familiar with the technical terminology and the special problems the experts are working on. On the other hand, magazines, because they are written for persons having a general educational background, usually avoid specialized terms and do not assume that readers possess an expert knowledge of the subject. The problem with magazines grows out of their effort to make complex ideas understandable. Simplifying sophisticated subjects often leads to some degree of distortion. Also, these magazines tend to leave out what could be important details from your point of view—complex examples, sophisticated theoretical explanations, and descriptions. What is true for this class of periodicals is even more likely to be true for newspapers.

You need to learn how to make the best use of both classes of periodicals if you hope to become a good research paper writer. Here are some guidelines that can help you handle the problems we just described.

If, like Anita Barrone, you were writing a paper for a science course, you would probably have to struggle with several journal articles. In that case, start your search for sources by looking through the *Readers' Guide* and a newspaper index. Magazine and newspaper accounts, which are usually very readable, will give you the general idea behind whatever recent discovery or theory your topic deals with. Then, when you move ahead to reading a journal article, you will be in a stronger position to cope with the technical vocabulary, and you will have become somewhat familiar with the subject.

If, however, your topic focuses on a current social problem, you may not have to resort to an academic journal. Social issues appeal to readers of varied interests, not just to experts in one field. For this reason, you can often find full discussions of an issue in newsstand magazines that are written for an educated but otherwise general audience. For example, the controversy over deployment of the neutron bomb, which destroys people but not buildings, can be understood without expert knowledge of how such a weapon is assembled or how a nuclear reaction takes place. Research into this topic would focus on sources that consider such matters as the bomb's value in the Cold War and the possible outcomes—social, environmental, and political—of its deployment. You don't have to be a nuclear physicist to understand the debate, so you might very well limit your search for periodicals to the *Readers' Guide* and a newspaper index. In any case, it is a good idea to ask your instructor what kinds of sources you will be expected to use, given your particular topic.

REVIEWING YOUR HYPOTHESIS

After skimming and evaluating the sources, review your notes to check the direction your hypothesis is taking. If you see that the sources do not fully support the hypothesis, make whatever modifications are needed to bring it into conformity with the sources. Do not plow straight ahead. Stop and consider what you have just learned through skimming. Revising the hypothesis will bring it into sharper focus and this will make the next step—reading the sources in depth—much easier.

Review Questions

1. What is a working bibliography? How does it differ from the final list of Works Cited?

2. Write out the information for the following sources as you would on a bibliography card:

   • a 1952 book published in New York by Harcourt, Brace, & World called A History of Western Philosophy and written by W. T. Jones.

- an article about the Japanese economy called How Japan Does It, written by Christopher Byron, published in Time magazine on March 30, 1981, and running from page 54 through page 60.
- an article in The Sixteenth Century Journal by N. M. Sutherland called Catherine de Medici: The Legend of the Wicked Italian Queen, running from page 45 through page 56 and published in volume 9 in 1978.

3. Briefly outline the different but related processes of skimming a book and skimming a periodical article.

4. Explain how you can tell whether a potential source is likely to be useful to you. Mention several specific criteria.

5. What signs might warn that a topic is probably too narrow? too broad? What steps can be taken to resolve both problems?

6. After you have found what seems to be an adequate *number* of sources, and you are *looking over the titles*, what should you be looking for if you are concerned that the list might not really be adequate?

Exercises

1. If you are presently working on a research project and have developed a topic and hypothesis, follow the suggestions in this chapter to put together a working bibliography and evaluate the potential sources by skimming them. Turn in your notes (annotated bibliography).

2. In a popular magazine of your choice, read an article about a topic of current interest, such as *new energy sources, genetic engineering, political problems in Central America,* or *space probes of distant planets.* Then, using an appropriate periodical index, find an article on the same topic in a professional journal, and read it. Write a paragraph or two contrasting the approaches used by the authors of the two articles.

3. Choose a nationally controversial topic, such as *the war on drugs, Medicaid payments for abortion, free agency in baseball, nuclear power plants, affirmative action programs,* or any important issue facing your area of the country. Find articles in two different periodicals (newspapers included) that take opposite sides on the issue. Write a summary that points out the major differences in their views and the general tone of each article.

5
Reading the Sources and Taking Notes

Taking good notes is not simply a matter of copying down as much information as you can, as fast as you can. You must be selective. Although you will surely end up with more information in your notes than will ultimately appear in your paper, you don't want to go too far in that direction. Yet you also want to be sure to record everything you will need when it's time to support whatever thesis your investigation leads to. For notes to be effective, then, it is essential to keep your hypothesis firmly in mind at all times.

Practical Aspects of Note-taking

When taking notes, you cannot know just how each piece of information will finally be used in the paper. One thing is certain, however: you will present your information in a different order from that in which you recorded it. Therefore, you will want a flexible method of note-taking that makes it easy to find the best possible arrangement of your information. We can offer two such methods, each having its own advantages.

PREFERRED METHOD

Use four-by-six-inch note cards, and record just one idea, or a small group of closely related facts, on each card. Write notes on only one side of each card, leaving the back free for bibliographic information. The main advantage of note cards is that you can spread the cards out on a table and rearrange them until you discover a satisfactory order. Another advantage is that the limited writing space available on a card will encourage you to avoid taking longer notes than you need.

ALTERNATE METHOD

If you still feel more comfortable using a notebook, perhaps because you are worried that a card is too easy to lose, write on just one side of each page and leave a fair amount of space between notes. This will allow you to cut each page into separate notes when you are ready to organize your paper.

Whatever method you use, be a big spender. Do not try to squeeze as many notes as possible into the space available. The satisfaction gained from being thrifty cannot compensate for the frustration of trying to untangle a tightly bunched, loosely connected set of facts and ideas.

ENTERING INFORMATION ON CARDS

We feel it is important to develop a single format for putting information on cards and then to follow it consistently. Later you will want to thumb through the stack of cards looking for a particular piece of information or looking simply to see if there's an appropriate piece of information that fits in with whatever you are doing at the moment. In either case, you want to know at a glance if a card has what you want. Using a set format makes this easy.

1. On the back side of each card, identify the author and title of the source, and be sure to add the numbers of the page or pages from which you are taking the information. We need to stress this seemingly minor point. If you forget to take down this information, you could lose hours retracing your steps.

2. Use only the front side when recording information. Don't be tempted to save a penny by finishing up on the back, for you may miss that piece of information when reviewing your notes.

3. Leave lots of white space to make it easier to review your notes. Main points should easily catch your eye. Minor points should be clearly subordinate to the major ideas they support, so you should use numbers more often than you normally do. Underline *major ideas*. Capitalize KEY WORDS. Use numbers or letters to indicate (1) subordination, (2) sequence. (See Figures 5–1 and 5–2.)

4. Think ahead to the organization of the paper and try to come up with a few likely subtopics. For example, the Cotton Mather topic

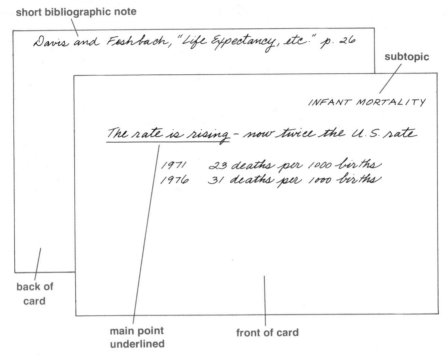

Figure 5–1. Front and back of a note card

might be broken down into: *involvement in Salem witch trials, religious beliefs, attitudes toward witches, complex personality.* The appropriate subtopic should be written in pencil at the top of each card, using more than one subtopic if a note refers to more than one. Most of the time, you will discover some subtopics while reading the sources. As soon as you see one emerging, start using it. Then, when you take a break from reading, go over the previous cards adding the new subtopic where it fits. Reviewing your earlier notes from time to time can also prove very helpful in keeping the scope of your project clearly in mind.

The Fine Art of Note-taking

As we have said, effective note-taking consists of more than copying relevant passages out of your sources. In fact, the more direct copying you do, the less useful your notes are likely to be. Here is why.

Note-taking for a research paper has three fundamental objectives:

- to record the general ideas that will form the backbone of your research paper,

- to record specific pieces of information that support the general ideas, and
- to preserve the exact wording of some statements in your sources that you may want to quote directly in the paper.

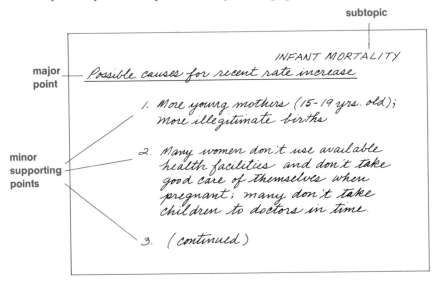

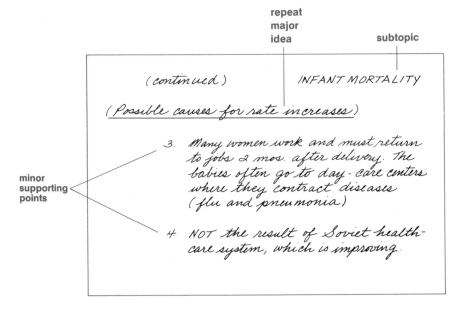

Figure 5–2. A series of notes continued on a second card
Note: Author, title, and page numbers appear on backs of *both* cards in case one becomes mislaid.

Many students waste time copying down long passages, even whole pages, word for word, because they believe, wrongly, that research papers must contain a large number of quotations. This is just not so. In fact, the opposite is true. For most research assignments, you should restrict the use of direct quotation to at most 20 percent of the paper. (This limit does not apply to literature topics for which you must quote from the literary works you are discussing as well as from secondary sources.) For some topics, especially in the natural sciences, excellent papers can be produced without using any direct quotations at all.

One important reason for limiting the amount of direct quotation is that by stating most of the ideas and information in the paper in your own words, you show your readers that you understand what you are talking about. Furthermore, the quotes will come from a wide variety of sources, each written in a distinctive style. Therefore, expressing the ideas in your own style, using consistent vocabulary and sentence patterns, will make it much easier for someone to read the paper. Finally, producing a convincing paper from a collection of quotations is almost impossible. Even though it might seem easier to quote than to paraphrase and summarize, the resulting ''paper'' would amount to a confusing, loosely related set of statements. Actually, it is easier to express most of the ideas and information in your own words than to try to piece dozens of quotations together into a smoothly flowing, coherent essay.

Paraphrasing

To paraphrase is to express another person's idea in your own words. The value of paraphrasing goes far beyond meeting the requirement that you find your own way of saying what you have found in your sources. For one thing, a good paraphrase usually takes fewer words than the original to convey the essential meaning. Even more important is the increased understanding that comes from trying to paraphrase what you are reading. Psychological experiments have shown that putting a difficult idea into your own words makes a stronger impression on your memory than merely copying the idea word for word. In fact, if you have trouble restating an idea, you probably do not thoroughly understand it. In general, therefore, paraphrase any ideas that go into your notes unless there is a good reason for quoting the exact words in the source. (Several common situations that call for quotation are discussed on pages 86–88.)

The following examples reveal two benefits to be gained from paraphrasing: brevity and clarity.

original	Will reputable scientists ever accept the claim that extrasensory perception and other "paranormal powers" really exist? It appears that many of them have.
paraphrase	Many scientists today believe in the reality of ESP and other paranormal powers.

The idea of "reputable" is not needed in your note; you know that you are looking only for real scientists—not those who simply call themselves scientists, as do some who work with ESP.

original	Contrary to popular belief, exercise has never been shown conclusively to prolong life.
paraphrase	No one has ever proved that exercise lengthens life.
poor paraphrase: too close to the original	Contrary to popular thinking, exercise has never been demonstrated conclusively to lengthen life.

There's no need to record "contrary to popular belief" if that is not the point you are interested in. Being careful to exclude unnecessary information from your paraphrase will help you avoid the sort of "partial paraphrase" that can slip into plagiarism, a serious problem discussed at length on pages 102–107.

original	Olfactory receptors for communication between different creatures are crucial for establishment of symbiotic relations.
two reasonable paraphrases	The sense of smell is essential to cooperation among different animal species. Cooperation between different animal species is made possible by their sense of smell.

The original, which comes from a biology journal, shows how difficult such periodicals can be. Obviously, the notetaker had already learned some of the specialized vocabulary of the field or had looked up the meanings of the technical terms. Notice that either paraphrase would be much easier to understand than the original when reviewing notes and organizing information into an essay.

Summarizing

A summary greatly reduces the length of what you have read, which might be anything from a long paragraph to an entire magazine article. Writing effective summaries requires good judgment, for you must decide what can be left out of your notes without losing or distorting the basic idea.

If you are working on a single paragraph, you may find that it contains a clearly stated topic sentence aptly supported by several details. In that case, you can simply paraphrase the main idea and then decide whether you need to note briefly any of the details, either for use in your paper or to reinforce your understanding of the main idea. In the following example, the main idea is stated in the first sentence, as is the case in much professional writing.

original

Zoologists define *species* as a category of animals whose members are capable of mating and producing offspring which are also able to reproduce. Thus, dogs constitute a species because even males and females of the most dissimilar breeds can produce mongrels that can, in turn, reproduce. However, the mating of a horse and a donkey, though the two are more similar in appearance than, let us say, a poodle and a boxer, yields a mule, which is always sterile. Thus, they are placed in separate species. A lion and a tiger, though of different species, can produce a ''liger'' or a ''tiglon,'' which in very rare cases may be fertile. This exception betrays a slight weakness in our definition of the term *species*.

summary note card

> *Species*
>
> Definition of species — mating
>
> Two animals are said to belong to the same species if they can produce fertile offspring.
>
> Ex: poodle + boxer but not
> horse + donkey (mule is sterile)

Whether or not you should include details in your note depends on your hypothesis. If your use for this source goes no further than the definition of *species,* you probably do not need the parenthetical examples. If you intend to develop the concept of *species* in your paper, you may need them. The example of the "liger" and the "tiglon" would be needed only if you planned to discuss the fact that a scientific term can be less precise than most of us believe.

Often your summary of a paragraph will consist of a general idea that you have derived from several details in the paragraph which directly relate to your hypothesis. Assume when reading the next example that you are gathering information related to the hypothesis, "Most scientists now believe that life probably exists on planets circling other stars in the universe."

original

> The sun is accompanied on its journey through space by a retinue of nine planets, thirty-two natural satellites revolving around the planets, hundreds of comets and thousands of asteroids. Do other stars have similar arrays of companions? At present there is no direct way of telling, because if such a collection of bodies were associated with a nearby star, the most powerful telescopes on the earth could not detect them. The feeble light reflected from the companions would be lost in the brilliant glare of the central star.

Helmut A. Abt, "The Companions of Sun-like Stars"
Sci. Amer., April 1977

LIFE-SUPPORTING PLANETS

Do systems like our solar system exist?

Other stars may have planets, but the strongest telescopes can't pick them out because of the brightness of the stars.

**summary
note card**

The background information at the beginning of the original paragraph has been left out of the summary because you do not need it to understand the main idea—that even if other stars have planets on which life might exist, these planets cannot be seen by our telescopes. This example illustrates another way to keep your notes brief. If some of the background information had been new to you, you might have been tempted to add it to your notes, just because it was unfamiliar. Doing so would not have helped you when you came to write your paper. Use your hypothesis to guide you in deciding whether such information is truly relevant to your purposes.

Quoting

Once you accept the principle that you should paraphrase or summarize most of the ideas that go into your notes, you will be better able to judge when quotation can be both appropriate and effective. There are four common reasons for quoting from your sources—*conciseness, accuracy, memorable language*, and *authority*.

Sometimes your best efforts at paraphrasing will produce a version that is either longer and clumsier than the original or else somewhat inaccurate. In either case, you should quote all or part of the original statement. On other occasions, a source may express an idea so brilliantly that you want to preserve its beauty and power. Finally, you may want to support an idea or one of your conclusions by quoting a key statement or two from an established authority on the subject. None of these reasons for quoting is, however, an excuse for avoiding the effort necessary to create a successful paraphrase. You must learn to recognize those special times when these reasons are likely to be valid.

Examples of four situations in which direct quotation is desirable are presented here, along with some further advice on when to quote rather than paraphrase or summarize. The examples consist of note cards and of excerpts from research papers that show how the quotations were eventually put to use.

Conciseness: *You find that you cannot paraphrase an idea without using many more words than the source.*

A common instance of this occurs when you decide to introduce a specialized term into your paper. You think it should be defined, but your attempts to paraphrase a definition are long and awkward. In that case, you should quote at least part of the definition from the source.

excerpt from paper   Noam Chomsky can be considered a reductionist--
someone who believes that "all complex phenomena
are ultimately explained and understood by
analyzing them into increasingly simpler and
supposedly more elementary components" (Pronko
497).

Works Cited entry   Pronko, N. H. <u>Panorama of Psychology.</u> Belmont, CA: Wadsworth, 1969.

(The note refers to the source of the definition, a textbook that the student used solely for the definition and not for any information related to Professor Chomsky. That textbook, however, must be included in the list of Works Cited for the research paper, and the student therefore made out a bibliography card for the source as well as a note card for the quotation.)

Accuracy: *You find that you cannot effectively paraphrase an idea without distorting the author's meaning.*

If, for example, a writer said that ''virtually all women have experienced fantasies in which they were born as men,'' any paraphrase is likely to be more or less inaccurate.

questionable
paraphrases

Most women wish they were men.

The majority of women have dreamed that they were men.

Almost every woman has a dream or daydream in which she had been born a male.

The first paraphrase grossly distorts the meaning; the second comes closer, but is not entirely accurate; the third is accurate but longer than the original. In such cases, you would do much better to quote the source and let your readers draw their own conclusions. Then, they can compare their interpretations with those you put forth in your paper.

Memorable language: *You believe that the words or ideas expressed by your source are so vivid or powerful that the meaning cannot be captured in a paraphrase.*

Restrain yourself in this matter; beware of quoting someone merely because you feel you cannot say it so well. An example of brilliant language that cries out for quotation comes from a speech by Winston Churchill, in which he refers to the behavior of Russia as ''a riddle wrapped in a mystery inside an enigma.''

In the same vein, you should quote famous remarks whether or not the word choice is brilliant or difficult to paraphrase. President Harry Truman once advised timid politicians, "If you can't stand the heat, get out of the kitchen."

Finally, you may come across a remark which is so startling that your readers deserve to see the original. The outstanding biologist J. H. S. Haldane described Albert Einstein as "the greatest Jew since Jesus." Such a striking comment would surely lose a great deal if paraphrased.

Authority: *You want to support a conclusion you have reached in your research by quoting the words of an expert on the subject.*

The authors of many of your sources are probably experts on their subjects, at least in the sense that their ideas have been thought authoritative enough to be published. Still, you need to be a little selective in this regard. Choose those writers whose credentials are known. A reporter for *Newsweek* or the *Washington Post* is an expert only on journalism, though he or she may be well informed on the topic you are dealing with. A person referred to in your other sources (or in a biographical sketch accompanying her article in *Scientific American*) as "a leading gerontologist" can be treated as an expert in the study of aging. In general, however, even experts should be quoted only when their words are more concise, accurate, or memorable than any paraphrase or summary you can make.

At any rate, remember that you cannot rely entirely upon expert opinion, whether quoted or paraphrased. You must also work to support your conclusions with hard facts and clear reasoning.

QUOTING OUT OF CONTEXT

Since you are always quoting just a small part of any source, you must take great care to see that everything *which you did not quote* agrees with the idea which you did quote. This principle applies to paraphrasing as well, of course. The next example shows how someone could read a passage hastily and then produce a serious misrepresentation of its author's meaning.

student's source   It is currently very fashionable among popular social critics to blame television for the recent widespread increase in juvenile crime statistics. The argument usually pursues this line of reasoning: Many parents today neglect their children by allowing them complete freedom in watching TV. The shows these children choose to watch often present violence in an attractive form, and some have even gone so far as to depict clever ways of committing crimes. Many of these children later re-enact the violent acts they have witnessed on TV in order to recapture the thrills.

I contend, however, that this widely accepted explanation of a serious social problem is too simplistic. . . .

Anyone who read that passage and then produced the following quotation would be grossly distorting the author's meaning.

quotation out of context

Sociologist Jane Doe joins those persons who denounce violence on TV as the primary cause of the sharp increase in the number of crimes committed by young people: "Many . . . children later re-enact the violent acts they have witnessed on TV in order to recapture the thrills" (41).

Apparently, the student missed the signal that tells the reader that the writer disagrees with the points listed. ("It is currently very fashionable among popular social critics . . ." carries a mocking tone.) Then, the student completely ignored the clear-cut assertion that opens the next paragraph: "I contend, however, that this . . . is too simplistic."

BLENDING QUOTATION WITH PARAPHRASE

The most effective way to avoid quoting too many words is to combine quotation with paraphrase. A good guideline says to quote only that part of a passage that relates directly to your hypothesis. Below, you can read the context surrounding Churchill's famous remark about Russia, and you will see the advantage of quoting just the most pertinent part of a source. Churchill was attempting to alleviate Britain's fears that Russia might not enter the war against Nazi Germany. Part of that speech is presented here, along with a note card showing how quotation can be blended with paraphrase or summary. (The student's hypothesis was, "Before and during World War II, Churchill demonstrated a clear understanding of other nations and the ways their leaders thought.")

original speech by Churchill

I cannot forecast to you the action of Russia. It is a riddle wrapped in a mystery inside an enigma; but perhaps there is a key. That key is Russian national interest. It cannot be in accordance with the interest or safety of Russia that Germany should plant itself upon the shores of the Black Sea, or that it should overrun the Balkan states and subjugate the Slavonic peoples of Southeastern Europe. That would be contrary to the historic life interests of Russia.

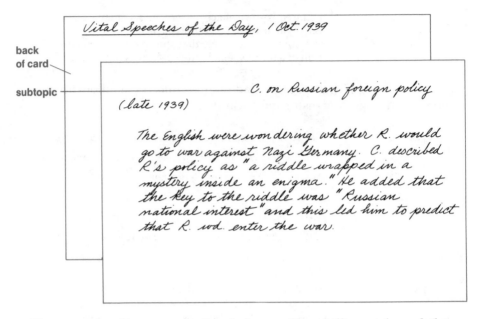

back of card

subtopic

Vital Speeches of the Day, 1 Oct. 1939

C. on Russian foreign policy
(late 1939)

The English were wondering whether R. would go to war against Nazi Germany. C. described R.'s policy as "a riddle wrapped in a mystery inside an enigma." He added that the key to the riddle was "Russian national interest" and this led him to predict that R. wd. enter the war.

The note supplies a connection between Churchill's words and the student's hypothesis—that when others were confused (in this case, about Russia), Churchill's intuition or plain old political savvy led him to the truth. The note shows this point better than a lengthy quotation from the speech.

ENTERING QUOTATIONS ONTO NOTE CARDS

When writing a note, you must be extremely precise in placing the quotation marks and absolutely accurate in recording the author's words. This need for accuracy when quoting can be better understood if we examine some problems that can occur when reviewing notes in preparation for writing the paper.

Problem 1   Since quotation marks are small, they can be overlooked when you are transferring information from your notes to your paper. To avoid missing a quotation mark or two, use very heavy strokes or even the marks « and » (guillemets). This will insure against your confusing quotations with paraphrases.

Problem 2   If a note summarizing several pages of a source includes a quotation, you must record the page number where the quotation appeared, as well as the page numbers of the full passage being summarized. Be sure to record the page number of each direct quotation.

back
of card

page numbers
of section being
summarized

Herman Arthur, "To Err Is Huperson; to Forgive, Divine," Amer. Educator, Winter 1980, pp. 30-32.

SEXISM

Correcting sexism in language

In getting rid of sexism, teachers must avoid awkward and ugly constructions such as he/she. « *Like badly tattered fig leaves, they call attention to what they are trying to conceal.* » (30).

Three suggestions (1) Do away with most feminine suffixes, such as -ess and -ette; (2) Provide substitutes for man and woman suffixes, ex: mail deliverer instead of mailman; (3) Avoid he/she and him/her constructions by using it when sex is not specified.

summary with
direct quotation
clearly marked

page number
of quotation

Problem 3

Sometimes, you will want to leave some words out of the middle of a quotation because they are not relevant to your purpose. A reader is entitled to know about such an omission, so you must use an *ellipsis*, which consists of three dots in place of the omitted words. The example on page 92 shows a quotation that was shortened by ellipsis. (The passage also demonstrates a smooth blend of quotation and paraphrase.)

student's source

Literature is slow to register its own historical moment. Only in the past few years has a literature announcing the end of the 1960s emerged. It isn't generally a literature *about* that decade; apart from the novels of Marge Piercy and a few scenes in Mary Gordon's *The Company of Women*, there isn't much description of the tableaux that represent the sixties: rock concerts, riots, campus demonstrations. Purposeful collective acts have given way to private anomie. The predominant mood in the novels and stories of Jayne Anne Phillips, Richard Ford, Mary Robison, Ann Beattie, and Raymond Carver—to mention five younger writers who have begun to command an audience—is indifference, depression, even criminality. Such is fiction's bleak requiem for that turbulent era.

omitted words

excerpt from student's
paper

The critic James Atlas believes that "a
literature announcing the end of the 1960s" has
only come into being as we move into the 1980s, and
it does not present those public events that
marked "that turbulent era," such as student
demonstrations against the war, riots in the inner
cities, and rock concerts. "Purposeful
collective acts have given way to private anomie.

ellipsis

The predominant mood . . . is indifference,
depression, even criminality" (96).

Works Cited entry

Atlas, James. "Less to Less." Atlantic Monthly
June 1981: 96-98.

The two partial quotations give readers the maximum chance to understand Atlas's points. The only word Atlas used to describe the 1960s was "turbulent." With so little else to go on, the student decided not to risk distorting the meaning by looking for a synonym for that word. The other partial quotation describes a theme of recent literature, represented metaphorically—we doubt these novelists actually said, "the 1960s are over!" The "end of the 1960s" refers to the end of a way of thinking about life and its problems. Conciseness and accuracy were the motives for quoting Atlas's major point.

Notice that you must leave spaces around the dots of an ellipsis. Also, occasionally, the ellipsis will fall at the end of your own sentence. When that happens, you must add a fourth dot, which is really the period that ends *your* sentence.

Problem 4

One last problem occurs when you want to quote a remark that was quoted by your source. The possible danger here is that when you review your notes you might become confused. You must clearly indicate whether the quotation marks enclosed your source's words or those of the person your source was quoting. Devise a format that leaves no doubt in your mind when you review the notes. We believe the easiest solution is to add a parenthetical note on your card if there is any chance of mistake.

student's source

Of all the Concord circle, Emerson was perhaps the most widely read in science. He was familiar with Sir Charles Lyell's work in geology and was well aware that Christian chronology had become a mere "kitchen clock" compared with the vast time depths the earth sciences were beginning to reveal. "What terrible questions we are learning to ask," brooded the man sometimes accused of walking with his head in the clouds. He saw us as already divesting ourselves of the theism of our fathers.

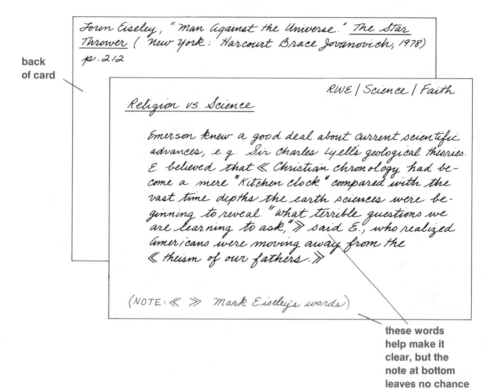

back of card

Loren Eiseley, "Man against the Universe." *The Star Thrower* (New York: Harcourt Brace Jovanovich, 1978) p. 212

RWE / Science / Faith

Religion vs. Science

Emerson knew a good deal about current scientific advances, e.g. Sir Charles Lyell's geological theories. E. believed that « Christian chronology had become a mere "kitchen clock" compared with the vast time depths the earth sciences were beginning to reveal. "What terrible questions we are learning to ask," » said E., who realized Americans were moving away from the « theism of our fathers. »

(NOTE: « » mark Eiseley's words)

these words help make it clear, but the note at bottom leaves no chance for error

An Extended Example of Effective Note-taking

To illustrate the process of note-taking, an article that served as a source for a paper on ESP follows. Accompanying the article is a full set of note cards derived from it. First, notice how the student's hypothesis limits the amount of information that has to be recorded. Also note the student's reasoning for deciding what to quote, paraphrase, or summarize.

Student's hypothesis: "Modern scientific techniques are being used to investigate ESP, and the results have convinced some leading scientists that parapsychology is a valid field of study."

Note: As mentioned in chapter 2, ESP is one of those subjects, like UFOs and the "Bermuda Triangle," which must be handled with great caution. Far too much of the writing in these areas consists of personal, *unverified* accounts. These cannot be taken as *proof* of any kind, and are *evidence* only of what some people are claiming, for a variety of reasons. This student stuck to verifiable materials, the work of professional scientists, trying to discover validity in some areas of ESP.

Arguing the Existence of ESP

By MALCOLM W. BROWNE

Browne's thesis takes the form of a question and its answer. The research that went into this article may have grown out of that question.

This is a restatement of the thesis, so no note is needed.

WILL reputable scientists ever accept the claim that extrasensory perception and other "paranormal powers" really exist?

It appears that many of them already have.

Not only do some of the world's most honored scientists believe in parapsychology, but a newly published survey suggests that a majority of American scientists accept at least the possibility that extrasensory perception really exists.

This states the controversy; no note needed.

A rash of new parapsychology experiments drawing ideas from the physics of atomic particles has rekindled an old controversy over whether parapsychology is a legitimate science or merely a pseudoscience created by charlatans to snare the naïve.

Results Are Reported

We are coming closer to specific details, but we can wait until the writer goes into them more precisely.

Some experimenters claim that the natural process of radioactive decay can be influenced by mental concentration, and that results of their latest work demonstrate the contention. Other experiments purport to show that mind power alone can change the temperature of supersensitive thermometers and the separation between objects. Some respected scientists have turned to meditation as a means of seeking truth.

Various laboratories have sought to either confirm or debunk the legitimacy of parapsychology since the controversial 1930s experiments by Dr. Joseph Banks Rhine of Duke University. Dr. Rhine had his subjects try to use supposed paranormal powers to "see" the designs on special cards concealed from them.

His results proved, he contended, that extrasensory perception permits subjects to pick the right cards significantly more often than chance alone would allow.

Conclusions Challenged

Other scientists challenged this conclusion, noting that Dr. Rhine and other parapsychologists routinely reject data from subjects who are not performing well. If all the data from extrasensory perception tests were preserved and reckoned into the statistics, critics say, the statistics would show a result no better than pure chance.

The parapsychologists have argued that paranormal abilities cannot be turned on or off like laboratory apparatus, and that it is fair to discard results from subjects who are not "on."

The dispute over this key question has never been resolved, and belief in parapsychology, like religion, remains a matter of faith. Despite that, belief by scientists in psychic phenomena seems to be far more widespread than many had suspected.

Dr. Mahlon Wagner, a psychologist at the Oswego campus of the State University of New York, recently published in the journal Zetetic Scholar the results of a poll he conducted. The journal, whose name is derived from the Greek word for skeptic, publishes scholarly papers, most of which attack claims of paranormal phenomena.

Dr. Wagner sent questionnaires to 2,100 professors at colleges and universities throughout the country, and received 1,188 responses. Of the natural scientists who responded, he said, 9 percent said they accepted extrasensory perception as

---

No note should be recorded. This information is interesting, but it is not directly related to the student's hypothesis.

No note is needed. The sentence merely restates the article's thesis.

See note cards 1 and 2.

This journal seems objective; that is the kind of evidence you are looking for.

The hypothesis points directly to such scientists and their views.

note
card 1

poll of scientists   re: ESP

poll sent to 2,100 professors across country
                1,188 answered

of the « natural scientists » who answered—

9% « accepted extrasensory perception as
    an "established fact" »
45% « described ESP as a "likely
    possibility." »

note
card 2

poll of scientists re: ESP

poll conducted by Dr. Mahlon Wagner, psychologist
      State Univ. of N.Y., Oswego

published in Zetetic Scholar, journal that
    often attacks claims of ESP.

Wagner: « "I used to be a total skeptic…
but I've become a little more accepting
because there are good, honest scholars
in the field." »
                ↳ (of parapsychology)
        (continued)

note
card 3

Scientists researching in parapsych.

1. Dr. Robert G. Jahn, dean of engineering
   and applied science at Princeton
   — can mental powers change a thermometer
   reading or the distance between objects?

2. Dr. Peter F. Phillips, physicist, Washington
   Univ. (St. Louis)
   received grant of $500,000 for « psychic
   research » from McDonnell Douglas
   Corp. foundation.

an "established fact," and 45 percent described ESP as "a likely possibility."

How does Dr. Wagner himself feel about his results?

"I used to be a total skeptic," he said, speaking of parapsychology, "but I've become a little more accepting because there are good, honest scholars in the field."

See note card 3.

Hypothesis focuses on modern scientific techniques, so this is valuable.

Research in parapsychology has been spurred by a number of recent financial grants.

Backed by private donors, Dr. Robert G. Jahn, dean of engineering and applied science at Princeton University, has undertaken a psychic research program based on some experiments that suggested mind power might change a thermometer reading or the distance between two objects.

Another physicist, Dr. Peter F. Phillips of Washington University in St. Louis, was awarded a $500,000 grant several months ago for psychic research. The grant, one of the largest ever made for psychic research, was from a foundation established by the McDonnell Douglas Corporation.

No note is needed. The information is interesting but not relevant to the student's hypothesis.

There have been hints that American intelligence organizations have experimented with ESP, and Soviet security officials interrogated and expelled an American news correspondent for allegedly receiving a secret research report on parapsychology.

See note card 4.

Once more we learn what tough-minded scientists are thinking.

At the annual meeting of the prestigious American Physical Society last year, a special session on parapsychology was held for the first time, and although most of those attending were deeply skeptical, some 500 scientists listened attentively to such parapsychologists as Helmut Schmidt of the Mind Science Foundation of San Antonio, Tex., an institution maintained by grants from William Thomas Slick Jr., a Texas oil magnate.

See note card 5.

More modern techniques.

Dr. Schmidt, a physicist by training, uses devices called random-number generators in his experiments. These machines are actuated by the random quantum-mechanical process of radioactive decay, producing a continuous series of numbers.

note
card 4

recognition of parasych. by
scientific world

American Physical Society

1979 annual meeting held special session
on parapsychology, though most
attending were skeptical.

Dr. Helmut Schmidt described his
experiments with ESP.

see Schmidt cards

note
card 5

Radioactive decay experiments
SCHMIDT

S. built machine in which radioactivity
randomly turns on lights, one at a
time. Lights are arranged in a circle.

« Subjects are asked to try to influence
the direction in which the lights
come on. »
Results —
« Significant correlation between subjects'
mental efforts and the observed
results. »

note
card 6

radioactive decay experiments
SCHMIDT

Criticism of Schmidt's conclusions

Paul Horowitz, physicist, Chairman of the
Amer. Physical Soc. parapsych. session —

Schmidt « probably wrong » but
H. believes that scientists should continue to investigate parapsych.

Describing his experiments in an interview, Dr. Schmidt said one of his machines has a ring of lights arranged like a clock dial, and the radioactive process randomly illuminates one of these lights at a time. Subjects are asked to try to influence the direction in which the lights come on. The results, he asserted, demonstrated a significant correlation between his subjects' mental efforts and the observed results.

See note card 6.

More modern techniques.

In another type of experiment, Dr. Schmidt said he gave subjects the same instructions, but unknown to them, the machine had already produced its random series of numbers the previous day. Electronic recordings had been made of the numbers and stored in a safe without being examined. Copies made from them were then played for the subjects, who believed they were watching the machine in action rather than a mere recording.

Again, Dr. Schmidt said, there was correlation between their mental efforts and the results, even though the results had been obtained beforehand. "The implication seems to be that the effect can work backward in time," he said, "and that is an outrageous idea from a conventional standpoint. But it may be that some quantum effects not yet understood could account for just such an outcome."

See note card 7.

Though this tough-minded scientist runs counter to hypothesis, you need his views to balance your research.

The chairman of the parapsychology session, Paul Horowitz of Cambridge, Mass., a physicist, asserted that Dr. Schmidt was "probably wrong." "But it's important that the investigation of parapsychology be kept within the structure of science where it can be examined critically," he said.

Some scientists are outraged by such thinking.

See note card 8.

This enemy of the believers causes you to realize that only "some" leading scientists believe there is something to be said for ESP.

Among them is John A. Wheeler, an American physicist specializing in the theory of gravitational collapse and "black holes."

Contending that parapsychology is a "pretentious pseudoscience," he has sought for the past year to have the Parapsychological Association, based in Alexandria, Va., deprived of its status as

note card 7

Radioactive decay experiments
SCHMIDT

Variation on experiment

Machine lit lights _before_ the people were asked to use their ES power, but people weren't told about it.

Results —
Same as on first test. Schmidt says this seems to show that ES power can work «"backward in time, and that is an outrageous idea from a conventional standpoint."» May be due to some «quantum effects» scientists don't understand.

note card 8

Scientists attack ESP

John A. Wheeler, physicist working on black hole theory

parapsych is a «"pretentious pseudoscience"» when its experiments are examined by rigorous scientific methods. They «prove nothing.»

Wheeler wd. like Parapsych. Assn. to lose status as Amer. Assn. for the Advancement of Science affiliate.

note card 9

Scientists attack ESP

John G. Taylor, mathematician at King's Coll., London, once believed but now does not. 1975 book, _Superminds_, supported parapsych.

T. had been convinced that Uri Geller, Israeli psychic, could bend spoons and move objects solely by mental power.

After Geller's tricks were exposed, Dr. Taylor wrote two papers recanting his earlier position.

See note card 9.

This case is especially relevant and interesting because he became a believer, then went back to his original skepticism.

See note cards 10 and 11.

Here are bona fide believers among the leading scientists.

No note is needed since scientists are expected to think rigorously.

an affiliate of the American Association for the Advancement of Science.

Dr. Wheeler and other scientific critics of parapsychology maintain that when results from psychic experiments are scrutinized according to accepted scientific and statistical tests they turn out to prove nothing.

Despite such objections, scientists are as often duped by charlatans and hoaxsters as are nonscientists, skeptics assert.

A case in point, they say, is that of John G. Taylor, a distinguished mathematician at King's College, London, who wrote a popular book in 1975 called "Superminds." The book, which was essentially a testimonial for parapsychology, recounted how Dr. Taylor had become convinced by the demonstrations of a self-styled psychic from Israel named Uri Geller. Mr. Geller claimed to be able to bend spoons, transport objects through the air and perform many other tricks by mental power alone.

Later, when Mr. Geller's feats were revealed as mere tricks of stagecraft, Dr. Taylor published two papers in the scientific journal Nature, recanting his earlier endorsement.

But many similar cases over the years have failed to shake the convictions of a number of distinguished scientists, including two giants of physics, Sir William Crookes and Wolfgang Pauli.

Dr. Brian Josephson, a 40-year-old British scientist who was awarded the Nobel physics prize in 1973, has increasingly turned toward parapsychology during the past 10 years in his research at Cavendish Laboratory, Cambridge University, England. (The latter institution awarded its first doctorate in parapsychology last year.)

In a telephone interview, Dr. Josephson said he was "99 percent convinced" of the reality of the paranormal effects, notably "remote viewing" and mental metal bending.

Dr. Josephson's mastery of quantum mechanics and other hard physical principles led him to discovery of the Josephson effect, by which electrical conductivity in an ultra-cold environment can be switched on or off with a mag-

note
card 10

> *Scientists support ESP*
>
> *Sir William Crookes*
> *Wolfgang Pauli*
>
> 《 *giants of physics* 》
>
> *Still believe in spite of numerous exposures of psychics like Uri Geller.*

note
card 11

> *Scientists support ESP*
> JOSEPHSON
> *Brian Josephson — Nobel prize in physics, 1973*
> *Cambridge Univ.*
>
> 《 *has increasingly turned toward parapsych. during the past 10 years in his research.* 》
>
> *is* 《 *"99% convinced"* 》 *that* 《 *"remote viewing"* 》 *and* 《 *metal bending* 》 *are real.*

note
card 12

> *Scientists support ESP*
> JOSEPHSON
> 《 *"to some extent . . . parapsych. lies within the bounds of physical law."* 》
> 《 *"but physical law itself may have to be re-defined . . . It may be that some effects in parapsych. are ordered-state effects of a kind not yet encompassed by physical theory."* 》
>
> *In this sense, the study of parapsych. is similar to the study of intelligence and consciousness.*

See note card 12.

Here you get a carefully measured acceptance of the belief without acceptance of many ESPers' specific claims.

netic field. Super computers of the coming decade are expected to be based on it. Is the rigorous technique of thought that discovered the Josephson effect compatible with parapsychology?

"You ask whether parapsychology lies within the bounds of physical law," Dr. Josephson said. "My feeling is that to some extent it does, but physical law itself may have to be redefined in terms of some new principles. It may be that some effects in parapsychology are ordered-state effects of a kind not yet encompassed by physical theory.

"My interest is not only in parapsychology but in the nature of intelligence and consciousness. These are also ordered processes which are not yet understood," he said. "It may be that an understanding of intelligence and consciousness lies outside the paradigm of physics. It may be that more can be learned about the nature of reality through meditative processes."

But he did not expect the results of such work to be universally persuasive.

"It is clear," he said, "that you can never satisfy a skeptic except by enrolling him directly in an experiment, and you can't do that with every skeptic."

The Problem of Plagiarism

The subject of plagiarism can be very perplexing because students often have trouble seeing it from the instructor's point of view. Many tend to feel that teachers exaggerate the seriousness of the offense, and some teachers think students treat the problem lightly because avoiding plagiarism sometimes takes too much effort. But the fact of the matter is that teachers do consider plagiarism a serious offense, and therefore, students need to beware of getting into trouble through carelessness.

The problem reduces to one of trust and personal integrity. Teachers want to believe that you will give proper credit where it is due, and they want to give you credit for your own judgments concerning the significance of the evidence you gathered. Readers assume that all ideas and judgments which are not accompanied by a note are yours. Only when a teacher has good reason to doubt that an idea is yours will he or she raise the question of plagiarism. As a matter of personal integrity, you must acknowledge any idea that comes from a source as well as the wording that was used to express that idea.

By "acknowledging sources" we mean that when you use an idea, for instance a critical judgment, that appeared in one of your sources, you must give that writer credit with a note telling readers who proposed the idea and just where you found it. Even if you arrived at the same judgment on your own, you need to acknowledge that the writer also came up with the idea.

It is possible to plagiarize by accident. In using an idea from a source, you might carelessly fail to insert a sourcenote, and so it would appear that you were trying to claim that idea was your own or that you had discovered the information through your own efforts. Such an oversight is easy to discover. Simply reread your paper, with your note cards at hand, and check each significant concept or fact against your notes to see whether you have given proper credit. Add any source citations you omitted. (Note: Chapter 8 provides specific guidelines for determining what kinds of information require notes.)

The problem of plagiarizing another author's language may not be so easy to deal with. Many of your notes will consist of paraphrases and summaries; therefore, you might accidentally treat one of your direct quotations as though it, too, had been written in your own words. If in taking notes you followed our suggestion and marked off the quotations with large quotation marks, or « and », then you can easily check your paper against your notes to be sure all quotations are identified as such. If the markings on your note cards are not clear, however, you must go back to the actual sources to determine which words in your notes are quotations and which are your own.

The problem of plagiarizing language, however, usually goes beyond copying full sentences or even paragraphs from a source without using quotation marks and notes. Some students find themselves suspected of plagiarism because the wording of their paraphrases is so close to that of the original passages that they are practically quoting. Only a few words are changed, and the sentence patterns are virtually identical to those in the sources. Here is an example.

This passage comes from a description of George Washington's plan for saving his forces from the British army, which had trapped him into defending a fortress on the shore of Long Island. The only means of escape required moving the men in small boats (source is Flexner, James T. *The Young Hamilton*. Boston: Little, Brown, 1978).

original passage   The other necessity, and this seemed the impossible one, was for Washington to find some way to get his army away without tremendous loss. The problem was that, when part of the force was on water, the rest, unable adequately to defend the fortifications, would become easy prey for the enemy. Unless he could somehow slip secretly away, Washington would have to sacrifice half his army.

a case of laziness or deliberate plagiarism?

The other need, which seemed to be impossible, was for Washington to discover some means of getting the army away without enormous losses. His problem was that, when some of the soldiers were on the water, the others would be unable to defend their land position adequately and could be easily defeated by the British. Unless Washington could manage to slip away in secret, he would lose half his forces (Flexner 110).

Perhaps the only crime here is laziness, but the fact remains that this student relied very heavily upon the original sentence structure and only "translated" the passage by finding synonyms for a few words. The flow of thought is a direct echo of the original. Although the note tells the reader where the information came from, there is no indication that the wording is not entirely the student's own work.

Perhaps this plagiarism was unintentional. The student may have thought that since the two versions are not *exactly* the same, no plagiarism occurred. But his version sounds too much like the original. In order to repair the damage, he would have to rewrite the entire paragraph, changing the sentence structure and finding different word choices. (Remember that a paraphrase restates the author's idea in your own words.)

acceptable paraphrase

Washington's brilliance as a field commander is shown by his plan for the army to escape by water before the British knew what was happening. Obviously, the soldiers could not simply board boats and sail away, because, if the British attacked in the middle of the operation, most of the troops would be in no position to defend themselves (Flexner 110).

This paraphrase is distinctly different from the source, as it should be. Of course, a note is still essential—to credit the author as the source of the information. (Remember that ideas, opinions, judgments, all must be acknowledged, even after you express them in your own words.)

It is not always easy to know how different from the original your paraphrase must be if you are to avoid plagiarism. A possible rule would be to enclose any words found in a source within quotation marks, but this could lead to absurdities in many common situations. For instance, how would you paraphrase the following sentence without using the italicized words?

original   The typical *Inuit igloo* offers superior insulation against *temperatures* that fall as low as − *50° F.*

There are no synonyms for most proper nouns, such as *Inuit*, just as there are no synonyms for most numbers (exceptions: *dozen* for *twelve*; *score* for *twenty*; *decade* for *ten years*). As for *igloo*, the substitution of *ice house* or *house made from blocks of hard-packed snow* would be either inaccurate or very clumsy, and *temperature* can only be replaced by a slightly different idea, such as *coldness* or *freezing weather*. If you put quotation marks around these words in your paraphrase, the result would look rather silly:

absurd use of   A well-made "Inuit igloo" can protect its
quotation marks   occupants even when "temperatures" outside reach
                            "-50° F."

Obviously, any rule must be flexible enough to prevent this ugliness. In general, then, you can safely repeat specific numbers (− *50° F.*, *21 percent*, *5,280 feet*, *7 million people*, *$524.52*), special terms for which there are no simple synonyms (*igloo, gross national product, income tax, influenza, touchdown, amphetamine*), and even very simple words that would require bizarre substitutions (*horse, ocean, atmosphere, lung, father, high school, temperature*).

Remember, however, that sometimes even a single word taken from a source requires quotation marks if it is especially colorful or represents the writer's judgment. The following summary of an article quoted just two isolated words, *ridiculous* and *absurd*.

student summary of   In 1912, H. H. Goddard, director of research at
article   Vineland Institute for Feeble-minded Girls and
                            Boys in New Jersey, was commissioned by the U.S.
                            Public Health Service to survey mental deficiency
                            among immigrant populations at Ellis Island.
                            According to paleontologist Stephen Jay Gould,
                            Goddard's study employed "ridiculous" criteria

which led to "absurd" conclusions regarding the
native intelligence of Jews and other unpopular
European minorities. Goddard's work played a
significant role in the passage of the Restriction
Act of 1924, which, according to Allan Chase,
author of The Legacy of Malthus, barred millions
of Jews from entering the United States and
thereby escaping the Nazi holocaust (Gould
14-15).

Works Cited shows   Gould, Stephen Jay. "Science and Jewish
                   Immigration." Natural History Dec. 1980:
                   14-19.

As you can see, the problem of plagiarism concerns not only individual words, but also the flow of thought and the presentation of ideas, all of which combine to give a piece of writing its style and originality. The research paper measures, among other things, your ability to express ideas effectively. Although this challenge can be frustrating at times, you are expected to maintain a personal integrity that will prevent your surrendering to the temptation to borrow even "just a little bit here and there" from your sources.

Review Questions

1. How does a hypothesis help you to read sources and take good notes?
2. What kind of information *must* be recorded on every note card to avoid problems at later stages in the process? Where should this information be entered on a card?
3. Why do successful notetakers keep each note as brief as possible?
4. What is the difference between a summary and a paraphrase? How are they similar?
5. What are the advantages of paraphrasing and summarizing rather than copying passages from sources?
6. When paraphrasing, do you have to change every word that appeared in the original? Explain your answer.
7. For what reasons might you quote rather than paraphrase a statement found in a source?

8. Why might plagiarism become a problem even for very honest writers of research papers?

Exercises

1. Take a full set of notes on the following excerpt from a lecture.* Be sure to follow the direction indicated by the hypothesis when deciding what information belongs in your notes. Remember not to put too much information on individual cards. If you quote something, mark it clearly, and, in parentheses, give a reason for quoting—accuracy, memorable words, conciseness, authority.

Topic: *the causes of violence in America today*

Hypothesis: "Although some observers blame violence on television and the economy, the cause may lie in our past, going back to the lawless West and to Prohibition."

It is commonly assumed that violence is part of our frontier heritage. But the historical record shows that frontier violence was very different from violence today. Robbery and burglary, two of our most common crimes, were of no great significance in the frontier towns of the Old West, and rape was seemingly nonexistent.

Bodie, one of the principal towns on the trans-Sierra frontier, illustrates the point. Nestled high in the mountains of eastern California, Bodie, which boomed in the late 1870s and early 1880s, ranked among the most notorious frontier towns of the Old West. It was, as one prospector put it, the last of the old-time mining camps.

Like the trans-Sierra frontier in general, Bodie was indisputably violent and lawless, yet most people were not affected. Fistfights and gunfights among willing combatants—gamblers, miners, and the like—were regular events, and stagecoach holdups were not unusual. But the old, the young, the weak, and the female—so often the victims of crime today—were generally not harmed.

Robbery was more often aimed at stagecoaches than at individuals. Highwaymen usually took only the express box and left the passengers alone. There were eleven stagecoach robberies in Bodie between 1878 and 1882, and in only two instances were passengers robbed. (In one instance, the highwaymen later apologized for their conduct.)

There were only ten robberies and three attempted robberies of individuals in Bodie during its boom years, and in nearly every case the circumstances were the same: the victim had spent the evening in a gambling den, saloon, or brothel; he had revealed that he had on his person a significant sum of money;

*Roger D. McGrath, "The Myth of Frontier Violence," *Harper's* Feb. 1985: 26–28, an excerpt from a lecture given November 1984 at California State University, Long Beach.

and he was staggering home drunk when the attack occurred.

Bodie's total of twenty-one robberies—eleven of stages and ten of individuals—over a five-year period converts to a rate of eighty-four robberies per 100,000 inhabitants per year. On this scale—the same scale used by the FBI to index crime—New York City's robbery rate in 1980 was 1,140, Miami's was 995, and Los Angeles's was 628. The rate for the United States as a whole was 243. Thus Bodie's robbery rate was significantly below the national average in 1980.

Perhaps the greatest deterrent to crime in Bodie was the fact that so many people were armed. Armed guards prevented bank robberies and holdups of stagecoaches carrying shipments of bullion, and armed homeowners and merchants discouraged burglary. Between 1878 and 1882, there were only thirty-two burglaries—seventeen of homes and fifteen of businesses—in Bodie. At least a half-dozen burglaries were thwarted by the presence of armed citizens. The newspapers regularly advocated shooting burglars on sight, and several burglars were, in fact, shot at.

Using the FBI scale, Bodie's burglary rate for those five years was 128. Miami's rate in 1980 was 3,282, New York City's was 2,661, and Los Angeles's was 2,602. The rate of the United States as a whole was 1,668, thirteen times that of Bodie.

Bodie's law enforcement institutions were certainly not responsible for these low rates. Rarely were robbers or burglars arrested, and even less often were they convicted. Moreover, many law enforcement officers operated on both sides of the law.

It was the armed citizens themselves who were the most potent—though not the only—deterrent to larcenous crime. Another was the threat of vigilantism. Highwaymen, for example, understood that while they could take the express box from a stagecoach without arousing

the citizens, they risked inciting the entire populace to action if they robbed the passengers.

There is considerable evidence that women in Bodie were rarely the victims of crime. Between 1878 and 1882 only one woman, a prostitute, was robbed, and there were no reported cases of rape. (There is no evidence that rapes occurred but were not reported.)

Finally, juvenile crime, which accounts for a significant portion of the violent crime in the United States today, was limited in Bodie to pranks and malicious mischief.

If robbery, burglary, crimes against women, and juvenile crime were relatively rare on the trans-Sierra frontier, homicide was not: thirty-one Bodieites were shot, stabbed, or beaten to death during the boom years, for a homicide rate of 116. No U.S. city today comes close to this rate. In 1980, Miami led the nation with a homicide rate of 32.7; Las Vegas was a distant second at 23.4. A half-dozen cities had rates of zero. The rate for the United States as a whole in that year was a mere 10.2.

Several factors contributed to Bodie's high homicide rate. A majority of the town's residents were young, adventurous, single males who adhered to a code of conduct that frequently required them to fight even if, or perhaps especially if, it could mean death. Courage was admired above all else. Alcohol also played a major role in fostering the settlement of disputes by violence.

If the men's code of conduct and their consumption of alcohol made fighting inevitable, their sidearms often made it fatal. While the carrying of guns probably reduced the incidence of robbery and burglary, it undoubtedly increased the number of homicides.

For the most part, the citizens of Bodie were not troubled by the great number of killings; nor were they troubled that only one man was ever convicted of murder. They accepted the killings and the lack of convictions because most of those killed had been willing combatants.

Thus the violence and lawlessness of the trans-Sierra frontier bear little relation to the violence and lawlessness that pervade American society today. If Bodie is at all representative of frontier towns, there is little justification for blaming contemporary American violence on our frontier heritage.

---

2. Take a full set of notes on this magazine article.* Be sure to follow the direction indicated by the hypothesis when deciding what information belongs in your notes. Remember not to crowd information on your cards. If you quote something, mark it clearly, and, in parentheses, give your reason for quoting—accuracy, memorable words, conciseness, authority. Also, make up bibliography cards for any potential sources you discover in this article.

Topic: *preservation of world's forests*

Hypothesis: "The continued loss of the world's forests will have disastrous effects on both nature and civilization."

The End of Eden

Man is fast destroying the rain forests.

Most Americans think of the environment—if they think of it at all—as whatever affects their own backyard. Oil spills, toxic-waste dumps, the Disneying of the national parks: all draw impassioned debate and criticism. In a broader context, however, such "parochial" concerns amount to not seeing the forest for the trees. The worst ecological disaster now facing mankind, as four timely new books attest, is the relentless eradication of the world's rain forests—those magnificent green expanses that are, as conservationist Norman Myers writes in *The Primary Source (399 pages. Norton. $17.95)*, "the finest celebration of nature ever known on the planet."

Until recently, no one really thought much about saving rain forests. Millions upon millions of acres of them girdled the equator, many unseen by human eye. In the last two decades, however, that seemingly infinite resource has dwindled at a terrifying speed. Every minute of every day, writes journalist Catherine Caufield in *In the Rainforest (304 pages. Knopf. $16.95)*, an exhaustively researched report from the front line, almost 30 acres vanish forever. Each year

*Annalyn Swan, *Newsweek*, 18 Feb. 1985.

an area the size of England, Scotland and Wales is razed. By the turn of the century, if this rate of destruction continues, most major rain forests (they exist primarily in Central and South America, the Congo basin and such eastern islands as Sumatra, Borneo and Papua New Guinea) may well be reduced to degraded patches. The war is on, waged by loggers eager for valuable timber, poor farmers hungry for land to call their own, Latin American ranchers who, often for the prestige of being a weekend *caballero*, clear vast tracts to run cattle.

It is hard for most people to envision what is being lost; few Americans will ever see a rain forest. Hence the value of books like Adrian Forsyth and Ken Miyata's *Tropical Nature (248 pages. Scribners. $16.95)*, which seeks "to provoke curiosity" about the forests—not just provide facts about them—and succeeds splendidly. Written by two biologists— one of whom, Miyata, was tragically killed on a fishing expedition before its publication—"Tropical Nature" evokes the magic and wonder of a world completely contained within itself.

On first seeing a rain forest, write the authors, the overwhelming impression is of green stillness and luxuriant life. Far above the ground is the forest canopy, through which little sunlight penetrates to the forest floor. Everywhere one looks are huge lianas or vines snaking toward the light. Tree trunks drip masses of epiphytes—ferns, mosses, orchids. There are thousands upon thousands of plant, animal and insect species, almost half the planet's species in only 2 percent of its area. Nothing is as it seems: in the high-stakes game of survival, many plants and insects have assumed the appearance or coloration of similar species that are inedible or even deadly. Some really *are* deadly, including the sinister pit vipers that use infrared sensors, located between their eyes, to track their victims through the darkness. At night, contrary to the Tarzan myth of a jungle echoing with screams and roars, the forest interior takes on a slightly foreboding stillness.

Drought: It's difficult to believe that such richness cannot be converted into prime farmland. The fact is, however, that most rain-forest soil is among the world's oldest and poorest. What's more, the forest acts like a giant sponge. If it is cut down, the result is not only flooding in the rainy season but drought in the dry; studies have shown that the forests retain and recycle as much moisture into the air as comes from the clouds. Destroy a rain forest and you wind up, at best, with a few years of crops gleaned from the temporary nutrients that come from burning trees. Then the soil is exhausted. And, since each species is interdependent with so many others in the great chain of being, the forest cannot easily regenerate itself. Where once there was exuberant life there is barren wasteland.

And still the misguided schemes to make the rain forest "productive" continue. In the forthcoming *Dreams of Amazonia (192 pages. Viking. $17.95)*, Roger Stone, a former Time-Life bureau chief in Brazil and now vice president of the World Wildlife Fund, chronicles one mistaken effort after another to turn Amazonia into El Dorado. The most famous venture of the 1970s was American billionaire Daniel K. Ludwig's ill-fated Jari, for which enormous paper mills were floated up the Amazon. Few people now remember Henry Ford's equally ambitious Fordlândia, which preceded Jari by four decades. This was a huge rubber plantation that limped along for years until Ford finally sold the land back to the Brazilian government in 1945. The most recent schemes, to resettle small farmers and clear vast tracts for cattle, have foundered on the poverty of the soil. Now the Brazilian government has launched a vast mining project, Grande Carajas, that dwarfs all of its predecessors. It will cover a sixth of Amazonia—the biggest rain-forest area left in the world—with huge mines and dams. The first, Tucuruí Dam, which is already under construction, will alone flood 800 square miles of virgin forest. It is far too big an area to clear; the trees will simply be left to rot. As for the Indians who have settled there, they'll be uprooted yet again and forced ever nearer to extinction.

Species: What's distressing about such destruction is not simply the loss of the world's most beautiful forests; it is the possibly disastrous side effects. At worst, the carbon released from the burning and decaying forest could have a "greenhouse effect" on the earth, melting part of the polar ice caps and causing floods worldwide. The world's gene pool will dwindle as species become extinct; wild plants are regularly interbred with domestic crops to strengthen them against blight and pests. Most tragic of all, perhaps, is the annihilation of species as yet undiscovered, which might well have proven invaluable to mankind. Of the plants known to have anticancerous properties, for example, more than 70 percent are rain-forest species. "Few environmental disorders cause irreversible damage to our biosphere," writes Myers in "The Primary Source." "But the extinction of species is a different ballgame. When a species is gone, it is gone forever."

Is there any way to save the forests, or at least significant chunks of them? Of the four books, "The Primary Source" is the most optimistic. Its proposals range from tree plantations planted with fast-growing species to limiting timber cutting to selected secondary, or previously logged, forest to a U.S. boycott of Central American beef. In the end, it is just as unlikely that Americans will deprive themselves of the cheap beef used by convenience-food giants as that rain-forest countries will welcome foreign intervention. In many countries, the destruction of the forest is a direct result of national poverty. In others, it is a matter of machismo or pride—"our moon shot," as one Brazilian proudly proclaimed to Stone. What chance does the forest stand against that? As an official of Eletronorte, the builders of the Tucuruí Dam, told Caufield, "Any dam is economic, most of all if you consider that the land is free. The only price is the environmental one." That price, sadly, will be paid by us all.

6

Preparing to Write
the Paper

You are now ready to enter the writing phase of the assignment, having completed virtually all the research and having read the sources. Of course, you may have to go back and reexamine one or more sources if you suspect you missed some useful information. Or, after you have begun to write the paper, you may hear of another possible source and want to check it out. Research is seldom a straightforward procedure. Retracing your steps is frequently necessary.

The writing of the paper is complicated by the large amount of information which must be organized into a logical sequence. In order to cope with this complexity, you must review all your findings to obtain a clear overview of what your research has uncovered.

Organizing Your Note Cards

An easy way to get such an overview is to lay all your note cards out on a table, arranging them into groups according to subtopics. Now you can see the advantage to having each note on its own card, for you can shift a note from one group to another as you try to find the best way to organize the information. By looking over the notes in this manner, you can begin to see possibilities for arranging the information into a coherent essay.

No one can tell how many subtopics you will end up with, but you can usually expect to find between ten and twenty groups of cards on the table. In order to come up with a rough outline of the paper, you should consolidate some of the small groups into fairly large ones representing major divisions of the essay.

For his paper on Cotton Mather, Fred gathered the cards he had assigned to relatively small groups and joined them to form one major subdivision of the paper:

> **Small Groups:** the Millennium's proximity; visits from an angel; Puritan colony and New Jerusalem; total system—God, Devil, angels, witches; Mather's belief in his closeness to God
>
> **Major Subdivision:** Mather's personal religious views

This was not Fred's final arrangement of this information. He later broke this silly division into two headings: Mather's special place in God's eyes; and the Puritan colony and the Second Coming. However, his later organizational changes depended upon his categorization of his notes into major subdivisions and small groups.

Another objective of this overviewing process is to determine whether your research is complete. If you feel you do not have enough evidence from which to draw a valid conclusion, you need to do more research—either find more sources or go back and get more information from sources you have already examined. A student writing on *dinosaur extinction* saw she had just one very brief note on a theory that is not widely held. Her research would not have been considered complete without a reasonably thorough account of that theory, which would give readers a fair chance to judge its validity. So back she went to the library.

Writing the Introduction

After you have arrived at your thesis and arranged your note cards into a rough, preliminary outline for the paper, your next step is to write the introduction. The introductory paragraph* not only states your thesis, but it also indicates the major subdivisions of the paper and the general nature of your sources. By putting together your major subtopics in what amounts to a preview of the whole paper, you gain a sense of control over the writing. This feeling of control will help you to see the significance of each detail as you try to find a place for it in the overall essay.

---

*For long essays, such as the sample paper on extending the human life span, two paragraphs may be needed.

Before writing the introduction, jot down the major points you expect it will include. In the case of Cotton Mather, the main points were:

Topic: *Cotton Mather's belief in witchcraft*

Major Subtopics: modern view—humane, not cruel; defense of the social order; possible antifeminism; personal religious views

Sources: modern historians

From these materials, Fred wrote a rough draft of his introduction:

> Many people today are amazed how strongly people in colonial New England believed in witches, and went so far as to burn or hang them out of fear. They especially wonder how intelligent, educated ministers could be so superstitious. Why would ministers believe witches were the agents of the Devil, and why would they be so afraid of some people as to accuse them of being witches? Many uneducated people might blame the Devil and witches for their bad luck, but educated religious leaders like Cotton Mather should have been setting them straight, not leading them on. No one seems to agree on the reasons why this prominent Puritan minister supported the witch-hunts, but most historians today say he was not just a cruel persecutor of innocent victims. They think he saw witches as part of God's creation and that he was concerned that the trials be conducted fairly. He was mostly worried that the witches could undermine the society, for they were supposed to be the Devil's secret agents.

Fred realized that this rough paragraph would have to be made a bit more elaborate and polished, but he also saw that it achieved the basic aims of an introduction—a clear view of the ideas he wanted to present. Fred did not write the final version, which grew to three short paragraphs, until he had written the rest of the paper. Take time to note the structure of this introduction.

In the first paragraph, Fred sets up the problem he was investigating: "Why did intelligent Christian ministers believe in witches to the extent of killing those accused of witchcraft?" The next paragraph provides several explanations for Mather's behavior. The third paragraph presents Fred's thesis: "Mather's belief in witchcraft stemmed from his perception of his own personal relation to God and that of the Puritans' place in God's master plan for humanity."

Thus, his introduction serves as an overview of the full paper.

introductory paragraph   In 1692, a series of trials held in Salem, Massachusetts, resulted in the execution of twenty people for practicing witchcraft. Over the years, many historians have tried to explain both the outbreak of witchcraft hysteria at that time and the motives of certain community leaders who played important roles in the hunting down and conviction of people who were considered to be

reference to source for background information   witches.[1] One such leader was Cotton Mather, a prominent Puritan minister and theologian, whose complex life and voluminous writings have provided historians with ample material for attempting to understand both the man and his times.

more background material—nature of sources for this paper   Early critics of Mather painted him as a cruel witch-hunter and tormentor of innocent people. And while this negative image of Mather has not entirely disappeared, modern historians have largely ruled out the interpretation that Mather's involvement in witch-hunting stemmed from a deliberate desire to inflict suffering upon innocent victims. Indeed, some historians have all but absolved Mather of any unusual responsibility for the trials. He was a person of the times, these writers argue; in late seventeenth-century America, it was a rare person who did not believe in and fear the existence of witches. Other historians see Mather's general support of the trials growing out of his desire to defend the authority of the civil judges and protect the Puritan social system. Yet another interpretation views Mather's role as that of a champion of the patriarchial social order. This idea may explain why Mather supported the trials of accused witches, the overwhelming majority of whom were women.

Cotton Mather was a complicated human being, and there may be some truth in all of these ideas. **narrowing of Fred's chief argument** However, the ultimate explanation for his behavior during this fascinating if terrible moment in American history may well lie in his unique view **statement of thesis** of himself and the Puritan colony. His belief in witches, along with his need to identify and punish them, seems to have supported both his belief that he enjoyed a special, personal relationship with God, and his view that the New England Puritan colony was destined to play the central role in God's plan for the future of humanity.

Constructing the Outline

Once you have drafted your introductory paragraph, your attention turns to the structure of the paper. An outline of some sort is essential if you hope to control all the information that lies spread out on the table in front of you. Outlining can be done in several stages, culminating in a detailed plan for the paper, in which each note card has been assigned to a specific point in the outline. There are several formats commonly used in creating outlines. Even for the rough outline of his Mather paper, Fred used the *sentence outline* form—he expressed all items in complete sentences.

The first attempt at an outline for a paper can be very short and simple—just take your main subtopics and figure out a reasonable order in which to present them. The first version of the outline for the Cotton Mather paper looked like this:

Introduction

1. The cruel portrait has been updated to show Mather's humaneness.

2. Mather tried to assure fairness of the trials.

3. Mather wrote and preached against witchcraft.

4. Several theories focus on Mather's defense of the social order.

5. One writer believes Mather was antifeminist.

6. Mather's personal religious views led to his belief in witches.

Conclusion

A short outline such as this gave Fred a chance to think about the shape of his paper without being confused by the details he had come across in his research.

As he thought over the items in this outline, he realized that point 2 is one of the examples of Mather's humaneness; that is, it is rightly a part of point 1. Fred also noticed that point 3 does not belong in the outline, for Mather's writings are referred to throughout the paper by the historians as they try to explain his character and motivation. However, he wanted to mention Mather's influence on the Salem community, so he reworded this item. Finally, point 5 refers to one aspect of the social order Mather was defending, so it belongs under point 4.

The revised short outline follows.

```
Introduction
1. Mather was more humane than originally portrayed. (Murdock;
   Hofstadter; Hansen; Levy)
2. Whatever his motives, Mather did influence the witch-hunting.
   (Silverman; Levin)
3. Mather was deeply committed to maintaining the Puritan social
   order. (Hansen; Levy; Karlsen; Pestana)
4. Mather's personal religious views necessitated his belief in
   witches. (Levin; Silverman; Levy; Middlekauff; Miller)
Conclusion
```

Notice that Fred listed the sources that contributed each idea to the development of this reasearch paper.

The next stage, constructing a detailed outline, depends on a careful evaluation of your materials. First, arrange the piles of note cards in the same order as the subtopics in your brief outline. Then, read through your notes again, to be sure they are both relevant and usable. You may want to eliminate a note that no longer seems relevant, to reassign a minor subtopic to a different major subtopic, or perhaps even to return to the library and look for information on an important subtopic about which you have not uncovered enough information.

Now you are ready to put your full set of cards in the precise order you expect to follow when writing the paper. Start by arranging the minor subtopics within the major subtopic to which you have assigned them. Then, arrange all the note cards within each minor subtopic in a logical sequence. By arranging your entire collection of notes in this way, you will have laid out on the table an organizational pattern for your paper. This is, in effect, a physical outline, and from it you can prepare the detailed written outline that will guide your writing of the first draft.

THE MATTER OF BALANCE

As you put your groups of note cards into sequence, look for possible imbalance. No subtopic should outweigh or overshadow other equally important subtopics. For example, suppose you were writing about Martin Luther King, Jr., and had arrived at the thesis, ''Martin Luther King's success resulted from three major factors—his courage, his intelligence, and his charisma.'' Your outline, which determines the shape of the paper, would be strongly unbalanced if you devoted one section to ''courage,'' one to ''intelligence,'' and then six sections to ''charisma.'' If your general impression from reading the sources was that all three factors contributed equally to King's success, then you would need to return to your sources or find new sources, looking for more information about the two briefly covered factors. If, however, you now realize that most of the sources had indeed emphasized charisma, you must revise your thesis. It might well read, ''Martin Luther King's success depended on three factors—courage, intelligence, and charisma—of which charisma was by far the most important.'' Whatever direction you take, be sure to correct an unbalanced outline before you start to write. You will find it much harder to make such a change later.

THE TRADITIONAL OUTLINE FORMAT

In constructing an outline, use whatever format you feel comfortable with, unless your instructor specifies a particular one. One of the most common formats combines letters and numbers to designate the various levels of classification. Even if you are already familiar with this format, take time now to be sure you understand the subtle distinctions between those levels.

This list indicates the relative difference between levels:

Roman numerals (I, II) represent major subtopics, each covering a large section of the paper.

Capital letters (A, B) represent minor subtopics, each occupying at least one, sometimes several paragraphs.

Arabic numerals (1, 2) represent major details that support a minor subtopic.

Small letters (a, b) represent minor details that support a major detail.

The longer the paper you are writing, the broader the area covered by the highest category (Roman numerals) and the greater the chance that you might need a fifth set of symbols to represent the smallest details in the paper (small Roman numerals—i, ii, iii).

Many writers follow two sensible rules for constructing outlines.

Rule 1: *Never break down a category into just one subdivision. To do so is illogical.*

wrong: only one detail supports subtopic A

    I. Difficulties faced by Diego Rivera in early years

        A. Childhood problems

            1. Grave illness from typhus and scarlet fever

        B. Adolescent problems

At some point, childhood problems must have seemed an important subtopic, but in this outline it looks trivial. Perhaps information about another childhood problem has been assigned to a different subtopic and could be moved into this one. Or perhaps another trip to the library would produce information about a second childhood problem accidentally omitted during note-taking. The outline might then look like this:

correct

    I. Difficulties faced by Diego Rivera in early years

        A. Childhood problems

            1. Grave illness from typhus and scarlet fever

            2. Dangers arising from father's radical politics

        B. Adolescent problems

On the other hand, if Rivera's only significant childhood problem had been illnesses, the outline might be revised to look like this:

correct

    I. Difficulties faced by Diego Rivera in early years

        A. Childhood illnesses

        B. Adolescent problems

(It is not necessary to add arabic numerals under *A* for the specific illnesses, unless your note cards treat them extensively and you mean to discuss them in detail.)

Rule 2: *Use the same grammatical form for words at the same level of classification. By doing so, you produce parallel structure; that is, a pleasing and easy-to-understand ordering of ideas.*

wrong; the
subdivisions are not
grammatically parallel

A. Symptoms of senility

   1. Forgetting recent events

   2. Mistakes in simple arithmetic

   3. Occasional hallucinating

   4. Inappropriate responses in social situations

correct; each
subdivision is a gerund
phrase

A. Symptoms of senility

   1. Forgetting recent events

   2. Making mistakes in simple arithmetic

   3. Hallucinating occasionally

   4. Responding inappropriately in social situations

SENTENCE OUTLINES

The outlines presented in the previous section are examples of *phrase outlines*, in which each category is expressed in a phrase. Some instructors may require you to submit a *sentence outline*, in which you must express each category as a complete sentence. A sentence outline usually takes more time to write than a phrase outline, but it offers you an important advantage. The sentences that make up the outline can often be used almost word for word when you start to write your full paper. Whatever outline form you use, be consistent. Do not mix phrases into a sentence outline or sentences into a phrase outline. (For an example of a complete phrase outline, see the sample student paper on Emily Dickinson in chapter 9.)

The following section of Fred's outline for his Cotton Mather paper is an example of a sentence outline. Note that in addition to using complete sentences, this outline also lists the source for each item discussed.

Cotton Mather's Necessary Witches

Introduction

   1. Historians have tried to learn Mather's role in witchcraft hysteria and the Salem trials.

   2. The old view of Mather as a cruel persecutor has given way to more favorable interpretations of his personality.

       3.   THESIS: Mather's belief in witchcraft was based on
private religious beliefs.

I. Historians' opinions of Mather's role in the witch-hunts and his
motives for playing that role have changed in recent years.

    A. Mather's belief in witchcraft was normal for the times, and
he was more humane than originally portrayed.

       1. The old harsh view of Mather was due to
misinterpretation. (Murdock)

          a. He was actually more humane than most people think.

          b. Almost everyone in seventeenth-century America
believed in witches.

       2. Modern historians may be biased against intellectuals of
that era. (Hofstadter)

          a. They "encouraged greater tolerance."

          b. They opposed unenlightened trial judges.

       3. Mather tried to ensure fairness of trials. (Hansen)

          a. He warned against dangers of accepting "spectral
evidence."

          b. He trusted judges to listen to him, but often they did
not.

       4. Witchcraft really works in communities where everyone
believes in it. (Hansen; long quotation)

       5. Mather also believed in witches because the Bible warns
against them. (Levy)

UNCONVENTIONAL OUTLINES

The major reason for constructing an outline is to organize your
thoughts and notes into a logical pattern before you write your research
paper. The conventional outline formats you have studied thus far have
been used for many years by many writers to organize their thoughts before undertaking an extensive piece of writing. However, some writers
prefer to devise their own approaches to outlining which both satisfy
their personal sense of organization and work well as guides to the creation of logical essays.

The following outline—developed by Anita Barrone for her research
paper "Increasing Maximum Life Expectancy: Myth or Reality?"—is an
example of an unconventional outline approach. As you look it over, you

may want to refer to the finished paper in chapter 9 now and again to see how Anita used her personal format to guide her writing of the paper.

Increasing Maximum Life Expectancy: Myth or Reality?

1. Introduction

    Make point that human beings have always dreamed of extending their life spans

    --Ponce de Leon example

    Today, we look to science, not magic

    Thesis: Gerontologists carrying out experiments that may or may not help to extend life span. Many are optimistic about being on right track.

2. Tell what gerontologists mean by "increasing life expectancy"

    --not just more people living longer

    --quote Rosenfeld on life span of Ancient Greeks--some Greeks lived ripe old ages, same as today

    --Use Alexander Leaf article to refute belief that people in certain areas of world have longer life spans

3. Explain "Hayflick limit"--quote Hayflick on "maximum proliferative capacity . . . rarely, if ever, reached by cells in vivo." (Explain difference between in vivo and in vitro)

    --according to Hayflick we may be dying prematurely, as it is

    --make point that gerontologists are working to overcome Hayflick limit

4. Use Walford's U.S. News interview to give list of hot theories about why we age

5. Immunologic Theory

    --Introduce/explain theory

    --talk about "autoimmunity" (quote Cromie)

    --problem for scientists: how to lower autoimmunity without lowering body's ability to fight infection (quote Rosenfeld)

    --drugs as anti-autoimmunity possibility--ex. thymosin (quote Kent)

    --diet as another anti-autoimmunity possibility (quote Walford and Watkin)

6. DNA Repair Theory

   --Introduce/explain theory

   --results of DNA damage (quote Schimke and Agniel)

   --DNA repair capacity helps us live longer than most animals
     (quote Kent)

   --Problem: DNA damage rate outpaces repair rate (quote Walford)

   --paramecia experiment by Sonneborn--maybe DNA repair can be
     increased

   --use "DNA Coils" as another example of scientists working to
     improve DNA repair

7. Free Radical Theory

   --Introduce/explain theory

   --damage caused by free radicals (quote Rosenfeld; Harman;
     Kurtzman and Gordon)

   --tell about attempts to counter effects of free radicals

   --Harman's experiment with rats; possible helpful effects of
     vitamins E and C; "SOD" article from Science Digest

8. Thymus Hormone Theory

   --Introduce/explain theory

   --thymus as "master gland" of immune system (quote Marx)

   --what is thymus? where located? (quote Rosenfeld)

   --why thymus aids immune system (Marx) T-cells

   --explain focus of research on thymus (Marx on hormones)

   --Walford and Adler on declining function of thymus

   --thymosin related to attempts to use drugs to continue work of
     thymus hormone(s)--(quote Kent)

9. Brain Programming Theory

   --Introduce/explain theory

   --the brain as location of "death clock" (quote Moment)

   --tell about attempts to locate "timing element" for aging in
     brain and to turn it off before it has too much effect on
     immune system

   --explain Denckla's theory of "biological clock" for mammals

   --bring up Walford's comment about hypothalamus as area of brain
     where death clock may well be located

   --introduce "neuroendocrinology" (quote Walford)

--use Finch to explain relationship between brain cell change
and neuroendocrine controls--how brain affects glands, which
affect aging process

--Denckla's theory of pituitary gland as gland that starts
aging process at command of the biological clock

--use Walford's comment on Denckla's attempts to isolate "death
hormone" and to make antidote to it

--explain work of scientists experimenting with brain
stimulators to keep information for body's controls from
becoming confused

--use work of Marshall and Berrios as example of experiments
with brain stimulators (apomorphine and L-dopa)

10. Where We Stand

--Make point that theories discussed in this paper may not lead
to success in drive to extend life expectancy

--other theories may arise that may lead to breakthrough

--bring up possibility that gerontologists may be engaged in a
war they cannot win

--refer to Fries, Crapo, Leaf, and Medawar as examples of
scientists who do not think life expectancy can be extended in
near future

11. Conclusion

Return to idea that life expectancy breakthrough will come--if
at all--through work of dedicated scientists

You no doubt noticed that Anita's outline was presented in rather loose form. Subtopics were not always clearly indicated; no real effort was made to distinguish the relative importance of ideas and details; dashes and parentheses were used—but not very systematically—to separate items, rather than the conventional letters and numbers systems of conventional formats; sentences were mixed with phrases to signal points of explanation under subtopics. In short, the overall format showed no consistent organizational approach. And you probably also noticed that some of Anita's entries read more like reminder notes to herself than like clarifying items in a logical pattern of organization.

And yet, despite its breaking the "rules," the outline guided Anita in writing a paper that supported her thesis and related her research findings in an acceptably organized essay.

Anita, a confident writer, explained that she finds it easier to organize her ideas effectively while actually writing an essay than to plan it very precisely before beginning to write. Anita prefers to spend extra time revising a rough draft because she gets a better sense of how to put ideas together after she has tried to organize them into a paragraph. Anita's outlines give her a general sense of direction and remind her of ideas and details she wants to include in her papers. In this sense, then, her outline represents both a plan and a rough, abbreviated first draft. This may explain Anita's frequent use of such directive terms as *explain*, *make a point of*, *use*, *tell about*, and *bring up*.

Other writers use mixes of the traditional outline formats. For example, a writer may use a very precise letter and number system to outline a section that includes many details and then switch to a sentence format to outline theoretical or explanatory sections.

What kind of outlining procedure is best for you? Obviously the one that best guides you in planning an effective essay—the kind of procedure that leads to a logical expression of your ideas and knowledge in essay form. Anita used an unconventional approach. Fred Hutchins and Susanna Andrews used more conventional formats. All three students produced successful research papers. You may have to do some experimenting before you hit upon an outlining approach that best suits your particular talents for planning and writing essays. In general, if you have had problems with writing well-organized essays in the past, then a tighter, more conventional form will probably serve you best. On the other hand, if you are the kind of person who finds that writing comes easily, then you might experiment with unconventional forms that allow you freer range in the planning and writing of your research paper. Your instructor can probably give you some good advice about which way you should go.

Review Questions

1. Why review and arrange all your note cards before beginning to write? What problems might you discover at this stage and how might you deal with them?

2. How do you arrive at a thesis for a paper?

3. What are the usual objectives of an introductory paragraph?

4. What is the function of an outline? What are some problems that you might encounter in constructing an outline?

Exercise

Read the following introductory paragraphs, keeping in mind that such a paragraph should state the thesis, identify the major subtopics for the paper, and describe the general nature of the sources used. Which paragraph best fulfills these objectives? Explain your choice. (Source notes have been left out.)

Topic: *Emily Dickinson's reluctance to publish her poems*

VERSION 1

Emily Dickinson was born in Amherst, Massachusetts, on December 10, 1830. She was the second of three children born to Edward and Emily Dickinson. She had an older brother, Austin, born in 1829, and a sister, Lavinia, who was born in 1833. "The three children were devoted to one another, but their home did not provoke gaiety." Dickinson went to school at Amherst Academy, and later spent a term at Mount Holyoke College. According to Clark Griffith, in 1858, "she began definitely and noticeably to seclude herself from the outside world." With rare exceptions, she spent the rest of her life in her father's house in Amherst. Emily Dickinson died in 1886, leaving behind over 1,700 poems. Only 7 of her poems were published while she was alive, and all of these were published anonymously. Today, she is considered to be a great poet. During her lifetime, however, she was reluctant to publish, and many people have wondered why.

VERSION 2

Great poets are never appreciated during their lifetimes. Emily Dickinson was a great poet. Yvor Winters, in fact, called her "one of the great lyric poets of all time." Actually, she was so far ahead of her time that she could not be appreciated while she was alive. Only 7 of her more than 1,700 poems were published during her lifetime, and even these appeared anonymously. Why should any poet try to become famous if fame means that she has to change her poems to conform to the unimaginative poetic standards of her day? To be a great poet requires great confidence in one's artistic ability. Unfortunately, the public is always too tradition-bound to recognize true art when it appears in an unfamiliar form. Emily Dickinson's work is no exception. The question is this: Are there any Emily Dickinsons today whose brilliance remains unappreciated due to our cultural blindness?

VERSION 3

Emily Dickinson, one of America's greatest poets, was all but unknown during her lifetime, for she allowed only a handful of her more than 1,700 poems to be published, and these appeared anonymously. Only after her death were her works discovered by her sister and brought forth to a warm public reception. Ever since then, the many persons who have written about this unusual genius have attempted to explain her reluctance to publish. The image created by literary critics and popular historians alike is that of a shy, reclusive, mystical dreamer--a sensitive soul deeply wrapped up in her personal joys and sorrows. However, a new picture of the poet has come forth from scholars working closely with her correspondence and with fresh biographical evidence. This view reveals an artist who felt so sure of her own worth that she deliberately kept her creations from a world she believed was incapable of understanding them and insensitive to their beauty.

7
Writing the Paper

After you have developed a logical outline and written an introductory paragraph, you are ready to write the paper itself. This task will consume a good deal of time, since you must plan to write at least three versions of your paper: a rough draft, a revised draft, and a polished final manuscript suitable for submission to your instructor. Many writers feel the need for even further revision, but three drafts are the absolute minimum.

Writing the Rough Draft

Writing the rough draft of a research paper can be thought of as "filling in the outline" because the outline provides a structure not just for your own ideas and conclusions but for the many research notes you have taken. If you try to write your rough draft by working only from the note cards, it will be much harder for you to keep in mind the relationships among them. Hardest of all is trying to write the draft from memory, off the top of your head. That approach may work well when writing essays based on personal experience, but if used for a research paper it absolutely guarantees mistakes and omissions.

While writing the rough draft, you may think of a better way to present your case than you had planned. If that happens, stop writing, go back and revise your outline or even construct a new one. Remember that if you change part of your outline, you will probably have to change other parts as well, in order to maintain balance and an orderly and logical presentation of ideas.

Since the first draft is not meant to be seen by anyone but yourself, don't worry if some sentences are weakly written, and some word choices are not as apt as you would like. Concentrate on expressing your ideas clearly. Let your ideas and sentences flow as freely as you can, getting everything down on paper in a form that reflects your thinking, however roughly. When you write the second draft, finding the right words for what you want to say will be considerably easier.

Here are three pieces of advice for the format of the first draft. *First,* leave plenty of space between the lines for later insertions and changes— about two lines of space for every line of writing. *Second,* don't slow yourself down by copying out each quotation, paraphrase, or summary from your cards. When you come to a place where you need to use a note, simply make a memo to yourself that says ''copy from card'' or ''see card.'' Or, before you start writing, you might take all of your note cards to a copy center or to the copying machine in the library and make photocopies. You can then cut and paste these copies right into the draft. *Finally,* be sure to note briefly in the margin the source of each note you use in the paper, no matter if the note is a direct quotation, a paraphrase, or a summary. You can simply note the author's name or a key word or two from the title, plus the page numbers. If you fail to make a note, you may later forget to add a source note.

INTEGRATING YOUR SOURCES

Though you are by now familiar with your notes, you are for the first time trying to blend them into a coherent whole. As you are writing the first draft, some situations may arise that cause special kinds of problems. The following occur fairly frequently.

No One Source Tells the Whole Story. Often you will have to draw details from different sources in order to deal with a subtopic as fully as you need to. Then you must be careful to keep track of which facts come from which sources. If you simply combine all the details into one account of the situation, with just one source note, your readers may not realize that the picture is a composite, its parts coming from various sources.

Several Sources Disagree over a Question of Fact. Here you have several options. You may simply report the disagreement, especially if you have no basis for trusting one source more than the others. Or you may choose one source if it seems more trustworthy than the others: it may be more fully documented, or merely be the most recent. Or you might try to verify the fact by further research. (The student writing about Emily Dickinson found that various sources said the number of poems published during the poet's lifetime was six, seven, or eight. Since the most exhaustive and best documented source said the number was seven, the student simply used that number in her paper and disregarded the other sources' claims. After all, she was in no position to verify the fact herself, and the exact number was not crucial to her thesis.)

Some Sources Disagree in Their Interpretation of a Fact or Facts. Such differences occur all the time; in fact, they are among the things that make research interesting. If the purpose of your paper is not to argue for a particular conclusion but to report the current state of knowledge, you may simply report the disagreement. If, however, your thesis states a definite position regarding your topic, you must not only report the disagreement but also draw your own conclusion as to which interpretation seems more soundly argued or based on more complete or more reliable evidence. In reporting the disagreement, you must be fair to the writers whose interpretations you reject by presenting their views with enough detail for your readers to be able to agree with your preference or not.

As you can see, writing the first draft involves a great deal of thinking about the ideas and information in your notes in order to draw reasonable conclusions about them. It is this thinking, and not the physical act of writing down your thoughts or keeping track of your sources, that makes the first draft a time-consuming and challenging task. This is also why we encourage you not to get bogged down trying to express your thoughts in exactly the right words. You have enough to do without worrying about that.

ENDING IT ALL

When the body of your paper is complete, you must compose a suitable conclusion. As a general rule, the conclusion should not introduce any new ideas or information. Instead, it should restate your thesis in terms that reflect the evidence that you have presented. (If you use the same words that you used to state your thesis in your introduction, your readers may feel that you haven't taken them anywhere.) Above all, your conclusion should bring your paper to a satisfying close with a statement that sums up what you think your research has shown. Don't be afraid to commit yourself in this respect: you ought to be able to stand confidently behind your research.

Now that you have completed a first draft of your paper, set the project aside for at least a few hours and do something else. It would be best if you could take at least a day's vacation from your paper. During the time you are not consciously working at the research project, your unconscious mind will be digesting, synthesizing, and generally working with what you have done. Then, as you tackle the second draft, not only will you feel refreshed, but you may also find yourself brimming with new ideas.

Revising the Rough Draft

Once you have brought your outline to life by writing a rough essay, the nature of your job changes significantly. You must now become your own toughest critic. Read what you have written closely, as if for the first time, so that you can find those parts that communicate most effectively as well as those that work poorly or not at all. Then you can become the author again, rewriting and, if necessary, reorganizing the weaker passages so that they become as strong as the best. Finally, you must examine the revised essay very closely in order to correct the spelling, punctuation, and other mechanical details.

Approach your revision in an orderly way, by thinking of the task on four levels of organization: the whole paper, paragraphs, sentences, and individual words and phrases.

First, reconsider the order of the major and minor subtopics as presented in your outline and see if this arrangement still serves your purposes well. Once you are satisfied that these larger elements of the paper have been presented in an effective sequence, re-examine the structure of each paragraph and revise where necessary. Then look for sentences that could use improvement. Long, cumbersome sentences, for example, can be broken down into simpler, more easily digested units, but sometimes your revision will work in the other direction—combining a series of short, choppy sentences into longer, smoothly flowing sentences. Still other sentences must simply be recast to make them clearer. Finally, read through the paper, checking your transitions between paragraphs and the details within each paragraph.

Changes in wording can be made at any stage of your revision, even when you are repairing weak paragraph organization or faulty sentence structure. But you should still give yourself one last chance to improve your choice of words just before writing the final, polished version.

RECONSIDERING THE ORGANIZATION

As you arranged your note cards and constructed your outline, you carefully thought about the best order in which to present the information and ideas that would support your thesis. While writing the first draft, however, you might have felt that your plan was not completely practical. Upon rereading your draft you may be more dissatisfied than ever. What can you do?

Perhaps you decided when constructing the outline to present the evidence supporting your thesis first and the evidence against it afterwards. This strategy is effective if your case is so strong that it will make the opposing arguments seem weak. On rereading your paper, however, you found that the opposing case did not seem weak; instead, it seemed to rebut much of your case point by point. One way to reverse that effect would be to switch the order of those subtopics, stating the opposing case first and rebutting it with your case. At this stage of the revision, you would not need to do any rewriting. You would simply cut the two passages out of the paper and tape or paste them back in the new order. Later you would rewrite them and revise the transitions to make the new order effective.

Rearrangements sometimes require more revision than simple adjustments in paragraph or sentence structure: you might occasionally find it a good idea to rewrite drastically and thereby produce a new "first" draft to work with. More often, however, you will find your outline a good guide, and no major reorganization will be necessary. You can then go on to revising the individual paragraphs.

REVISING PARAGRAPHS

Think of a paragraph as a group of sentences that work together to support a controlling idea—the idea expressed in the *topic* (or *main idea*) *sentence*. Ask yourself if a reader would be able to grasp easily the controlling ideas in your paragraphs, either because you have provided clear topic sentences or because you have so carefully constructed your paragraphs that the controlling ideas can be inferred readily from all the sentences taken together. Although you should not feel that you must impose a single rigid concept of paragraph structure on your writing, you should be certain that your paragraphs contribute to a logical progression of ideas in your paper. To the extent that they do not, you must revise.

If you think that one or more of your paragraphs might be confusing to a reader, the first thing to do is to see if the rewriting (or addition) of a topic sentence will clarify your thoughts. If a paragraph remains confusing even after you have improved its topic sentence or created a new topic sentence for it, you must focus on two additional features of paragraph structure:

1. the order in which you have presented the details in support of your topic sentence;
2. the smoothness with which you have moved from one sentence to the next or from one idea to another.

As you review your work, try to read each paragraph as though you were a reader unaware of what the writer intended to say. If you find a paragraph confusing, rearrange the details until you have found the most effective order for them. If the progression from one detail to the next still is not smooth, pick up your composition book or rhetoric and read about achieving coherence, or logical sequence, in paragraphs. Pay special attention to what the book says about using *transitional words and phrases* and other *devices for linking ideas* smoothly and logically. A short review of this kind can enable you to improve the flow of thought within your paragraphs and throughout your paper as a whole.

REVISING SENTENCES

Writing effective sentences is primarily a matter of style, and style develops only through a great deal of practice. Even when you recognize that a sentence calls for improvement, you may have trouble deciding just what changes would make it better. As you revise your paper, you can help yourself by being alert to a few common weaknesses in sentence construction. Pay particular attention to sentences in your rough draft that may be either too complex or too simple and to patterns of construction that may be monotonously repetitive.

First, check the length of your sentences. Some may be too long and complicated for readers to follow comfortably. Usually such sentences can be broken down into more easily digested sentences, as the example illustrates.

too long a sentence   Throughout the war, many Southerners came to think
of Lincoln as a power-hungry autocrat, who, in
spite of the public speeches in which he advocated
peace and reconciliation, was in reality
determined to destroy anyone, in the North or
South, who stood in the way of his gaining
absolute control of the nation he had been elected
to govern.

improvement   Throughout the war, many Southerners came to think
of Lincoln as a power-hungry autocrat, in spite of
the public speeches in which he advocated peace
and reconciliation. They believed that he was in
reality determined to destroy anyone, in the North
or South, who stood in the way of his gaining

absolute control of the nation he had been elected
to govern.

Short sentences are easy to understand, but a series of five or six very short, choppy sentences actually may be more difficult to read than two or three sentences of average length. When you find such a series in your draft, consider combining several of them into longer sentences. Save your short sentences until they can be used most effectively—for example, when emphasizing or summing up a particularly important point.

too many short sentences	Throughout the war, many people detested Lincoln. They considered him to be power-hungry. His speeches called for peace and reconciliation. But these people did not believe him. They included Northerners as well as Southerners. They believed that he intended to destroy anyone who opposed him. They thought he desired to gain absolute control of the country. They saw his election as part of his plan to rule as a dictator.
improvement	Throughout the war, many people detested Lincoln, whom they considered power-hungry. Although his speeches called for peace and reconciliation, these people did not believe him. Both Northerners and Southerners thought that he intended to destroy anyone who opposed him and sought dictatorial control of the country he had been elected to govern.

Also check the patterns of your sentences to see if you have repeated one pattern monotonously. Such repetition may needlessly bore your readers.

repetitive pattern	Hartman says that . . . Anna Freud states that . . . Mahler claims that . . . And now Kohut states that . . .
improvement	Hartman says that . . . Further support comes from Anna Freud . . . Mahler agrees, for the most part,

```
claiming that . . . Recently, Kohut added further
support to this idea when he stated . . .
```

The second example is an improvement over the first not only because it is more varied but also because the writer has taken a set of ideas from different sources and blended them into a smoothly flowing passage that shows how these ideas relate to each other.

REVISING WORD CHOICE

When you revise your word choice, there are three elements you should keep in mind:

1. *variety*—Find appropriate synonyms for words that appear often, except for technical terms, which do not allow substitutes.
2. *accuracy*—Avoid vague, loose terms that may be misinterpreted.
3. *slang*—Avoid words that are not appropriate to the formal context of a research paper.

Finding Variety. This example illustrates monotonous repetition of terms:

lacking variety

```
A young, idealistic anthropologist, on first
venturing into a primitive society, is likely to
suffer severe disillusionment. For one thing,
most such societies live under physical
conditions that no one coming from American
society can possibly anticipate. But far more
dispiriting is the fact that these societies often
practice customs radically opposite to the ideal
life in nature that naive students like to
imagine: a society of simple folk, yes, but a
society that knows the true value of love,
kindness, sharing, and mutual respect. The
Yanomamo society provides an example that could
try the soul of any young idealist searching for
simple, natural virtues. Their social practices
include . . .
```

improvement

A young, idealistic anthropologist, on first venturing into a primitive society, is likely to suffer severe disillusionment. For one thing, most such people live under physical conditions that no one coming from America can possibly anticipate. But far more dispiriting is the fact that these communities often practice customs radically opposite to the ideal life in nature that naive students like to imagine: a society of simple folk, yes, but one that knows the true value of love, kindness, sharing, and mutual respect. The Yanomamo tribe provides an example that could try the soul of any young idealist searching for simple, natural virtues. Their social practices include . . .

Avoiding Vagueness. Here are some examples illustrating the emptiness of vague words.

vague

Napoleon was a great man.
Sarah Bernhardt was an outstanding actress.
Einstein was a fantastic thinker.
Oedipus Rex is a first-rate play.

improved

Napoleon was a brilliant military strategist.
Sarah Bernhardt played a wide variety of roles to perfection.
Einstein's theories reshaped the world of modern physics.
The play Oedipus Rex provides meaningful insights into human behavior.

Of course, you cannot entirely avoid vague terms, but you can keep them to a minimum and use them with care. In short, say exactly what you mean, or at least come as close as possible.

Avoiding Slang and Colloquialisms. The following are examples of word choices not appropriate to the formal context of a research paper:

inappropriate	The women in Rubens's paintings are very sexy.
	The CIA has been blasted recently for failing to perform its duties with sufficient restraint.
	The prosecutor called upon a well-known shrink to testify that the defendant was not really crazy.
improved	The women in Rubens's paintings are very sensuous.
	The CIA has been sharply criticized recently for failing to perform its duties with sufficient restraint.
	The prosecutor called upon a well-known psychiatrist to testify that the defendant was not legally insane.

When revising word choice, be careful if you decide to use a *thesaurus*, or collection of synonyms. Books of synonyms can be valuable in helping you to remember a word whose meaning you know well; they can be dangerous if you use them to select high-sounding words that are unfamiliar to you. The connotations of such words may not be appropriate to the contexts in which you place them. You may find a *dictionary of synonyms* more useful than a thesaurus because the former defines and illustrates the different shades of meaning between synonyms.

SOME SAMPLES OF REVISION

Here is how Anita Barrone moved from rough draft through the various revisions of her opening paragraphs.

Increasing Maximum Life Expectancy:

Myth or Reality?

opening paragraph **rough draft**	For a long time, people have dreamed of extending their life spans. In fact, Juan Ponce de

Leon discovered Florida in 1513 when he was
searching for the Fountain of Youth. By now we have
pretty much given up hope that there is a fountain
of youth or a marvelous herb that can extend our
life spans. But gerontologists (people who study
aging processes) are working on the problem. They
are carrying out experiments that may or may not
help us to extend our lives. However, many
gerontologists are optimistic that they are on the
right track.

Anita realized that this opening paragraph was not particularly effective as an introduction to her paper. The reference to Ponce de Leon—intended as an "interest grabber"—was left hanging, leaving it to the reader to determine precisely why she had used this reference. She saw the possibility that some readers might interpret "For a long time" as meaning from 1513 to the present, when she had actually intended to suggest that the desire to extend life span has been a dream of human beings for as long as there have been human beings. In addition, she saw that the "problem" gerontologists are working on could be interpreted by some readers as the problem of finding a fountain of youth or a marvelous herb. The last two sentences, intended as her thesis statement, were vaguely worded and did not help to pull the paragraph together. All in all—she concluded—a paragraph badly in need of rethinking and rewriting.

After some thought, Anita decided to write a two-paragraph introduction. In the first she would expand upon the Ponce de Leon reference to create a broad introduction to her topic and to generate reader interest. In the second she would introduce her topic more specifically and present a clearer statement of her thesis. This strategy differed somewhat from her original plan for the paper, but Anita saw that the change was necessary to ensure that her paper got off to a good start.

revised opening paragraph

Every American schoolchild learns that Juan
Ponce de Leon discovered Florida in 1513 while
searching for the Fountain of Youth. He believed
the waters of the fountain would make him young
again. But he never found the fountain. Instead he

found death by an Indian arrow. Today we know how
silly Ponce de Loan was for believing in a fountain
of youth provided by a beneficent nature. But his
dream of extending his life span was one that many
people have had throughout the ages. It is still
very much with us today.

Now Anita felt that she had used her Ponce de Leon example successfully to present a broad introduction for her paper. She had not been too
concerned with her writing style because she was mainly interested in
improving the organization and content of the paragraph. Her next step
was to take a closer look at her sentences and her word use to see if the
writing itself could be improved. Her self-criticism, along with some advice from her instructor, led her to make the following changes.

a bit more accurate—Ponce de Leon did not want to be restored to childhood

sentence combining for variety and to lessen repetition of "fountain"

Every American schoolchild learns that Juan Ponce de
Leon discovered Florida in 1513 while searching for the
Fountain of Youth, *whose waters, he believed,* ~~He believed the waters of the fountain~~
~~*restore him to youthful manhood. Unfortunately,*~~
would, ~~make him young again. But,~~ he never found the fountain.
Instead he found death by an Indian arrow. Today we *smile*
at the naivete of ~~know how silly~~ Ponce de Leon ~~was~~ for believing in a fountain of
youth provided by a beneficent nature. But his dream of
extending his life span, was one that many people have had
, and it is a dream that is
throughout the ages, ~~It is~~ still very much with us today.

"unfortunately" word better than "but" to prepare reader for following sentence

"silly" isn't a fair word to describe the explorer's search— in his day, many people believed that nature held the secret to extended life

again, combining for variety and to clarify "it" as referring to "dream"

Satisfied with her first paragraph, Anita turned next to writing the
new second paragraph for her paper, using some of the ideas and wording that she left out of her revised first paragraph. This second paragraph, with Anita's critical revisions, follows.

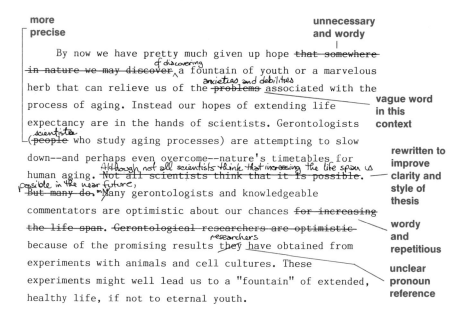

more   unnecessary
precise   and wordy

By now we have pretty much given up hope ~~that somewhere~~
~~in nature we may discover~~ ^of discovering^ a fountain of youth or a marvelous
herb that can relieve us of the ~~problems~~ ^anxieties and debilities^ associated with the
process of aging. Instead our hopes of extending life   **vague word**
expectancy are in the hands of scientists. Gerontologists **in this**
~~(people~~ ^scientists^ who study aging processes) are attempting to slow **context**
down--and perhaps even overcome--nature's timetables for   **rewritten to**
human aging. ^Although not all scientists think that increasing the life span is^ **improve**
~~Not all scientists think that it is possible.~~ **clarity and**
^possible in the near future,^   **style of**
~~But many do.~~ ^m^Many gerontologists and knowledgeable   **thesis**
commentators are optimistic about our chances ~~for increasing~~
~~the life span. Gerontological researchers are optimistic~~ **wordy**
                                              ^researchers^   **and**
because of the promising results ~~they~~ have obtained from **repetitious**
experiments with animals and cell cultures. These   **unclear**
experiments might well lead us to a "fountain" of extended, **pronoun**
healthy life, if not to eternal youth.   **reference**

Writing the Polished, Final Draft

Equipped with a carefully revised draft, you are ready to produce the polished, final version of your research paper. As you write the final version, you may continue to make changes in wording to improve the clarity of your paper. You may also make minor alterations in your paragraphs and sentences in order to improve the flow of thought. However, if at this time you find yourself making major changes in the organization or the content of your paper, then you have embarked upon the final draft without being fully prepared. If this is the case, consider this draft as another revision and work out your problems before again attempting to produce the final draft.

There are two more jobs you must do before you begin to prepare the manuscript of your paper. You must write a complete set of notes acknowledging the source of each quotation or paraphrase in the paper, and you must prepare a final version of your bibliography. The next chapter discusses the form and placement of these source citations.

Review Questions

1. At least how many versions of a research paper must you write? Why?

2. What should you do when your sources disagree?

3. Briefly outline the steps in revising a rough draft.

Exercise

Revise three consecutive paragraphs in your rough draft until you are satisfied with the entire sequence. Show every stage of your revision and explain your reasons for making each change.

8

Documenting Your Sources

After the paper has been written, revised, and polished, one essential step remains: documenting the sources. Documentation consists not only of listing all your sources under Works Cited, but also of inserting notes within the text to tell readers where you found the various ideas and information that form the backbone of your research paper. This final task serves several important purposes.

First of all, notes tell your readers where to find further information about your topic. You may have raised some questions that would send a curious reader back to your source for answers. Or a reader might want to verify your interpretation of what you read. For instance, someone might want to be certain you had not quoted out of context. Another reason for providing notes is to give knowledgeable readers some idea of how authoritative a particular statement is—that is, whether the source's author is an expert in the field or simply a reporter summarizing recent developments for the general public.

Another significant feature of the notes is the date of initial publication. For instance, Sigmund Freud spent more than forty years developing the psychoanalytic theory of personality, and over that period, he revised some of his earlier ideas considerably. Therefore, a well-informed reader might want to know just when Freud made some statement that was quoted in your paper. For this reason, you must be careful to find out the year the source was first published. Don't stop when you learn the year in which the book was *printed*, for many books are printed more than once and by more than one publisher.

Most important, the documentation gives readers an overall sense of how thoroughly you carried out your research. The list of Works Cited reveals at a glance the range of your investigation of the topic; the notes indicate how thoroughly you have read the sources.

The notes themselves can take one of two forms: *parenthetical notes* or *numbered notes*. This book concentrates on the Modern Language Association's 1988 format, which uses parenthetical notes. For an example of this system, see the paper on Emily Dickinson at the beginning of chapter 9. The traditional numbered endnote/footnote format, which many history instructors prefer, is briefly explained (see pp. 167–171) and then illustrated in the paper on Cotton Mather, also found in chapter 9. A third system, devised by the American Psychological Association and used in most of the social sciences is discussed on pages 171–177 and exemplified by the third paper in chapter 9. One further system—the numbered system for scientific research—is briefly explained on pages 177–178.

What to Document

While writing the rough draft, you noted in the margins the sources of all ideas and information that came from your note cards. Now you must add notes to your text, clearly indicating those sources for your reader. Before we discuss how to go about placing these notes in the paper, an important question needs to be answered:

Is it necessary to document the source of every piece of information that goes into your paper?

For instance, you might wonder whether it is essential to state where you came across simple facts such as these:

the Battle of Chickamauga was fought on September 19 and 20, 1863;

nitrogen makes up 78 percent of Earth's atmosphere;

the capital of the African nation Chad is Ndjamena.

Depending on the nature of your research topic, identifying the source of every such fact could clutter the paper with distracting and unhelpful notes. To prevent this, it is generally agreed that you do not have to identify the sources for information that is considered ''general knowledge,'' that is, information readily available in the reference section of any library, even a small one. The facts regarding Chickamauga, nitrogen, and Ndjamena clearly fall under the heading of general knowledge.

Naturally, you will sometimes be unsure whether a particular fact is general knowledge. In that case, to be safe, insert a note. The best thing to do before you begin any research paper, however, is to ask your instructor what kinds of information do not call for documentation.

Looking at the problem the other way around, we can say: *Documentation is required for any information that falls into one of these categories:*

1. opinions, judgments, theories, and personal explanations;
2. "facts" that are open to dispute, and virtually all statistics regarding human behavior;
3. factual information gathered by a small number of observers, no matter how expert they may be (for example, the results of a recent scientific test).

OPINIONS, JUDGMENTS, THEORIES, AND PERSONAL EXPLANATIONS

Encyclopedias are filled with facts that are considered general knowledge, but that does not mean that all information found in an encyclopedia can go into your paper without a note. In the following encyclopedia entry, the annotated passages constitute opinions and would therefore require notes if you used them in your paper.

"influenced by her . . . French contemporaries" is an inference; "greatly" indicates a judgment	CASSATT, Mary (1845–1926). American figure painter and etcher, b. Pittsburgh. Most of her life was spent in France, where she was greatly influenced by her great French contemporaries, particularly Manet and Degas, whose friendship and esteem she enjoyed. She allied herself with the impressionists early in her career. Motherhood was Cassatt's most frequent subject. Her pictures are notable
"refreshing simplicity," "vigorous treatment," and "pleasing color" reflect personal observations and judgments	for their refreshing simplicity, vigorous treatment, and pleasing color. She excelled also as a pastelist and etcher, and her drypoints and color prints are greatly admired. She is well represented in public and private galleries in the United States. Her best known paintings include several versions of *Mother and Child* (Metropolitan Mus.; Mus. of Fine Arts, Boston; Worcester, Mass., Art Museum); *Lady at the Tea-Table* (Metropolitan Mus.); *Modern Women*, a mural painted for the Women's Building at the Chicago Exposition; and a portrait of the artist's mother. See catalog by A. D. Breeskin (1970); biography by J. M. Carson (1966).

"FACTS" OPEN TO DISPUTE

This category includes commonly accepted "facts" based largely on inference. When new evidence is discovered, new inferences may have to be made. For example, the significance of a particular fossil bone is definitely a matter of judgment, and the astronomical phenomenon known as a "black hole" is by no means as factual as many popular accounts suggest.

Much of the work done by behavioral scientists consists of collecting statistical information (the average number of children in Chinese-American families, the rate of juvenile crime in Boston, and so on). Although the statistics you encounter in your research may seem to be hard facts, these facts can be disputed. Indeed, theories and conclusions based on such facts are continually debated by the experts. Therefore, almost all information in the behavioral sciences must be documented except historical facts about individual persons and events in the field.

FACTUAL INFORMATION GATHERED BY A SMALL NUMBER OF OBSERVERS

Information gathered by observation and experimentation is subject to dispute. The results of similar experiments may vary, or different researchers may interpret identical results differently. Accordingly, such information should be documented so your readers know its source.

For example, you might read in a newspaper or magazine this week that "scientists at the Murphy-Weiss Laboratories in Ipswich, Maine, have shown that cola drinks cause liver cancer in rats and monkeys." The headline might even have read: "Soda Pop Causes Cancer." The experiment may have been honestly and carefully executed, and the information may *eventually* be accepted as fact. But until other scientists have duplicated these scientists' work and arrived at the same results, this information is just a "possible" fact, and therefore, it definitely needs to be documented.

Now for one last question: Is it necessary to provide source notes for ideas and information which you were already aware of before undertaking the research paper?

If the information falls into one of the three categories just discussed, you must take the time to locate a source for it. Readers have a right as well as a need to know of a reliable source for the information in question. Furthermore, finding a source protects you against misremembering what you had previously heard or read. Thus, it is always wise when reading sources to take notes on everything that is relevant to your hypothesis, even when you are familiar with the information.

The MLA System of Parenthetical Notation

Because scholars in various fields have not yet agreed upon a standard system of documentation, for every paper you are assigned be sure to ask your instructor which system is preferred, and then consult a guide-book such as this for the proper format. Since most instructors of language and literature follow the system devised in 1988 by the Modern Language Association (MLA), we will describe and illustrate that system in detail.

In general, you will identify the source for any idea or information you discovered through research by placing a brief parenthetical reference within the appropriate sentence, most often directly following the words being cited. Such a note will contain the page number(s) on which the information was found, plus any additional information needed to identify the source, such as the author's name or the title of the work. The amount of information required in a parenthetical note depends on what you have said about the source within the text.

1. If you have mentioned the author's name in your text, the note usually consists of just the page number(s) on which the information was located.

   This fact led the critic Owen Thomas to conclude that Emily Dickinson ''was well aware of the world outside her little room, that in fact she used the language of this outside world to create some of her best poetry'' (523).

2. If you have not mentioned the author's name, then the note must include that information.

   But an economist who predicted the depression of 1981 a year in advance fears the price of gold will decline slowly for at least ten years (Goodserve 143).

3. If the author has written more than one of the sources in your Works Cited, your note must include a shortened form of the particular title unless it is mentioned in your text.

   Chomsky claims that all humans inherit the same basic linguistic structural framework upon which their community's particular language is fitted (Language 29-41).

   The Works Cited in this case also includes Chomsky's *Syntactic Structures*.

4. If the author is unknown, as in many newspaper accounts, the title must appear in the note, if not mentioned in the text. (Titles may be shortened.)

Only Mayor McCarthy expressed the least optimism toward the city's
fate ("Rebirth" 2).

The Works Cited for this source shows: "Rebirth of a City." *News-Times* [Danbury, CT] 6 Sept. 1977: 2.

SPACING AND PUNCTUATION

1. Leave one space before the opening parenthesis. If a punctuation mark follows the citation, place it *outside* the closing parenthesis, and leave one space after a comma, semicolon, or colon, and two spaces after a period, question mark, or exclamation point.

   Morgan believes the whale stands for God (132), whereas Kay claims
   it "embodies all that is evil" (19-20). This controversy derives
   largely from . . .

2. The parentheses are placed *inside* a sentence, directly following the quotation or paraphrase they refer to, and *outside* quotation marks. (See previous example.)

3. When a quotation ends with a ? or a !, the ? or ! goes *inside* the quotation marks. Note: A period is still needed *after* the parentheses.

   Dickinson's letter to Higginson contained a question: "Are you too
   deeply occupied to say if my Verse is alive?" (Letters 2: 403).

4. If you quote more than four lines from a source, set the quotation off from the rest of the text by *indenting ten spaces* from the margin. Then, place the parenthetical note *after* the final mark of punctuation, separated by two spaces.

   Catton also suggests that Davis's attempt to lead his people to
   independence was somehow doomed to failure from the start.

   > He had done the best he could do in an impossible job, and
   > if it is easy to show where he made grievous mistakes, it
   > is difficult to show that any other man, given the
   > materials available, could have done much better. He had
   > courage, integrity, tenacity, devotion to his cause, and
   > like Old Testament Sisera, the stars in their courses
   > marched against him. (279)

NUMBERED NOTES FOR SPECIAL PURPOSES

Once in a while, you will find something that might interest your readers but is not essential to whatever idea you are developing in the paper at that point. If that happens, you may insert a note number directing readers to a footnote or an endnote. Endnotes, if you use them, are placed on a separate page, coming between the end of the paper and the Works Cited.

Insert the note number immediately after the final mark of punctuation for the sentence which led you to think of adding the ''comment for interested readers.'' Raise the number half a line.

```
Literary critics, serious biographers, and writers of fictionalized
accounts of her life created an image of Emily Dickinson as a timid,
reclusive, mystical thinker, who was too absorbed in personal sorrows
and ecstasies to be concerned with literary recognition. And this
image persists, to a great extent, in the public mind today.[1]
```

The endnote page would show:

```
    [1] For a full discussion of sources leading to the ''Emily myth,''
see Ferlazzo: 13-21.
```

(This note offers readers more information than they could get from the simple parenthetical note: ''Ferlazzo 13-21.'')

Variations on the Basic MLA Format

SOURCES HAVING MORE THAN ONE AUTHOR

If the source was written by more than one person, you would need to give the names of all the writers or possibly use the first author's name and *et al.* if there were more than three.

```
Davis took the position that ''the President was entrusted with
military leadership, and he must exercise it'' (Randall and Donald
271).

A recent investigation of iridium levels in the Dolomites revealed
traces insufficient to justify Alvarez's hypothesis (Sapperstein et
al. 12).
```

Works Cited would show:

```
Randall, J. G., and David Donald. The Divided Union. Boston:
    Little, 1961.

Sapperstein, M. L., Jonathan Kohn, Natalie Sachs, and R. L. Davis.
    "Iridium Levels in the Dolomites." Astronomy Today Sept.
    1983: 12-15.
```

TWO OR MORE SOURCES FOR ONE NOTE

Sometimes a piece of information or an idea will appear in more than one of your sources. Usually, especially with purely factual information, you choose one of the sources and refer only to it. However, occasionally, when each source offers some interesting additional commentary that a curious reader might enjoy investigating, you should mention each of them in your note, separating them with semicolons.

```
Many of Davis's personal troubles grew out of his ill health (Catton
121-22; Nevins 3: 86-89).
```

INDIRECT SOURCE: A SOURCE QUOTES ANOTHER WRITER

Frequently, your source will quote another writer's work, and you may want to quote that second writer. When this happens, you must make every reasonable effort to find the original source in order to verify the accuracy of the quotation. For one thing, you should check to be certain it was not "quoted out of context" (see pp. 88–89). When you have seen that source, you can add it to your list of Works Cited and refer directly to it in a parenthetical note.

However, sometimes you will find it very difficult, or even impossible, to locate the original source. In that case, you will be forced to rely on your first source, but your parenthetical reference must indicate that you worked with an indirect source by using the abbreviation *qtd.* (for *quoted*).

In this example, the author was quoting from an out-of-print book, *Criminal Man,* that was written in Italian.

```
Lambroso's racism becomes apparent in his remark that "[criminals']
physical insensibility well recalls that of savage peoples who can
bear, in rites of puberty, torture that a white man could never endure.
All travelers know the indifference of Negroes and American savages
```

to pain: the former cut their hands and laugh in order to avoid work;
the latter, tied to the torture post, gaily sing the praises of their
tribe while they are slowly burnt'' (qtd. in Gould 18).

The Works Cited page would show:

Gould, Stephen Jay. ''<u>Criminal Man</u> Revived.'' <u>Natural History</u>
    Mar. 1976: 16-18.

REFERENCE TO AN ENTIRE WORK

If you refer to an entire source by way of a summary or a paraphrase of
its thesis, then you do not need a parenthetical note as long as you mention author and title.

Gore Vidal's <u>Lincoln</u> presents a very readable reconstruction of the
president's approach to problems, both personal and political.

SUMMARY OF A CHAPTER OR AN ESSAY

Occasionally, you will make a statement that summarizes a major idea
from an article or essay or a chapter in a book. For a chapter, you may
use the chapter number instead of page numbers.

Chomsky claims that all humans inherit the same basic linguistic
structural framework upon which their community's particular
language is fitted (<u>Language</u> ch. 2).

For an essay or an article, do not use a note. Just mention the author
within your text. A reader can tell from the nature of your statement that
it covers a good deal of ground and will expect no note.

Gould settled the perplexing question as to whether a Portuguese man-
of-war is an organism or a colony by approaching the problem from a
new point of view, that of overlapping, evolving categories rather
than rigidly fixed definitions.

The author's name is enough to lead a reader to the right source in your
Works Cited:

Gould, Stephen Jay. ''A Most Ingenious Paradox.'' <u>Natural History</u>
    Dec. 1984: 20-29.

QUOTATION FROM LITERARY WORKS

When writing on literary topics, you will usually quote from the plays, poems, or prose works under discussion. For works of prose reprinted in many editions (novels, short stories, and most plays), indicate the page numbers, as with other sources, but also include chapter, book, act, or scene number, so readers can locate the quoted material in any edition. For poems and long poetic works that consist of ''books'' or ''cantos,'' indicate the quoted material not by page numbers but by line numbers. For long poems, like *The Iliad*, give the canto or book number plus the line numbers. For verse drama, use act/scene/line notation.

novel

It would seem that Captain Ahab has forever rejected God as he commences his final soliloquy in <u>Moby Dick</u> with, ''I turn my body from the sun . . .'' (468; ch. 135).

poetry

Along the same lines, given her deliberate decision to forgo publication rather than compromise her art, the first lines of another poem become significantly clear: ''Publication-- is the Auction / Of the Mind of Man'' (lines 1-2). And there can be no doubt that when she wrote the following stanza, Emily Dickinson had accepted the fact that true fame would not be hers in her lifetime.

> Some--Work for Immortality--
> The Chiefer part, for Time--
> He--Compensates--immediately
> The former--Checks--On Fame-- (lines 1-4)

drama

(reference to *Othello*)

Once again, Shakespeare deftly shifts images, this time in Othello's speech over the sleeping Desdemona, from lightness of color (Desdemona as compared to Othello) to light as a symbol of life (5.2.3-13).

If you do not mention the title of the verse drama or long poetic work in your text, add the title—which you may abbreviate—to the note.

(quotation from *Doctor Faustus*)

```
I see there's virtue in my heavenly words;
Who would not be proficient in this art?
How pliant is this Mephistophilis,
Full of obedience and humility!
Such is the force of magic and my spells:
Now, Faustus, thou art conjuror laureate,
That canst command great Mephistophilis.
(Faustus 1.3.30-36)
```

long poetic work (quotation from *Paradise Lost*)

```
Thus Adam to himself lamented loud
       . . . on the ground
Outstretcht he lay, on the cold ground, and oft
Curs'd his Creation, Death as oft accus'd
Of tardy execution, since denounc't
The day of his offence. Why comes not Death,
Said he, with one thrice acceptable stroke
To end me? (PL 10.845-56)
```

Note the difference between the punctuation of this note and the punctuation for volume and page numbers: *10.845–56* reads "book ten, lines 845–56"; *3:203* reads "volume 3, page 203."

Some Advice about Using Parenthetical Notation

This system of documentation encourages you to name your sources as you refer to them in the essay and to put as little information as possible in the parenthetical notes. Keep in mind that your notes should avoid, as far as possible, breaking a reader's concentration. The example shows how an obtrusive parenthetical note can be made less obtrusive.

obtrusive

```
Certainly then, the woman who has been called
"one of the greatest lyric poets of all time"
(Winters 40) was all but unknown as a poet during
her lifetime.
```

less obtrusive
```
                    Certainly then, the woman Yvor Winters has called
                    "one of the greatest lyric poets of all time"
                    (40) was all but unknown as a poet during her
                    lifetime.
```

Notice that the parenthetical note was placed directly after the quoted phrase. If it had been put at the end of the sentence (to reduce the interruptive effect), the note would seem to cover the whole idea, not just the part that belonged to Yvor Winters.

When paraphrasing, you will sometimes find it difficult to slip in the source's name, especially when the paraphrase deals with factual matter rather than a judgment, as in this example.

```
During her later years, Emily Dickinson had virtually no direct
contact with anyone outside her immediate family. While she was
still connected to her circle of friends, the poet made at least one
tentative attempt to find an audience for her poetry. But only a
handful of verses were published anonymously, most of them in a local
newspaper, and these were subjected to considerable editing. Upon
the poet's death at fifty-six, her sister discovered over one
thousand poems and initiated an effort to publish them. Beginning
four years later, in 1890, these poems finally appeared in print
(Sewall 1: 4-11).
```

Clearly, you would have had no reason to introduce Sewall's name in the text, since the information is both factual and very general; nothing seems to be particularly the work of a specific biographer.

Both of the next examples are well-constructed passages using the same sources; both make good use of the parenthetical note format. The differences are due to a shift of purpose on the writer's part. The comments that follow the examples explain the effect of the variation.

```
1. Recent studies show that anorexia can be successfully treated by
   psychotherapy (Kline; Evans et al.; Yaster and Korman). These
   studies dealt mostly with young persons who came to therapy
   voluntarily and continued treatment for at least six weeks. The
   authors of the studies concluded that anorexia is a "socially
   induced disorder" (Kline 214) and not a biologically caused
   illness.
```

2. Recent studies show that anorexia can be treated successfully by
   psychotherapy. Kline achieved an 85 percent cure for twenty cases
   in adolescent women. A group of Illinois therapists found that
   "most victims underwent marked improvement following four
   sessions" (Evans et al. 35). In California, Oscar Yaster and
   T. G. Korman, working with a population of males and females ages
   16-30, produced "significant remission rates" among those
   completing five sessions or more of group and individual
   treatment (17-18).

Notice that in (1) the writer did not intend to make a specific statement about each of the sources. Therefore, she cited all three of them after the introductory sentence of the paragraph. However, when she decided to quote a phrase from one of the three sources, which she felt spoke for all three, she then cited that one study.

If, on the other hand, the writer had wanted to say something about each source, she might have constructed the second paragraph. In that case, she would delay citing the sources until she got to each one individually. No special note was needed for Kline because the writer was summarizing the full study. But with Evans et al., she introduced a quotation, and that called for a note indicating the page number. Although the last of the three sources was quoted very briefly, a note was still needed to show where the phrase could be found. (Putting that note directly after the quoted phrase would have created an unnecessary interruption.)

General Guidelines for Listing Sources in Works Cited

A list of all your sources must appear at the end of your paper, in a section titled *Works Cited*. Arrange the items alphabetically according to the authors' last names. If a source has no known author, list it alphabetically according to the first word of its title (ignoring *A*, *An*, or *The*). See the Works Cited list for the paper on Emily Dickinson, on pages 203–204.

Do not inflate your list of Works Cited by including items that were not direct sources of the information in your paper. This means that, as a rule, no item should appear among your Works Cited unless at least one note in the paper refers to it.

To be useful to your reader, a bibliography or list of Works Cited must answer several basic questions about each source.

What is its full title?

Who wrote or created it?

Where and when was it published? And by what publisher?

And for articles in periodicals and for essays in books, on what pages can it be found?

Occasionally other kinds of information will have to be added. For books, there may be translators and editors, or volume numbers; for periodicals, the handling of dates and of volume and issue numbers varies according to the type of periodical (annual, monthly, weekly, daily); and for nonprint sources, such as films, recordings, television programs, yet other kinds of information must be included.

Our list of sample entries in this section covers the most common variations, dividing them into three categories: *books*, *periodicals*, and *other kinds of source materials*. Later in your college career, advanced research may lead you to rarer kinds of publications. At such times you may need to check the *MLA Handbook for Writers of Research Papers*, 3rd edition, for the correct format. But of course you will often discover these unusual sources through specialized indexes or in bibliographies attached to other sources, in which case, you would see the correct entry form before you picked up the source.

Group One: Sample Entries for Books

BASIC FORMAT

Pay close attention to spacing and punctuation in each case. In general, however,

1. The first line of each entry starts flush with the left margin; each subsequent line indents five spaces.
2. Periods separate main parts of an entry—author. title. publisher & date.
3. Each period is followed by *two* spaces.
4. Titles of books are underlined.
5. Quotation marks are used to indicate titles of essays and other short works contained within books or periodicals. (Exception: See "Critical Review," page 163.)
6. Use a shortened form of the publisher's name, dropping any *Inc.*, *Co.*, *Publishers*, or *Press*. Use only the first surname when the publisher's name is made up of one or more individual's name: *Norton* for *W. W. Norton and Company*, *Farrar* for *Farrar, Straus and Giroux*. For university presses, abbreviate *University* and *Press: Oxford UP, U of Chicago P.*

A SINGLE AUTHOR

Author of a Book

note punctuation and indentation; *Viking* is a shortened form of *The Viking Press*

Thomas, Lewis. The Lives of a Cell. New York:
Viking, 1974.

Author of an Essay in a Collection

Ed. stands for *editors*, the compilers of the book's essays or other writings; pages on which full essay appears are shown, even if only a page or two are used as sources

Frake, Charles O. ''How to Ask for a Drink in
Subanum.'' Directions in Sociolinguistics.
Ed. John J. Gumperz and D. Hymes. New York:
Holt, 1972. 127-32.

Note: If all the essays in a collection are by the same author, you do not need to include the individual essay title in the Works Cited entry. But if the collection contains essays by various authors—as in the second example here—the essay title should be cited.

TWO OR MORE AUTHORS

authors' names in the order in which they appear on title page of source

Bar-Adon, Aaron, and Werner F. Leopold. Child
Language. Englewood Cliffs: Prentice, 1971.
Dugan, James, Robert C. Cowen, Bill Barada, and
Richard M. Crum. World Beneath the Sea.
Washington: Nat. Geographic Soc., 1967.

TWO OR MORE SOURCES HAVING SAME AUTHOR

line of three hyphens is used in place of author's name for all entries after the first works listed alphabetically by title

Thomas, Lewis. The Lives of a Cell. New York:
Viking, 1974.
---. The Medusa and the Snail. New York: Viking,
1979.

AUTHOR OF SEVERAL SOURCES HAVING DIFFERENT COAUTHORS

coauthored books follow singly authored books alphabetically by coauthor

Chomsky, Noam. <u>Syntactic Structures</u>. The Hague:
Mouton, 1957.

Chomsky, Noam, and Morris Halle. <u>The Sound
Pattern of English</u>. New York: Harper, 1968.

Chomsky, Noam, and George A. Miller. <u>Analyse
formelle des langues naturelles</u>. No. 8 of
<u>Mathematiques et sciences de l'homme</u>. The
Hague: Mouton, 1971.

Special Cases

AFTERWORD

A commentary coming at end of some books: see ''Preface,'' page 160.

ANONYMOUS AUTHOR

Classical Literature

<u>The Song of Roland</u>. Trans. Frederick B. Luquines.
New York: Macmillan, 1960.

Unsigned Pamphlet

both writer and publisher unknown

<u>Push for Pot</u>. Ann Arbor: n. p., 1969.

THE BIBLE AS A SOURCE

No need to list this work in Works Cited unless you use a version other than the King James. Just provide the book, chapter, and verse numbers in your parenthetical note (Gen. 3:14–20).

CORPORATION AS AN AUTHOR

could also be entered by title; choice is yours

Phillips Petroleum. <u>66 Ways to Save Energy</u>.
Bartlesville, OK: Phillips Petroleum, 1978.

EDITOR

Editor's Ideas Were Cited

> Gardner, Martin, ed. <u>The Annotated Alice. Alice's</u>
> <u>Adventures in Wonderland and Through the</u>
> <u>Looking Glass</u>. By Lewis Carroll. New York:
> Potter, 1960.

The Work Itself Was Cited

> Carroll, Lewis. <u>The Annotated Alice. Alice's</u>
> <u>Adventures in Wonderland and Through the</u>
> <u>Looking Glass</u>. Ed. Martin Gardner. New York:
> Potter, 1960.

ENCYCLOPEDIA ARTICLE

although article's title is "Isaac Newton," it is entered under "Newton," under which a reader would look it up; second example shows form for signed article; publisher's name is not necessary

> "Newton, Isaac." <u>The New Columbia Encyclopedia</u>.
> 1975.
>
> Kaufmann, Walter. "Friedrich Nietzsche."
> <u>Encyclopaedia Britannica</u>. 1969.

ENLARGED EDITION

See "Revised Edition," page 160.

FOREWORD

A commentary at the beginning of some books: see "Preface," page 160.

GOVERNMENT AS AUTHOR

could also be entered by title; choice is yours

> Federal Council for Science and Technology. <u>First</u>
> <u>Annual Report of Ad Hoc Committee on</u>
> <u>Geodynamics</u>. USIGP-F476, Washington, 1978.

PREFACE, FOREWORD, INTRODUCTION, OR AFTERWORD

reference here is to
Edel's rather than
Wilson's writing; had
Wilson's text also been
cited, book would be
entered twice, once
under each author's
name

Edel, Leon. Foreword. <u>The Thirties</u>. By Edmund
    Wilson. New York: Farrar, 1980.

REPRINT

note distinction
between reprint and
revised edition; revision
means that changes
were made, and date
given is that of the
changes; reprint leaves
everything as in the
original; important date
is that of the first
writing

Boys, C. V. <u>Soap Bubbles and the Forces Which
    Mould Them</u>. 1916. New York: Doubleday, 1959.

REVISED OR ENLARGED EDITION

editions other than first
must be identified

Chomsky, Noam. <u>Language and Mind</u>. Enl. ed. New
    York: Harcourt, 1972.

TITLE WITHIN A TITLE

Especially in the field of literary criticism, titles of books and essays often contain titles of other works.

When a book's title includes the title of another *book*, do not underline the interior title.

<u>The Theological Underpinning of</u> Moby Dick.

When a book's title includes the title of a *poem* or *essay*, underline the interior title and place it within quotation marks.

<u>The Anthropological Background of ''The
Wasteland'' of T. S. Eliot</u>.

TRANSLATOR

Translator's Ideas Are Cited

> Fitzgerald, Robert, trans. The Iliad. By Homer.
> Garden City, NY: Anchor, 1974.

Only the Work Is Cited

> Homer. The Iliad. Trans. Robert Fitzgerald.
> Garden City, NY: Anchor, 1974.

VOLUME NUMBERS

For works that are published in more than one volume, you must indicate which volume(s) you used in your paper.

More Than One of the Volumes Was Cited

bibliographic entry indicates that all three volumes have been used

> Dickinson, Emily. The Poems of Emily Dickinson.
> Ed. Thomas H. Johnson. 3 vols. Cambridge,
> MA: Belknap P-Harvard UP, 1955.

Just One Volume Was Cited

> Wellek, René. A History of Modern Criticism:
> 1750-1950. Vol. 2. New Haven: Yale UP, 1955.

a volume will often have its own title; if that title is prominent in its own right, it is cited first

> Nevins, Allan. The Organized War, 1863-64. Vol. 3
> of The War for the Union. New York:
> Scribner's, 1971.

Group Two: Sample Entries for Periodicals

A periodical entry contains two titles: that of the article (within quotation marks) and that of the periodical (underlined, like the title of a book).

Volume numbers are needed for periodicals that do not carry specific dates—month, or day and month. Academic journals are especially likely to go by volume and issue rather than a date.

Page numbers of the full article are placed at the end of the entry.

BASIC FORMAT

Pay close attention to spacing and punctuation for each case. In general, however,

1. Periods separate main parts of an entry—author. article title. periodical title & date. Page numbers are preceded by a colon.
2. Each period is followed by TWO spaces.
3. Names of periodicals are underlined.
4. Quotation marks are used to indicate titles of articles.

A SINGLE AUTHOR

> Bethell, Tom. "Agnostic Evolutionists."
> Harper's Feb. 1985: 49-61.

ARTICLE IN AN ANNUAL, SEMIANNUAL, OR QUARTERLY PERIODICAL

when author's name is not given, source is listed by title

> Moore, John B. "The Role of Gulliver." Modern
> Philological Quarterly 25 (1928): 169-80.
> "Do Cities Change the Weather?" Mosaic 5 (Summer
> 1974): 29-34.

ARTICLE IN A MONTHLY PERIODICAL

volume number is generally unnecessary; "+" indicates article continues at end of magazine

> Premack, Anne James, and David Premack.
> "Teaching Language to an Ape." Scientific
> American Oct. 1972: 92-99.
> Sahgal, Pavan. "Idiot Geniuses." Science
> Digest May 1981: 12-13+.

ARTICLE IN A WEEKLY PERIODICAL

issue is identified by date, month, and year

> Dorschner, John. "Look Out! Here Comes the
> Sahara!" Tropic 29 Dec. 1974: 34-45.

"Women's Bank: A Modest Profit." <u>Newsweek</u> 20
Apr. 1981: 16.

ARTICLE IN A DAILY NEWSPAPER

when only writer's initials are known, they follow normal order (not "K., J."); note quotation marks within quotation marks in the third example; section number or letter, if there is one, is included; when the paper's title does not include the name of the city, that information is shown in brackets (the *Daily Worker* was a national newspaper)

Roughton, Roger. "Barber's Bust with Loaf on
Head." <u>Daily Worker</u> 8 Apr. 1936: 7.

J. K. "Explodes an Illusion." <u>Daily Worker</u> 30
Dec. 1936: 7-8.

"Presidential Panel Holds Hearings on 'Right to
Die.' " <u>New York Times</u> 12 Apr. 1981, late
ed., sec. 1: 24.

"Rebirth of a City." <u>New-Times</u> [Danbury, CT] 6
Sept. 1977: 2.

Special Cases

CRITICAL REVIEW OF ANOTHER WORK

Chomsky, Noam. Rev. of <u>Verbal Behavior,</u> by B. F.
Skinner. <u>Language</u> 35 (1959): 26-58.

(Note that the title of the review itself title is neither underlined nor enclosed within quotation marks.)

ISSUE NUMBERS

Some journals do not publish in "volumes"; they assign issue numbers only. Treat the issue number exactly as you would a volume number. In this example, 94 is the issue number.

Pritchard, Allan. "West of the Great Divide: A
View of the Literature of British Columbia."
<u>Canadian Literature</u> 94 (1982): 96-112.

REPRINT OF A JOURNAL ARTICLE

```
Mazzeo, Joseph A.  "A Critique of Some Modern
     Theories of Metaphysical Poetry."  Modern
     Philology 50 (1952): 88-96. Rpt. in
     Seventeenth-Century English Poetry.  Ed.
     William R. Keast.  New York: Oxford UP, 1962.
     63-74.
```

TITLE WITHIN A TITLE

Underline the titles of books, plays, and long poems (The Iliad).

```
"Hawthorne's Reaction to Moby-Dick."
```

Place single quotation marks around the title of an essay, short story, or short poem.

```
"A Psychoanalytic Interpretation of 'The Emperor
     of Ice Cream.'"
```

Group Three: Sample Entries for Other Material

COMPUTERIZED INFORMATION, FROM DATABASE SOURCE

```
"Thomas Jefferson." Academic American
     Encyclopedia, 1981. CompuServe record no.
     1823.
```

COMPUTER SOFTWARE

```
Connections.  Computer software. Krell Software,
     1982.
```

FILM

can be entered either by title or director, depending on how used as a source: when

```
A Clockwork Orange.  Dir. Stanley Kubrick.  Warner,
     1971. Based on Anthony Burgess's  A Clockwork
     Orange.
```

studying director's work, name is given first; when studying film itself (as art form or as adaptation of a novel) title is used

Kubrick, Stanley, dir. <u>2001: A Space Odyssey</u>. MGM, 1969.

INFORMATION SERVICE MATERIAL

Use the format for a book, adding the code numbers used by the service (e.g., ERIC ED 187 864) at the end. (ERIC stands for Educational Resources Information Center.)

INTERVIEW

Moynihan, Patrick, Sen. Personal interview. 17 March 1983.

LECTURE

Thomas, Lewis. "Notes of a Biology Watcher." Lecture at the Princeton Club of New York, 21 Feb. 1978.

LETTER

Entwhistle, Jacob, M.D. Letter to the author. 28 May 1980.

MICROFILM OR MICROFICHE

Just be sure to add in parentheses at the end of the entry the word "microfilm" or "microfiche."

RECORDING

again purpose dictates order in which information is presented: when topic is music, second form

Leadbelly (Huddie Ledbetter). <u>Rock Island Line</u>. Notes by Frederick Ramsey, Jr. Folkways, FA 2014, 1956.

is used; when artist is topic, his/her name is entered; when artist or author is identified by nickname or pseudonym, supply the true name in parenthesis

"Black Girl." <u>Rock Island Line</u>. Sung by
   Leadbelly (Huddie Ledbetter).
   Folkways, FA 2014, 1956.

TELEVISION PROGRAM

Marshall was program's narrator

"Gorilla." <u>National Geographic Society</u>. Narr.
   E. G. Marshall. PBS. WNET, New York. 15
   Apr. 1981.

TESTIMONY, OFFICIAL

note absence of underlining or quotation marks

Bell, Mark. Testimony before the Subcommittee on
   the Environment and the Atmosphere.
   Committee on Science and Technology, House of
   Representatives, 22 May 1975.

Documentation of Illustrative Materials

A final matter regarding documentation concerns the layout and labeling of graphs, tables, and other illustrative materials.

Tables are referred to as "Tables," but graphs, pictures, diagrams, and other kinds of illustration are all referred to as "Figures" (usually abbreviated *Fig.*). Each kind of item is numbered consecutively throughout the paper with arabic numerals (Table 1, Table 2; Fig. 1, Fig. 2, Fig. 3).

Table 1
U.S.-Japan Merchandise Trade: 1975-78

Year	U.S. domestic exports to Japan	U.S. general imports from Japan
1975	$ 9,421,000,000	$11,268,000,000
1976	10,027,000,000	15,504,000,000
1977	10,422,000,000	18,550,000,000
1978	12,689,000,000	24,458,000,000

Source: U.S. Bureau of the Census, <u>Statistical Abstract of the United</u>
   <u>States: 1979</u> (Washington: GPO, 1979) 920.

Figure 1

U.S.-Japan Merchandise Trade: 1975-78

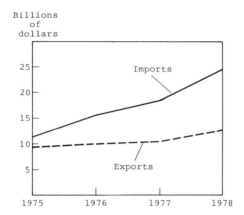

figure shows same information as preceding table; captions below the figure are sometimes used instead of titles above

Source: U.S. Bureau of the Census, Statistical Abstract of the United States: 1979 (Washington: GPO, 1979) 920.

The Endnote/Footnote System of Documentation

Some instructors, particularly those in the fields of history, philosophy, political science, and religion, may prefer that you document your sources by inserting numbers in your text to refer to notations on a separate page of endnotes or at the foot of each page. These guidelines should prove helpful for such situations.

Insert a single number slightly above the line at all points where you would have used a parenthetical note. These numbers must run in sequence throughout the paper: 1, 2, 3, and so on. If you find you have left out a note after inserting all the numbers within the text, you must change all the succeeding numbers. Do not create "5a," for instance, when inserting an entry between 5 and 6.

After all the numbers have been placed within the text, make a list of "endnotes." Next to each number, enter the bibliographic information that precisely identifies the source of the quotation, paraphrase, or summary. On rare occasions, an instructor may ask you to place footnotes at the bottom of each page, rather than compile a list of endnotes. The rules for punctuating and spacing footnotes are the same as those for endnotes.

Insertion of Numbers Within the Text

1. Each number is typed *half a space* above the line, and directly (no space) after the final punctuation of the sentence it refers to.
2. For quotations that end in the middle of a sentence, place the number directly after the final quotation mark.
3. Always skip TWO spaces after each number that falls at the end of a sentence.

Here are examples in which numbers replaced parenthetical notes in the paper on Emily Dickinson.

> Dickinson sent Higginson four poems, along with a letter containing this question: "Are you too deeply occupied to say if my Verse is alive?"[8] This . . .

> Certainly then, the poet Yvor Winters called "one of the greatest lyric poets of all time"[2] was all but unknown as a poet during her lifetime.

> Paul Ferlazzo, for example, infers that Higginson's response to her first letter must have included some recommendations for altering, or "regularizing," her poems, along with a request for more of her work.[9]

> The general reading public that asked for meter that is smooth, rhythm that is easy, and words that are limited to only one obvious meaning interested her not at all. She was willing to wait.[15]

When you quote from a literary work, use an endnote for the first reference, identifying the specific edition you used and informing your readers that all subsequent notes will be in-text parenthetical notes. After the first note, simply insert the pages or, as in the following quotation from *Paradise Lost*, the book and line numbers.

> Evil into the mind of God or Man
> May come and go, so unapprov'd, and leave
> No spot or blame behind: Which gives me hope

That what in sleep thou didst abhor to dream,

Waking thou never wilt consent to do.

(PL 5.117-21)

BASIC ENDNOTE FORMAT

This format differs from that of the Works Cited, although the same basic questions are answered—Who? What? Where? When?

Works Cited   Bernstein, Jeremy. Einstein. New York: Vintage-

Random, 1973.

Endnote   1 Jeremy Bernstein, Einstein (New York: Vintage-

Random, 1973) 79.

Here is the basic endnote format:

1. The first line of each note indents five spaces; each subsequent line flushes with the left margin.
2. Author's name is given in normal order.
3. Commas and spaces replace the periods and two spaces used in Works Cited.
4. Parentheses surround publishing information.
5. Page number(s) are added at the very end. Do not use **p.** or **pp.** No colon or comma comes between parentheses and page number(s).

A few samples of the most common situations should give you an idea of how to handle this system.

EDITOR AND TRANSLATOR

1 Martin Gardner, ed., The Annotated Alice.

Alice's Adventures in Wonderland and Through the

Looking Glass, by Lewis Carroll (New York: Potter,

1960) iv-vi.

2Feodor Dostoevsky, Crime and Punishment,

trans. Jessie Coulson, ed. George Gibian (New

York: Norton, 1964) 142.

ESSAY IN A BOOK OF ESSAYS

3 Charles O. Frake, ''How to Ask for a Drink in Subanum,'' <u>Directions in Sociolinguistics</u>, ed. John J. Gumperz and D. Hymes (New York: Holt, 1972) 129-30.

INTRODUCTION, FOREWORD, AFTERWORD, PREFACE

4 Leon Edel, foreword, <u>The Thirties</u>, by Edmund Wilson (New York: Farrar, 1980) vii.

PERIODICALS

5 Stephen Jay Gould, ''A Most Ingenious Paradox,'' <u>Natural History</u> Dec. 1984: 20.

(Note the colon between date and page number, unlike the format for books.)

6 William Howard, ''Emily Dickinson's Poetic Vocabulary,'' <u>PMLA</u> 72 (1957): 227.

(Note use of parentheses around the date *when volume number is given.*)

7 John Dorschner, ''Look Out! Here Comes the Sahara!'' <u>Tropic</u> 29 Dec. 1974: 38.

(No comma after title that ends with ? or !)

8 ''Presidential Panel Holds Hearings on 'Right to Die,' '' <u>New York Times</u> 12 Apr. 1981, late ed., sec. 1: 24.

SHORTENED FORM FOR SECOND AND FURTHER REFERENCES TO SAME SOURCE

After you have produced one complete note for a particular source, you can use a shorter form for all subsequent references to the same source.

```
10 Bernstein 231.
```

(No comma between author and page.)

DO NOT use *ibid.* or *loc. cit.* or other Latin abbreviations you may see in journals or books.

If the author wrote more than one of your sources, you have to put the title (in a shortened form) in the note. In the next example, earlier notes would have given the complete bibliographic information for Freud's *The Interpretation of Dreams* and his *Moses and Monotheism.*

```
16 Freud, Dreams 303.

17 Freud, Moses 68.
```

(Comma goes between author and title only.)

In this system, as in the 1988 MLA parenthetical system, mentioning the source or the author in the text affects the amount of information that appears in the note.

```
Jehovah was originally the god of a local volcano,

according to Freud.19

      19 Moses 23.
```

Don't carry this too far, however. Always mention either the author or the title in the shortened notes. Never give just the page number(s).

For a full example of this system of documentation, see the sample paper by Fred Hutchins in chapter 9.

The APA (Author/Year) System of Documentation

Many behavioral science instructors will ask you to follow the system devised by the American Psychological Association (APA), which uses parenthetical notes in the text that correspond to sources listed at the end of the paper under *References.* The APA system is similar in form to the 1988 MLA system; the major difference lies in the basic contents of the parenthetical notes.

- In the APA system, you generally give the year of publication in the note, whereas in MLA, you never put the date in the note.
- In the APA system, you give the page numbers only for a quotation, not for paraphrases or summaries, as in MLA.

These differences are not trivial. The APA believes the most important information is the time the idea was presented to the world; the MLA is primarily concerned with precisely locating the information within the source.

The APA system is a variant on a general approach called the author/ year system. (Some disciplines within the behavioral sciences have arrived at their own slightly different versions of author/year. Several of these are briefly illustrated at the end of this section.)

PUNCTUATION OF NOTES

1. As in MLA, parenthetical notes are included within the sentences to which they refer.
2. Commas separate name from date when both appear inside a note.
3. An ampersand (&) is used instead of *and* between authors' names, when more than one name appears in a note. (But use *and* when you mention coauthors in your text.)
4. The abbreviations p. and pp. are used to indicate *page* and *pages*, except after volume and issue numbers.

BASIC FORMAT

Insert the parenthetical note immediately after the name of the author. You are strongly encouraged to mention the author's name in your text rather than in the parenthetical note. The note contains just the year of publication.

> Robinson (1980) asserted that child abuse in
> upper-middle-class homes manifests itself in
> subtler ways.

If a source has two authors, mention them both.

> Martin and Elder (1969) demonstrated that abusive
> parents were usually themselves abused.

If, for stylistic reasons, you do not mention the authors' names in your text, then place them inside the note.

> It was shown in the late sixties (Martin & Elder,
> 1969) that abusive parents were usually
> themselves abused.

You can avoid using a note by mentioning both author and date in your text.

> In 1969, Martin and Elder demonstrated that
> abusive parents were usually themselves abused.

When you quote a source directly, use a note to indicate the page number as well as the date and author if they are not already clear in the text.

> Rogers (1979) believes that "virtually all female
> abusers suffered from primary splitting" (p. 67).
>
> One theorist believes that "virtually all female
> abusers suffered from primary splitting"
> (Rogers, 1979, p. 67).

When a source has more than three but less than six authors, use the first author's name and *et al.* after the first full citation. If a source has more than six authors, use the first author's surname and *et al.* for the first and subsequent citations. But watch out for the situation when two of your sources have several authors with the same person heading both series of names.

> Gold, Bache, Cohen, and Arnach (1978) found
> that . . .
>
> Gold et al. (1978) were not so sure that . . .
>
> Marx, Walcott, Blau, and Johanssen (1975)
> said . . .
>
> Marx, Martin, and Schuster (1980) were convinced
> that . . .
>
> A study completed ten years ago (Marx, Walcott, et
> al., 1975) concluded that . . .

If two authors have the same last name, use initials to distinguish them, both in notes and within the text.

> J. Prescott (1983) tried testing infants . . .
>
> A later study (D. Prescott, 1985) could find
> no . . .

If the "author" is a corporation or government agency, place the full name in the first note and the abbreviation in brackets; abbreviate thereafter.

> The government (National Institute of Mental
> Health [NIMH], 1981) took a strong interest
> in . . .
>
> A hotly contested government survey (NIMH, 1981)
> came to the conclusion that . . .

If an author contributed more than one source to your list, and two of them were published in the same year, small letters are added to the year numbers.

> Freud (1923a) first announced . . .
>
> In a now-famous essay (Freud, 1923b), the idea
> of . . .

When a source has no author, use a short form of the title in the parenthetical note.

> One source ("Supergene cluster," 1982) predicted
> that . . .

The References page listed this article as follows:

> Supergene cluster fights aging. (1982, August).
> Science Digest, p. 91.

If one of your sources mentioned the work of another author, and you want to refer to that other work, use this form:

> Ashkenazi's work (cited in Beatty, 1982)
> showed . . .

Note: Be sure to list Beatty's work, not Ashkenazi's, in your list of References, for that is where you found the information.

LISTING SOURCES UNDER REFERENCES

Punctuation

1. Underline book titles and periodical names and volume numbers.
2. Do not use quotation marks around titles of essays and periodical articles. (And do not underline them.)
3. Capitalize only the first word, proper nouns, and proper adjectives in essay and article titles. But capitalize all main words in names of periodicals.
4. Use commas between authors' surnames and initials and between authors. With more than one author, use an ampersand (&) before the last author's name.

Format

1. Sources are listed alphabetically by their authors' names, or when author is not known, by the first word of the title, excluding **A**, **An**, **The**.
2. No first names given for authors, just initials (unless two persons have same last names and initials).
3. When a source has multiple authors, all authors' names are entered by last name, followed by initials.
4. The year of publication (inside parentheses) follows the author's name. When two or more sources have the same author, list the sources chronologically. If two or more articles appeared in the same year, use letters (a, b, c) to distinguish them and list them alphabetically. Repeat the author's name in each case.

(In this sample list, only authors and titles are shown, so you can concentrate on the above points.)

```
            Freud, A. (1951). An experiment in group
               upbringing. . . .
            Freud, S. (1905). Three essays on the theory of
               sexuality. . . .
            Freud, S. (1910a). Five lectures on psychoanal-
               ysis. . . .
            Freud, S. (1910b). Leonardo da Vinci and a memory
               of his childhood. . . .
```

```
Freud, S. (1931). Female sexuality. . . .
Goldstein, J., Freud, A., & Solnit, A. J. (1979).
    Before the best interests of the child. . . .
Klein, M. (1961). Narrative of a child anal-
    ysis. . . .
```

Note also the following list of standard abbreviations for common bibliographical terms.

chap.	ed. (edition)	
Vol. 4	Ed. (editor)	Trans. (translator)
4 vols.	rev. ed.	rpt. (reprint)
No. (number)	2nd ed.	

SAMPLE LIST OF REFERENCES

```
Arlow, J. A. (1981). Theories of pathogenesis.
    Psychoanalytic Quarterly, 50, 488-514.
Maccoby, E., & Jacklin, C. (1974). The psychology
    of sex differences. Stanford, CA: Stanford
    University Press.
Epstein, A. (1982). Teen parents: What they need
    to know. High/Scope Resource, 1(2), 6-7.
Kohn, M. L. (1980). Job complexity and adult
    personality. In N. J. Smelser & E. H. Erikson
    (Eds.), Themes of work and love in adulthood
    (pp. 193-212). Cambridge, MA: Harvard
    University Press.
Steinem, G. (1981, May). The politics of talking
    in groups. Ms., pp. 43-45+.
Murphy, K. (1989, April 17). The long arm of RICO--
    is it reaching too far? Los Angeles
    Times, pp. 1, 19.
Freud, S. (1966). Introductory lectures on
    psychoanalysis (J. Strachey, Trans. and
    Ed.). New York: W. W. Norton. (Original work
    published 1917)
```

Berkowitz, M. S. (Ed.). (1985). Peer conflict and
    psychological growth. San Francisco: Jossey-
    Bass.

Foulks, E. F., Persons, J. B., & Merkel, R. L.
    (1986). The effect of patients' beliefs
    about their illnesses on compliance in
    psychotherapy. American Journal of
    Psychiatry, 143, 340-344.

Supergene cluster fights aging. (1982, August).
    Science Digest, p. 91.

FORMATS FOR OTHER KINDS OF SOURCES

Ritchie, M. (Director). (1972). The candidate
    [Film]. Warner.

Wilson, J. Q. (1987). Libel & the media [Review of
    Reckless disregard: Westmoreland v. CBS et
    al., Sharon v. Time]. Commentary, 83(3),
    70-74.

Kaminsky, J. (1987, June). [Interview with John
    Roach, chairman of Tandy Corp.]. Consumer
    Electronics, pp. 45-50.

See also the sample paper by Anita Barrone in chapter 9.

The Numbered System of Documentation

A fourth system, sometimes called the *numbered* system, is employed
primarily in chemistry, physics, and engineering. It, too, uses parenthetical notes, but the sources are assigned numbers in the list of References,
and these numbers are what readers see within the parentheses, instead
of page numbers or years.

Widlow (1) discovered that cells injected
    with . . .

Breitenstein and Forester (2) attempted to con-
    vert . . .

```
Morgan (3) and Stanley (4) both argued that
    stress . . .
```

Even if you do not mention the author within your text, place only the number assigned to it in the note. If you refer to more than one source at the same time, include the number assigned to each source.

```
Recent experimentation (6, 7, 8) seems to indi-
    cate . . .
```

In these sciences, writers rarely quote their sources directly; however, if you quote, the page number must be included in the note.

```
As Elsasser stated (6, p. 18), "The outcome
    depended on . . . "
```

Listing Sources under References

Some disciplines ask for alphabetical listing by author, with each item assigned a number. Other disciplines want the sources listed in the order in which they are cited in the paper. Check for your instructor's preference. The above set of examples followed the "order cited" format, as you can see.

Format Preferences for Various Academic Disciplines

Be sure to look for the differences in these areas:

- placing of publication date;
- use of underlining and quotation marks and capitalization for titles;
- abbreviation of periodical names;
- treatment of publisher's location and name.

SCIENCES

Biology uses the numbered system and lists references in alphabetical order.

first words in titles and
proper nouns are
capitalized; when

```
1. Bernal, J. D., and I. Frankuchen. X-ray and
    crystallographic studies of plant virus
```

article appears on just one page, page number is repeated; date follows all other information

 preparations. J. Gen. Physio. 25:111-165; 1941.

2. Crick, F. H. C. Is α-keratin a coiled coil? Nature. 170:882-882; 1952.

3. Judson, H. F. The eighth day of creation. Simon & Schuster, New York: 1979.

Botany and *Zoology* use the author/year system and list references in alphabetical order.

first words in titles and proper nouns are capitalized; volume numbers are underlined

Hairston, N. G., F. E. Smith, and L. B. Slobodkin. 1960. Community, structure, population, control, and competition. American Naturalist 94: 421-425.

Muller, W. H. 1974. Botany: a functional approach. Macmillan, New York.

Chemistry uses the numbered system and lists references in the order in which they are cited in the paper.

note omission of titles for periodical articles and use of quotation marks for book titles

(1) T. Raptolinsky, ''Chemists and the New Technology,'' Mills Ltd., Manchester, 1976, pp. 102-109.

(2) R. Johnstone, J. Am. Chem. Soc., 89, 405-412 (1978).

(3) L. Pauling, R. B. Corey, and H. R. Branson, Proc. N. A. S., 37, 205-211 (1951).

Engineering uses the numbered system and lists references in the order in which they are cited in the paper.

normal capitalization

1. Keenan, J. H., and Keyes, F. G. Thermodynamic Properties of Steam, Wiley, New York, 1936.

2. Cook, E. G. ''Stress Patterns in Danbury Bridge,'' ACBL 42, August 1979.

Geology uses the author/year system and lists references in alphabetical order.

follows same format as botany and zoology, except that order of publisher and city is reversed

Purrett, L. A. 1972. Before Pangaea—what? Science News 102: 220-222.

Sullivan, W. 1974. Continents in motion. New York, McGraw-Hill. 399 p.

Mathematics uses the numbered system and lists references in alphabetical order.

note that all titles are underlined

[1.] Petr Beckmann, A History of Pi, New York, St. Martin's, 1976.

[2.] Paul Bennacerraf, God, the Devil, and Goedel, Monist 51 (1967), 9.

[3.] J. R. Lucas, Minds, Machines, and Goedel, in Minds and Machines, ed. A. R. Anderson, Englewood Cliffs, NJ, Prentice-Hall, 1964.

Physics uses the numbered system and lists references in the order in which they are cited.

page numbers for books tell which pages are relevant to paper

1A. Baker, Modern Physics and Anti-physics (Addison-Wesley, Reading, MA, 1970), pp. 45-49, 102-10.

titles of articles are not given; titles of periodicals are not underlined

2J. M. Jauch, Are Quanta Real? A Galilean Dialogue (Indiana University Press, Bloomington, 1973), pp. 72-77.

3D. R. Hofstadter, Physical Review B, 14, no. 6, 45-64 (1976).

SOCIAL SCIENCES

Economics uses the author/year system and lists references in alphabetical order.

note that last item, although numbered like a periodical, is a pamphlet or small book and no page numbers are given

R. Easterlin, "Does Money Buy Happiness?" The Public Interest, Winter 1973, 30, 1-17.

E. E. Lawler II, Pay and Organizational Effectiveness: A Psychological View, New York, 1971.

United States Department of Commerce, <u>Survey of</u>

<u>Current Business</u>, July 1979, 59, no. 7.

Education uses either the MLA format or the author/year system and lists references in alphabetical order.

preferred form

Bruner, Jerome S., ''The Growth of Mind,'' <u>Amer.</u>

<u>Psychol.</u> 20: 1007-17; Oct. 1977.

Jones, Richard M., <u>Fantasy and Feeling in</u>

<u>Education</u>. New York: New York Univ. Press,

1968. 276 p.

History follows the MLA format or the numbered footnote system.

Political Science usually follows the MLA format.

Psychology commonly uses the author/year system, but some journals use the numbered system. Both systems follow alphabetical order when listing references. Ask your instructor which to use.

preferred form

Blos, P. (1962). <u>On adolescence</u>. New York: Free

Press.

Erikson, E. H. (1956). The problem of ego

identity. <u>J. Amer. Psychoanal. Assn.</u>,

<u>4</u>: 56-121.

Mahler, M. S., Pine, F., & Bergman, A. (1975). <u>The</u>

<u>psychological birth of the human infant</u>.

New York: Basic Books.

Sociology uses the author/year system and lists references in alphabetical order. Book and journal titles are not underlined and article titles are not capitalized (after the first word) or enclosed in quotation marks. Your instructor's preferences may vary this somewhat.

preferred form

Gumperz, John J. (1971). Language in social

groups. Stanford, CA: Stanford Univ. Press.

Maranda, Elli (1971). Theory and practice of

riddle analysis. Jour. Amer. Folklore 84

(July): 51-61.

Review Questions

1. Why do research papers include parenthetical notes? Is the answer the same for all disciplines?

2. When might you use a traditional footnote number while working with the MLA system of parenthetical documentation?

3. Explain why you would or would not cite a source for each of the following pieces of information.

   - the definition of *palindrome*
   - the names of Emily Dickinson's father and mother
   - the latest census data about the size of the average American household
   - the poet T. S. Eliot's interpretation of the river in *Huckleberry Finn*
   - Dr. Elizabeth Kübler-Ross's concept of the appropriate attitudes toward dying patients
   - author Willa Cather's date and place of birth
   - results of a recent study of caffeine's effect on sleep
   - the population of Saigon, Vietnam, before and after the Vietnam War
   - American patriot Nathan Hale's last words, ''I regret that I have but one life to give for my country.''

Exercise

Construct a Works Cited page for the following sources, putting all of the information in the correct order according to the MLA format.

If you need help getting started, the first five of the following items appear in the bibliography for the Dickinson paper in chapter 9.

1. Your research led you to a book titled Emily Dickinson: A Collection of Critical Essays, in which you found an essay called Emily Dickinson and the Limits of Judgment. The book was edited by Richard B. Sewall, and the essay was the work of Yvor Winters. The essay began on page 38 and ended on page 56. The book was published in 1963 by Prentice-Hall, located in Englewood Cliffs, New Jersey.

2. Your research uncovered an essay, Father and Daughter: Edward and Emily Dickinson, which was published in a journal, American Literature, in January 1960. This was volume 40, and the essay covered pages 510 to 523. The writer was Owen Thomas.

3. When quoting Emily Dickinson's poetry, you used a collection called The Complete Poems of Emily Dickinson, which was published in 1960 by Little, Brown and Company, located in Boston, Massachusetts. The person who edited the poems was Thomas H. Johnson.

4. When quoting the poet's letters, you used a three-volume collection called The Letters of Emily Dickinson, which was published in Cambridge, Massachusetts, by the Harvard University Press in 1958. The editors were Thomas H. Johnson and Theodora Ward.

5. You read a book written by the critic Paul J. Ferlazzo in 1976. The book was titled Emily Dickinson and was published by Twayne Publishers, which is located in Boston, Massachusetts.

6. You read a tribute to the poet, called The First Lady of Mt. Holyoke, which appeared in the South Hadley (Massachusetts) Gazette on December 10, 1980. This unsigned essay appeared on the second and third pages of the second section of the newspaper.

7. You also wrote a letter to a professor at Mt. Holyoke College, Joanna Caldwell, who is an authority on the poet and her works. You quoted a remark from her reply to you, which was written on November 4, 1980.

8. You read an article in the magazine Psychology Today, written by John Forsyte, Joanna Caldwell, and Edgar Polishook. The article, titled Emily Dickinson: Inhibited Genius?, appeared in the July 1979 issue on pages 68 to 80.

9. You read a review of Ferlazzo's book (see item 5), written by Joanna Caldwell, which was published in PMLA, volume 65, pages 343 to 345. This issue was published in May 1980.

9

Preparing the Final Manuscript

As you no doubt already know, appearances count. After investing so much time and energy in the research assignment, you would be foolish to hand in a paper containing numerous typographical errors, insertions, and corrections. A messy manuscript could easily mislead your reader to think you had done the whole job in haste. Be sure, therefore, to leave enough time for preparing a clean, attractively designed manuscript.

First and foremost, type the paper, at all costs. Most instructors will insist that you type research papers, but even if you find one who accepts handwritten papers, you would be wise to get the paper typed, even if you believe your script is exceptionally neat and easy to read.

Follow precisely whatever format your instructor specifies. If none is recommended, however, the advice given here will meet most instructors' standards.

The Mechanics of Manuscript Preparation

MATERIALS

1. Use 8½- by 11-inch white paper, twenty-pound bond.

2. Do not use erasable paper—it smudges easily. Do not use onionskin paper, either, except for your own carbon copy if you choose to

make one. (You must always keep a copy when you hand in a man-uscript.)

3. Type on just one side of each page.
4. Use a *new* ribbon, black only.

SPACING AND MARGINS

1. In general, leave a one-inch margin at the top and bottom of each page and on the left-hand side. Of course, you cannot know where lines will end on the right-hand side, but you should try to leave a one-inch margin there, as well. Break up long words with hyphens before they extend into the margin.
   Exception: The top of the first page looks a bit different. Type the ti-tle two inches from the top; then double-space twice before the first line of your text.

2. Double-space lines throughout the paper, including long quota-tions indented from the margin and pages listing Endnotes, Works Cited, or References.

3. Indent each paragraph five spaces. Long quotations—more than four lines long—should be indented ten spaces and double-spaced. When indenting a long quotation, do not enclose the quotation in quotation marks. (See page 195ff.)

PAGE NUMBERING

Starting with the second page, type the page number in the upper right-hand corner, one-half inch from the top. The Works Cited and any endnote pages are usually given numbers. It is a good idea to type your name next to each page number and on the unnumbered pages to pre-vent confusion if your paper should become mixed up with someone else's. If your instructor requires you to follow APA style, type the first word (or first two words) of your title, rather than your name, next to the page number.

TITLE PAGE

The following information appears on the title page: the title, your name, your instructor's name, the course and section numbers, and the date on which the paper is submitted. Use a title page whenever you submit an outline along with your paper. If your instructor requires you to follow MLA style, do not use a title page. Instead, type your name, your instructor's name, the name of the course, and the date, each on its own line in the upper left-hand corner, double-spaced. Then double-space to your title, and double-space again to begin your text.

BINDING

In order to keep the pages of your paper together, use an extra large paperclip. Do not staple your pages together. Do not use a plastic folder or other kind of binding.

CORRECTIONS

Proofread the final draft with extreme care. If the paper contains a few errors, these may be corrected neatly *in ink*. Make your changes above the lines in which they occur. Do not use the margins for this purpose. Insert a word or phrase neatly above a caret, as in this sentence.

insertion

```
         Most historians today conclude that Jefferson

         Davis, despite his personal shortcomings,
                        probably
         was the most capable president the South could
             ^
         have chosen.
```

Three Sample Research Papers

Here are three sample student research papers. These papers were selected as samples not only because they demonstrate competence in the research techniques described in this book, but also because the students were writing for different academic disciplines and therefore used slightly different approaches to their projects. The first paper, ''Emily Dickinson's Reluctance to Publish,'' illustrates MLA documentation style and procedures; the second paper, ''Cotton Mather's Necessary Witches,'' illustrates the traditional numbered endnote (footnote) method of documentation; the third paper, ''Increasing Maximum Life Expectancy: Myth or Reality?,'' illustrates the author/year system of the American Psychological Association (APA), a system used by researchers in various scientific and social science disciplines.

Emily Dickinson's Reluctance to Publish

by

Susanna Andrews

English 102; American Literature

Section 3c

Professor Ann Leigh

June 2, 19--

OUTLINE

Emily Dickinson's Reluctance to Publish

Introductory paragraph, including thesis statement

I. Background of the "myth of tragic Emily"

   A. Life in brief

      1. Retreat from social life

      2. Tentative effort to find an audience

      3. Eventual publication of her work

   B. After death

      1. The myth's genesis

      2. Its revision in recent years

   C. Refutation of "unworldly" image through
analysis of poems

      1. The vocabulary (Thomas; Howard)

      2. The content (Griffith)

II. The correspondence between Dickinson and
Higginson

   A. The beginnings of their dialogue

      1. Higginson's article

      2. Dickinson's approach

   B. Higginson's first letter to the poet

      1. "Surgery" advised

      2. Request to see more poems

    C. Higginson's second letter

       1. Further revision advised

       2. Dickinson's response--disavowal of
          ambition

    D. Interpretations of Dickinson's reaction

       1. Disavowal questioned

       2. Higginson's blindness apparent

III. Dickinson's view of herself as an artist

    A. Her state of mind

       1. Self-confidence

       2. Realization that the world was not ready

       3. Refusal to compromise

    B. Dickinson's real reason for approaching
       Higginson

       1. Need for special kind of advice

       2. The painful first publications

    C. Higginson's effect on Emily Dickinson

       1. His limitations recognized

       2. His confusion in face of genius

       3. Her rejection of his advice

 IV. Evidence from Dickinson's poetry

    A. Choice between fame and popular recognition

       1. Kher's interpretation of poem

       2. Poem's suggestion of her choice

Andrews iii

    B. Choice between publication and artistic
       integrity
       1. Dickinson's decision to forgo publication
       2. Opposition of immortality and time

Conclusion

Emily Dickinson's Reluctance to Publish

At her death in 1886, Emily Dickinson left behind over 1,700 poems, of which only 7 were published-- anonymously--while she was alive (Johnson, Poems 1: 1x). Certainly then, the woman Yvor Winters called ''one of the greatest lyric poets of all time'' (40) was all but unknown as a poet during her lifetime. For many years after her poems first appeared in 1890, her reluctance to publish was attributed to a supposed unconcern for worldly matters, including literary fame. Literary critics, serious biographers, and writers of fictionalized accounts of her life created an image of Emily Dickinson as a timid, reclusive, mystical thinker, who was too absorbed in personal sorrows and ecstasies to be concerned with literary recognition. And this image persists, to a great extent, in the public mind today.[1] Since the late 1950s, however, a new view of the poet has been emerging. This view, based on close studies of Dickinson's life, letters, and poetry, reveals an artist well aware of her worth, who deliberately chose to withhold her poems from the world until they could be

Introductory paragraph

Note includes title because Johnson authored several Works Cited

Question behind this research

The traditional view

Readers offered extra information in an endnote

Nature of sources

Thesis statement

valued as unique artistic creations, even if this meant postponing fame until after her death.

Subtopic: background of the myth

Beginning in her mid-twenties, Emily Dickinson gradually retreated from the many stimulating personal relationships that had filled her early life. By her late thirties, her retirement was complete; she passed the rest of her days living with her parents and her younger sister, who managed the household. During her later years, Emily Dickinson had virtually no direct contact with anyone outside her immediate family. While she was still connected to her circle of friends, Dickinson made at least one tentative attempt to find an audience for her poetry but only a handful of verses were published anonymously, most of them in a local newspaper, and these were subjected to considerable editing. Upon the poet's death at fifty-six, her sister discovered over one thousand poems and initiated an effort to publish them. Beginning four years later, in 1890, these poems finally appeared in print (Sewall 1: 4-11).

Note refers to the entire paragraph, summarizing source

Over the years, as her following grew, Emily Dickinson became the subject of a number of highly romanticized biographies. Her admirers were trying to establish a connection between her cloistered

existence and the powerful passions that course through
much of her finest poetry. Only after scholarly
editions of her letters and poetry appeared in the
1950s were literary critics in a good position to
produce an accurate picture of the poet's life and her
attitude toward her art. Even so, a good deal of the
mystery remains with us.

    The idea that Emily Dickinson knew very little of
the real world has been disputed by recent studies of
her life and works. One biographer and critic, Owen
Thomas, finds a remarkable number of legal, political,
and financial words and expressions in her poetry. This
fact leads him to conclude that Dickinson "was well
aware of the world outside her little room, that in fact
she used the language of this outside world to create
some of her best poetry" (523). In the same vein,
William Howard points out that the largest group of
specialized words in Dickinson's poems reflects the
scientific and technological discussions of her day
(230). Further disagreement with the image of the poet
as a shy, unworldly creature comes from Clark Griffith,
who sees her as a person whose sensibility was
"responsive to the brutalities which life imposes on
the individual, and acutely aware of the nothingness

Subtopic: refutation of myth

Note clearly refers to Thomas's work

New source, identified in text

Andrews 4

Connection of subtopic with thesis

with which existence seems surrounded'' (5-6). If we reject the image of Emily Dickinson as a mystical recluse who had little interest in the real world, we must also question the theory that she did not publish her poems out of the same lack of interest.

Subtopic: correspondence with Higginson

Perhaps the most substantial evidence regarding Dickinson's reluctance to publish can be found in her letters to a professional writer and social reformer named Thomas Wentworth Higginson. This correspondence began in 1862, after Higginson published an article in the April issue of the Atlantic Monthly, entitled ''Letter to a Young Contributor,'' which offered some practical advice for beginning writers seeking to publish. As a result of reading this article, Dickinson sent Higginson four poems, along with a letter containing this question: ''Are you too deeply

Reference to primary source; *Letters* are clearly Dickinson's

occupied to say if my Verse is alive?'' (Letters 2: 403). This and other early letters in their correspondence reveal the poet's interest in gaining recognition. Later correspondence with Higginson seems, however, to have dampened her hope of achieving critical praise.

Unfortunately, almost all of Higginson's letters to Emily Dickinson have been lost. Nevertheless, the main points of his answers to her early letters have

Andrews 5

been inferred by numerous critics, using the poet's
replies to Higginson as the basis for these
conclusions. Paul Ferlazzo, for example, infers that
Higginson's response to her first letter must have
included some recommendations for altering, or
"regularizing," her poems, along with a request for
more of her work (136). Ferlazzo bases this judgment on
Dickinson's second letter to Higginson, which says, in
part, "Thank you for the surgery--it was not so painful
as I supposed. I bring you others--as you ask--though
they might not differ--" (Letters 2: 404). The
"surgery" surely refers to some changes recommended
by Higginson, and Ferlazzo thinks it is significant
that the poet admits that she was sending him more of
the same kind, for this indicates that she did not
intend to follow his advice (137).

    In a second letter to Dickinson, Higginson must
have recommended that she not try to publish for the
present time, perhaps suggesting that she rewrite her
poems along the lines he had prescribed. This can be
inferred from her reply to this letter, which reads, in
part:

        I smile when you suggest that I delay "to
        publish"--that being foreign to my thought,
        as Firmament to Fin--If Fame belonged to me,

**Quotation from
Letters interrupts
reference to
Ferlazzo; otherwise,
one note at end of
paragraph [(136-37)]
would be sufficient**

Support for thesis

Andrews 6

> I could not escape her--if she did not, the
> longest day would pass me on the chase--
> . . . My Barefoot--Rank is better. (<u>Letters</u>
> 2: 408)

Note referring to long, indented quote comes *after* concluding punctuation and is preceded by two spaces

Those critics who believe that Dickinson's reluctance to publish was a deliberate choice on her part do not take at face value her avowal to Higginson that publishing was "foreign" to her. Instead, they see Higginson's inability to recognize the genius in her work as a major factor in her decision to renounce her desire to publish. As Richard Sewall says it, Dickinson's

> . . . disavowal about publishing can hardly
> be taken literally. After all, she had sent
> him [Higginson] the poems in response to his
> article on how young writers could get their
> work published. . . . What she said . . .
> about publishing could perhaps mean that, in
> view of Higginson's hesitance, she was
> renouncing her ambition to be a public poet
> . . . perhaps in the hope that some far-off
> Tribunal would render different and
> unequivocal judgment. . . . (2: 555)

Extended quotation; student felt it was necessary to identify "him" in brackets

Subtopic: Dickinson's view of herself as an artist

In suggesting that Dickinson chose obscurity after Higginson's "hesitance," Sewall does not mean

Andrews 7

to imply that she was unsure of herself as a poet
because of his criticism. On the contrary, Sewall
states that "in her exalted conception of herself as a
poet and in her confidence in her powers, she had no
. . . reason to be deferential to Higginson . . . and

Support for thesis

she knew it" (2: 555). Thus, it was not a sense of
inferiority that moved the poet to her decision.
Rather it was the realization that her poems would not
be accepted in the forms she had created for them and
that public recognition would require her to alter them
to meet public expectations. Robert Spiller, in
finding that Dickinson "failed to publish" because
she would not accept compromise as a path to
recognition, makes much the same point as Sewall:

**Two sources
connected**

> The general reading public that asked for
> meter that is smooth, rhythm that is easy,
> and words that are limited to only one
> obvious meaning interested her not at all.
> She was willing to wait. (Spiller 127)

In this same regard, Johnson remarks that,
although Dickinson's early letters to Higginson do
indicate an interest in publication, she is also asking
for a special kind of advice. "At the time she wrote
Higginson," Johnson explains in his biography of the
poet, "she does not seem to be trying to avoid

**Reader could be
confused because
Sewall's name
precedes quotation,
so Spiller's name is
added to the note**

publication as such; she is inquiring how one can
publish and at the same time preserve the integrity of
one's art'' (11). This inquiry, Johnson continues, was

Mixture of paraphrase and quotation

a real concern for Dickinson because prior to her
writing to Higginson, two of her poems had been
published anonymously in the Springfield Daily
Republican, an influential newspaper of that time, and
both poems had been altered radically by editors to
suit their sense of regularity.

Modern critics and biographers are in almost
universal agreement that she was disappointed in
Higginson's response to her poetry. They also agree
that, as Ferlazzo puts it, the man ''lacked discernment
as to her purpose as an artist'' (139). Thomas Johnson,
in his appraisal of their correspondence, concludes
that Higginson, though somewhat impressed by the
wording and thoughts in Dickinson's poems, ''literally

Here and below it would be difficult to work "biography" into the text smoothly

did not understand what he was reading'' (Biography
111). By this, Johnson means that Higginson was
confronted with the work of an ''original genius'' and
was bewildered as to what to make of it. Throughout his
correspondence with her, Higginson was apparently
attempting to get her to write more traditional poetry,
or as Johnson observes: ''He was trying to measure a
cube by the rules of plane geometry'' (Biography 107).

Andrews 9

There is no evidence, however, that she ever followed
any of Higginson's suggestions, despite the fact that
she maintained a friendly correspondence with him for
many years.

For Emily Dickinson, then, the idea of revising
her creations for the sake of achieving quick--and
probably fleeting--recognition was what was "foreign"
to her, not recognition based on acceptance of her poems
as unique works of art. This conviction comes through
clearly in several of her poems; for example:

> Fame is the one that does not stay--
> Its occupant must die
> Or out of sight of estimate
> Ascend incessantly--
> Or be that most insolvent thing
> A Lightning in the Germ--
> Electrical the embryo
> But we demand the Flame.
> (lines 1-8)

In commenting on this poem, Inder Nath Kher says
that it does not mean that Dickinson is "averse to
genuine fame." It means, he continues, "that she does
not wish to be considered as writing simply for the sake
of some cheap glory" (128). Reinforced by this poem--

Subtopic: evidence from poetry

Reference to primary source

Support for thesis

assuming "we" in the last line refers to the poet--is
the conclusion that Dickinson would rather have had
"the Flame" of her artistic integrity than the
"insolvent thing" called popular recognition.

Along the same lines, given the deliberate
decision to forego publication rather than compromise
her art, the first lines of another poem become

References to primary sources

significantly clear: "Publication--is the Auction/Of
the Mind of Man" (lines 1-2). And there can be no doubt

Support for thesis

that when she wrote the following stanza, Emily
Dickinson had accepted the fact that true fame would
not be hers in her lifetime.

> Some--Work for Immortality--
> The Chiefer part, for Time--
> He--Compensates--immediately
> The former--Checks--on Fame--
> (lines 1-4)

She chose to maintain her artistic integrity and await
that immortality.

Conclusion

The personality of Emily Dickinson will continue
to fascinate those who enjoy speculating about
brilliant artists whose lives were cloaked in privacy.
Since she said so little about herself outside of her
somewhat enigmatic poetry and her letters, the popular
image of a mystical, romantic Emily is likely to co-

Andrews 11

exist for many years with scholarly appraisals of her
life and work. Her poetry, however, does more than
create an aura of mystery about its author; it reveals a
dedicated genius moved by deep, religious reverence for
her craft. Yet Emily Dickinson, gifted with the power
to create extraordinary works of art, also felt
compelled to preserve the uniqueness of her creations
by refusing to compromise in order to attain public
recognition. She was willing to trust that future
generations of readers would award her the fame her
work deserved.

Restatement of the thesis

Andrews 12

Note

1 For a discussion of the sources of the ''Emily myth,'' see Ferlazzo 13-21.

Works Cited

Dickinson, Emily. The Complete Poems of Emily
    Dickinson. Ed. Thomas H. Johnson. Boston: Little,
    1960.
---. The Letters of Emily Dickinson. Ed. Thomas H.
    Johnson and Theodora Ward. 3 vols. Cambridge,
    MA: Harvard UP, 1958.
---. The Poems of Emily Dickinson. Ed. Thomas H.
    Johnson. 3 vols. Cambridge, MA: Belknap P-
    Harvard UP, 1955.
Ferlazzo, Paul J. Emily Dickinson. Boston: Twayne,
    1976.
Griffith, Clark. The Long Shadow: Emily Dickinson's
    Tragic Poetry. Princeton: Princeton UP, 1964.
Howard, William. "Emily Dickinson's Poetic
    Vocabulary." PMLA 72 (1957): 225-48.
Johnson, Thomas H. Emily Dickinson: An Interpretive
    Biography. Cambridge, MA: Harvard UP, 1955.
---, ed. The Poems of Emily Dickinson. 3 vols.
    Cambridge, MA: Belknap P-Harvard UP, 1955.
Kher, Inder Nath. The Landscape of Absence: Emily
    Dickinson's Poetry. New Haven: Yale UP, 1974.

Sewall, Richard B. The Life of Emily Dickinson. 2
    vols. New York: Farrar, 1974.

Spiller, Robert E. The Cycle of American Literature: An
    Essay in Historical Criticism. 2nd ed. New York:
    Free, 1967.

Thomas, Owen. "Father and Daughter: Edward and Emily
    Dickinson." American Literature 40 (1960):
    510-23.

Winters, Yvor. "Emily Dickinson and the Limits of
    Judgment." Emily Dickinson: A Collection of
    Critical Essays. Ed. Richard B. Sewall.
    Englewood Cliffs: Prentice, 1963.

Cotton Mather's Necessary Witches

by
Fred Hutchins

History 57; Witchcraft in America
Professor Alfred Wintrol
November 13, 19--

OUTLINE

Cotton Mather's Necessary Witches

Introduction

1. Historians have tried to learn Mather's role
   in witchcraft hysteria and the Salem trials.

2. The old view of Mather as a cruel persecutor
   has given way to more favorable
   interpretations of his personality.

3. THESIS: Mather's belief in witchcraft was
   based on private religious beliefs.

I. Historians' opinions of Mather's role in the witch-
   hunts and his motives for playing that role have
   changed in recent years.

A. Mather's belief in witchcraft was normal for the
   time, and he was more humane than originally
   portrayed.

1. The old harsh view of Mather was due to
   misinterpretation. (Murdock)

   a. He was actually more humane than most
      people think.

   b. Almost everyone in seventeenth-century
      America believed in witches.

2. Modern historians may be biased against
   intellectuals of that era. (Hofstadter)
   a. They "encouraged greater tolerance."
   b. They opposed unenlightened trial judges.
3. Mather tried to ensure fairness of trials.
   (Hansen)
   a. He warned against dangers of accepting
      "spectral evidence."
   b. He trusted judges to listen to him, but
      often they did not.
4. Witchcraft really works in communities
   where everyone believes in it. (Hansen;
   long quotation)
5. Mather also believed in witches because the
   Bible warns against them. (Levy)

B. Whatever his motives, Mather played a critical
   role in the witch-hunts.
   1. Mather's influence as preacher and writer
      may have encouraged the witch-hunting.
      (Silverman)
   2. However, witch-hunts began as local events,
      and probably would have occurred without
      Mather's pronouncements. (Silverman)
   3. Mather did not oppose the trials as such,
      and that implied approval. (Levin)

C. Mather was deeply committed to maintaining the
   Puritan social order.

   1. Mather's book, <u>Wonders</u>, expressed concern
   for the Puritan church and the Devil's
   attempt to ruin it.

     a. He defended his friends, the judges.
   (Hansen)

     b. He later admitted some judges erred, but
   he never said the trials were wrong.
   (Levy)

   2. Mather may have been an antifeminist.
   (Karlsen)

     a. History shows that accused witches were
   mainly women.

     b. He writes of "woman's complicity" in the
   Devil's plot against the Puritans.

   3. Salem trials were symptomatic of women's
   problems in colonial America. (Karlsen)

     a. A "new woman" was called for; she should
   take care of the home so her husband could
   be free to succeed in business.

     b. Many women asserted their spiritual
   equality with men, based on Puritan
   creed.

      c. Men feared this equality might threaten their social dominance.

    4. By defending the church against the Devil, Mather was defending male superiority. (Karlsen)

    5. Puritans closely linked "church, state, and family," and saw the Devil attacking all three. (Pestana)

II. Mather's personal religious views necessitated his belief in witches.

  A. Mather believed he enjoyed a special relationship with God.

    1. Mather had to believe in witches to support belief in good supernatural beings.

      a. Witches were as real as angels. (Levin)

      b. Witches, angels, spirit, God are all linked. (Silverman)

    2. Denying witches meant denying his whole faith.

      a. Mather believed he had been visited by an angel, who assured him he was righteous. (Levy)

      b. Witches proved atheism and doubt are evil. (Silverman)

   B. Mather believed New England had a special part
      in God's plan.

     2. Mather saw the New England Puritan colony as
        the place where Christ would return to
        Earth. (Levy)

        a. The Bible said the Millennium would be
          preceded by evil days.

        b. So, the witchcraft outbreak seemed to
          signal Christ's immediate return.

     2. Mather focused on the American Puritan
        church's special role in God's plan for the
        world. (Middlekauff)

        a. It was purer than the English Puritan
          church.

        b. It deserved to be the site of Christ's
          return.

     3. The witchcraft epidemic brought good and bad
        news. (Miller)

        a. It pained individual sufferers.

        b. It foretold Christ's Second Coming.

Conclusion

     1. All the social perspectives have some merit,
        but the role of Mather's personal beliefs
        seems to have been the basic source of his
        attitudes toward witches.

2. Afterthought: Mather may have found the
   conflict between the Devil's agents and
   God's followers a ''thrilling'' spectacle to
   participate in. (Starkey)

Cotton Mather's Necessary Witches

Introduction of topic

In 1692, a series of trials held in Salem, Massachusetts, resulted in the execution of twenty people for practicing witchcraft. Over the years, many historians have tried to explain both the outbreak of witchcraft hysteria at that time and the motives of certain community leaders who played important roles in the hunting down and conviction of people who were

Reference to source for background information

considered to be witches.[1] One such leader was Cotton Mather, a prominent Puritan minister and theologian, whose complex life and voluminous writings have provided historians with ample material for attempting to understand both the man and his times.

More background material

Early critics of Mather painted him as a cruel witch-hunter and tormentor of innocent people. And

Nature of sources for this paper

while this negative image of Mather has not entirely disappeared, modern historians have largely ruled out the interpretation that Mather's involvement in witch-hunting stemmed from a deliberate desire to inflict suffering upon innocent victims. Indeed, some historians have all but absolved Mather of any unusual responsibility for the trials. He was a person of the times, these writers argue, and in late seventeenth-century America, it was a rare person who did not believe in and fear the existence of witches. Other historians see Mather's general support of the trials growing out of his desire to defend the authority of the civil judges and protect the Puritan social system. Yet another interpretation views Mather's role as that of a champion of the patriarchial social order. This idea may explain why Mather supported the trials of accused witches, the overwhelming majority of whom were women.

Cotton Mather was a complicated human being, and there may be some truth in all of these ideas. However, the ultimate explanation for his behavior during this fascinating if terrible moment in American history may well lie in his unique view of himself and the Puritan colony. His belief in witches, along with his need to identify and punish them, seem to have supported both his belief that he enjoyed a special, personal relationship with God, and his view that the New England Puritan colony was destined to play the central role in God's plan for the future of humanity.

The commonly accepted description of Cotton

Narrowing of paper's chief argument

Statement of thesis

Subtopic: Mistaken views of Mather

Mather shows a "bloodthirsty persecutor" who fanned the flames of the witchcraft hysteria that swept through New England during the last half of the seventeenth century. However, historians today claim that this inaccurate picture of Mather was based upon early misinterpretations of Mather's role in the proceedings. Kenneth Murdock, for example, says that

Mixture of paraphrase and quotation

Mather's writings and recent research "prove him to have been not less but more humane than his contemporaries."[2] Murdock accepts that Mather believed in witches, and he attributes that belief to the simple fact that most of Mather's contemporaries believed in them.[3]

Further support for mistaken view of Mather

In the same vein, Richard Hofstadter sees an anti-intellectual bias in the way Mather and other educated leaders of that era have been treated by the "modern liberal mind." The charge that intellectual ministers were the "prime movers" of the Salem witch-hunts does not take into account the social complexities of that

Summary with partial quotations

period. According to Hofstadter, there is "ample evidence" that these ministers, including Cotton Mather, used their influence to "encourage greater tolerance" in the New England colony. In fact, in Hofstadter's view, these ministers wished to oppose the

unenlightened actions of the civil judges who
conducted the trials.[4]

   The idea that Cotton Mather served as a moderating
influence during the trials comes from a number of
warnings he issued concerning the conduct of the
trials. He said it was dangerous for a court to accept
"spectral evidence" as decisive proof that a person
was guilty of having made a contract with the Devil.
Chadwick Hansen defines spectral evidence as "the
appearance of the specter of a suspected person in the
hallucinations of the afflicted."[5] People who claimed
to be suffering from the torments of a witch would say
in court that they could see the ghostly form of the
person who was tormenting them. Although the form
remained invisible to everyone else in the courtroom,
at many trials this testimony was accepted as evidence
against the accused. Mather reasoned that if spectral
evidence were accepted as proof that someone was
"trafficking with the Devil," then the way was clear
for anyone to be accused by a personal enemy or a
dreamer, with very little chance of refuting such
evidence. Mather trusted in the wisdom of the civil
judges to minimize the value of spectral evidence when
evaluating the total evidence against an accused.

Quoted definition

Student's explanation of definition

Summary of source material related to note 6

However, the judges were far more willing to accept
spectral evidence than Mather had expected, and as a
result, the number of imprisonments and executions
increased.[6]

Hansen's discussion of witchcraft revolves around
the idea that witchcraft <u>does</u> exist in societies that
strongly believe in it. As Hansen explains it:

Long, direct quotation indented

> We must bear in mind that in a society which
> believes in witchcraft, it works. If you
> believe in witchcraft and you discover that
> someone has been melting your wax image over a
> slow fire or muttering charms over your nail
> parings, the probability is that you will get
> extremely sick. To be sure, your symptoms
> will be psychosomatic rather than organic.
> But the fact that they are obviously not
> organic will make them only more terrible,
> since they will seem the result of malefic and
> demonic power. So it was in seventeenth-
> century Europe, and so it was in seventeenth-
> century Massachusetts.[7]

From this point of view, Cotton Mather was a product
of his society; for Mather and the Salem community, the
strange behavior of the people who claimed they were

Hutchins 6

being attacked by witches could only be due to the
influence of the Devil. And, as Babette Levy says,
Mather would have taken seriously the warnings in the
Bible against witches and recognized the need to put
such sinners to death.[8]

It appears, then, that Cotton Mather's belief in
witches reflected the commonly accepted beliefs of
seventeenth-century New England. And, to the extent
that he tried to influence people's attitudes toward
the judgement of accused witches, he was more
enlightened and humane than most Puritans of that time.

However, the evidence also indicates that Mather
was not simply a person of his times who got caught up
in a sudden awareness of the Devil's activity in New
England. Kenneth Silverman, one of Mather's
biographers, says that Mather may have contributed to
the outbreak of witch-hunting. For many months before
the witchcraft trials, Mather "kept calling public
attention to the existence of devils and witches." As
the leader of a large congregation, Mather preached
frequently, and he was a prolific writer. The wide
circulation of his ideas could have led to the general
fear of an evil "invisible world" that threatened the
very existence of the Puritan colony.[9]

Silverman, however, suggests that the persecution

Student summarizes paper to this point

Subtopic: Mather heavily involved in witchcraft events

of witches stemmed from a number of factors. Such
outbreaks were "distinctly community events," in that
members of the community had to start accusing each
other of being witches. And, taking these accused
witches to trial and punishing them could only occur
with the consent of the community as a whole. Thus, the
witchcraft mania might have broken out in New England
at that time whether or not Cotton Mather had spoken out
against the danger.[10]

David Levin, in another biography, offers a
stronger criticism of Mather. Levin asserts that a
study of Mather's role "will not allow even the most
sympathetic biographer the pleasure of casting Mather
as a defeated hero in this affair." Levin points out
that even though Mather criticized the courts for
relying on spectral evidence as grounds for
convictions, he did not strongly oppose the witch-
hunts, thereby allowing the hunts to continue with his
apparent approval. Levin warns against viewing Mather
as a noble hero challenging the established order over
the issue of spectral evidence. Instead, we should
realize that Mather's doubts about the conduct of the
trials were clearly secondary to deeper religious
beliefs that touched his personal sense of God and of
the way God's will works in the world.[11]

**Mather's
involvement tended
toward approval of
the trials**

Hutchins 8

In 1692, Cotton Mather wrote Wonders of the
Invisible World, an account of five witchcraft trials.
In this book, he expresed great concern for New England
and its Puritan church, saying that his goal was "to
countermine the whole Plot of the Devil against New
England, in every Branch of it, as far as one of my
darkness can comprehend such a work of darkness."[12]
Without doubt, Mather showed concern for the colony and
the Puritan church, but Chadwick Hansen senses another
purpose behind this book. He regards Wonders as a
defense of the court, in which Mather went out of his
way "to defend his friends," the judges of the court,
from the increasing criticism of their methods. In
this view, Mather becomes the "chief apologist" for a
group of men whose methods he had earlier criticized.[13]
Later in life, Mather acknowledged that the judges had
made some mistakes that resulted in innocent people
being hanged; however, as Levy explains, Mather
attributed those errors to human weakness, not to
"intentional evil." Yet, despite questioning the
judges' methods and admitting their mistakes, Mather
never repudiated his belief that the witchcraft peril
had been substantial and that therefore the trials were
fully justified.[14]

Carol Karlsen also sees Wonders as Mather's

Subtopic: Mather as
defender of Puritan
social order

Another aspect of
Mather's defense of
social order

defense of the social order, but from a slightly
different point of view. Calling <u>Wonders</u> Mather's
"chief" justification for the witchcraft trials and
executions,"[15] Karlsen goes on to connect the events
at Salem to the history of witchcraft, which she sees as
"primarily the story of women." She places
considerable emphasis on the fact that throughout
history a great many more women than men were executed
as witches.[16] Further, Karlsen traces a long tradition
of female suppression in Christianity, starting with
the concept of Eve as the "main symbol of woman-as-evil
. . . in many ways, the archetypal witch."[17] Applying
this view of history to her evaluation of Cotton Mather,
Karlsen claims that he focused in <u>Wonders</u> on "women's
complicity" in the Devil's plot to destroy the Puritan
church.[18]

     Karlsen regards the Salem trials as a symptom of
problems growing out of the role of women in the New
World. The growth of capitalism in the New England
colony had led its leaders to call for a "new woman,"
one who would relieve her husband of most domestic
responsibilities so he could direct his energies toward
success in business. It was woman's duty to bolster her
husband's sense of self-importance.[19] Back in England,

Summary of source material

Hutchins 10

and during the earliest days of the colony, women had
come to assert that they were the spiritual equals of
men, basing their argument on parts of the Puritan
creed. However, once the Puritan church became
established in New England, church leaders questioned
this idea of spiritual equality because they feared it
would spill over into the social order as well and call
into question the tradition of male superiority, a
tradition which, according to the male leaders, was
divinely ordained.[20]

    Mather, in his defense of the "True church"
against the Devil's assaults, was, according to
Karlsen's interpretation, equally ready to defend the
Puritan social structure against the Devil's wily
attempts to use women as tools for subversion of that
social order. The divine order that began with God, the
all-knowing, all-powerful father, established the
model for men as fathers on earth, both within the
family and within the church. This order had to be
preserved at all costs, in Mather's view, and
witchcraft, which was primarily a woman's crime,
threatened that order.[21]

    Surely the question of what role the fear of
women's influence upon the social order played in the

Church and social order linked

Depths of Puritan regard for social order supported

Salem witch trials will continue to be investigated, but Karlsen's study serves to call our attention to the close connection between the religious and the civil power structures in the Puritan colony. Along these lines, Carla Pestana shows how the Puritan leaders had "shaped all their social institutions--the church, the state, the family--into weapons to be used in the cause of good." The Puritans, says Pestana, "expected Satan to attempt to undermine their holy commonwealth in countless ways," and as a result, they were constantly on the alert for his disciples and agents, who could appear in their midst at any time.[22]

Student's interpretation

These various interpretations of Cotton Mather's role in the tragic occurrence at Salem leave us with the fundamental question, "How did Mather come to believe so strongly in the Devil and witchraft?" Levin tells us that Mather's belief in the Devil was derived, through a kind of religious logic, from his belief in good supernatural entities. For Mather, "denial of the Devil's power in this world implied the denial of other

Ellipsis

spirits, including angels. . . ."[23] Such denials would, of course, strike at the heart of Mather's religious beliefs and destroy the faith upon which his whole life was based. Kenneth Silverman expresses much

Hutchins 12

the same idea in saying that Mather thought that a

disbelief in witches "threatened to deny the reality

of Spirit itself." As Silverman states: "No witches,

no Spirit, no God."[24]

In fact, as Babette Levy points out, for Mather to

deny the existence of witches, he would have to deny his

"totality of faith." And that would mean denying that

he had been visited by his "guardian angel" on a

number of occasions following extended periods of

fasting and prayer.[25] Mather needed to believe the

angel's appearances were real because those visits

assured him that he was predestined for salvation and

that he was performing his clerical duties in a manner

that was pleasing to God. Belief in angels compelled

him to believe in witches, for both are part of the

supernatural world in which good and evil spirits

operate in inexplicable ways. Silverman notes that

Cotton Mather looked upon instances of witchcraft as

"Letters of Thanks from Hell"--signs of a

supernatural order that disproved atheism and theories

of religious doubt.[26]

To a large extent, then, Cotton Mather wanted to

believe in witches. Their existence justified both

his view of himself as a God-chosen person and the

Support for thesis

Support for thesis

Subtopic: Mather's special relationship to God

Student restates thesis

traditions of his Puritan faith. In addition, as part
of this system of belief, Mather had formed a concept of
the Puritan colony's special role in God's eternal
plan.

Further support for thesis

According to Levy, Mather believed that New
England was a "likely site for the New Jerusalem," the
place where "Christ would rule the Earth in a kingdom
with his saints for a thousand years before the final
Day of Judgment," as foretold in Revelation. This last
book of the New Testament spoke of signs that would
appear when the Millennium (Christ's thousand-year
reign) was close at hand. The major sign would be a
"period of deepening corruption . . . when the Devil
would make more violent assaults than usual" on

Mixture of paraphrase and quotation

humankind. In the 1690s, Mather and other Puritan
leaders thought the Millennium was about to begin,
probably in the early 1700s. The outbreak of
witchcraft fit neatly into this view.[27]

New England's special place in God's plan
dominated Cotton Mather's thinking throughout most of
his life, according to Robert Middlekauff. The Puritan
church in New England was the "true church," having
escaped from the corruption of the original Puritan
church in England, as well as from the corruption that
plagued all other religions. Mather believed it was his

duty to "preserve the Church," and thus the "true
faith," until Christ returned to make all things right
and just.28

But if the Devil's assault on New England through
witchcraft was painful to witness and called for a
courageous counterattack, the situation also offered
opportunity for optimism, since it meant Christ would
be returning soon. In analyzing Wonders, Perry Miller
notes that "the discourse plunges into chiliastic
ecstasy. The witches are signs of the times, of the
death pangs of the Devil; mischievous powers prevail
for the moment, but only because his rule is nearing
extinction."29 Thus, for Cotton Mather, the outbreak
of witchcraft was bad news and good news at the same
time.

It seems, then, that Mather was a complicated
person, and in all likelihood, the beliefs of his time,
his concept of social and religious order, and his view
of women's place within that order all played parts in
shaping his attitude toward witchcraft and the Salem
trials. However, these factors seem to provide only
secondary motives for his belief in witches and for his
general support of the witchcraft trials. Looked at
one way, the witches represented Satan's insidious plot
to throw the Puritan church and its community into

Further support for thesis

Conclusion

Restatement of major points of paper

Student's summary of his research

Hutchins 15

disorder. On the other hand, the witches' presence
confirmed Mather's concept of a supernatural world
populated with good and bad spirits, a concept that
supported Mather's understanding of his personal
relationship with God. From yet another viewpoint, the
Devil's use of witches marked the final days before
Christ's glorious return to Earth to reign in New
England, the New Jerusalem.

Interesting afterthought

Speculating on Mather's "dramatic" view of the witchcraft events

In addition, recognizing that the Salem
witchcraft crisis provided a time of high excitement
for the New England colony, and that Cotton Mather was
profoundly involved in the event, intellectually,
emotionally, and spiritually, one might wonder, along
with Marion Starkey, about the poetically dramatic
"thrill" that may have been "unconsciously
submerged" in this great religious figure as he
witnessed "a collision between heaven and hell."[30]

Notes

[1] For an overview of a number of the more current interpretations of causes leading to the New England witchcraft outbreak, see: David D. Hall, "Witchcraft and the Limits of Interpretation," The New England Quarterly 59 (June 1985): 253-81.

[2] Kenneth B. Murdock, ed., introduction, Cotton Mather: Selections, by Cotton Mather (1926; New York: Hafner, 1965) xv.

[3] Murdock xvi.

[4] Richard Hofstadter, Anti-intellectualism in American Life (New York: Knopf, 1963) 62-63.

[5] Chadwick Hansen, Witchcraft at Salem (New York: Braziller, 1969) 101.

[6] Hansen 101-04.

[7] Hansen 10.

[8] Babette M. Levy, Cotton Mather (Boston: Twayne, 1979) 59-60.

[9] Kenneth Silverman, The Life and Times of Cotton Mather (New York: Harper, 1984) 87-88.

[10] Silverman 89-90.

[11] David Levin, Cotton Mather: The Young Life of
the Lord's Remembrancer (Cambridge, MA: Harvard UP,
1978) 200.

[12] Cotton Mather, Wonders of the Invisible World
(1693; rpt. in Narratives of the Witchcraft Cases 1648-
1706, ed. George Lincoln Burr, 1914; New York: Barnes
1975) 211.

[13] Hansen 171.

[14] Levy 64.

[15] Carol F. Karlsen, The Devil in the Shape of a
Woman: Witchcraft in Colonial New England (New York:
Norton, 1987) 180.

[16] Karlsen xii.

[17] Karlsen 177.

[18] Karlsen 179.

[19] Karlsen 180.

[20] Karlsen 172.

[21] Karlsen 181.

[22] Carla G. Pestana, "The City upon a Hill under
Siege: The Puritan Perception of the Quaker Threat to
Massachusetts Bay, 1656-1661," The New England
Quarterly 56 (Sept. 1983): 353.

[23] Levin 200.

[24] Silverman 92.

[25] Levy 59.

[26] Silverman 92-93.

[27] Levy 33-34.

[28] Robert Middlekauff, <u>The Mathers: Three Generations of Puritan Intellectuals, 1596-1728</u> (New York: Oxford UP, 1971) 200.

[29] Perry Miller, <u>The New England Mind from Colony to Provinces</u> (Cambridge, MA: Harvard UP, 1962) 203.

[30] Marion L. Starkey, <u>The Devil in Massachusetts: A Modern Inquiry into the Salem Witch Trials</u> (1949; New York: Anchor, 1969) 239.

Bibliography

Hall, David D. "Witchcraft and the Limits of
    Interpretation," The New England Quarterly 59
    (June 1985): 253-281.

Hansen, Chadwick. Witchcraft at Salem. New York:
    Braziller, 1969.

Hofstadter, Richard. Anti-intellectualism in American
    Life. New York: Knopf, 1963.

Karlsen, Carol F. The Devil in the Shape of a Woman:
    Witchcraft in Colonial New England. New York:
    Norton, 1987.

Levin, David. Cotton Mather: The Young Life of the
    Lord's Remembrancer. Cambridge, MA: Harvard UP,
    1978.

Levy, Babette M. Cotton Mather. Boston: Twayne, 1979.

Mather, Cotton. The Wonders of the Invisible World.
    1693. Rpt. in Narratives of the Witchcraft Cases
    1648-1706. Ed. George Lincoln Burr. 1914. New
    York: Barnes, 1975.

Middlekauff, Robert. The Mathers: Three Generations of
    Puritan Intellectuals, 1596-1728. New York:
    Oxford UP, 1971.

Hutchins 20

Miller, Perry. <u>The New England Mind from Colony</u>
    <u>to Provinces</u>. Cambridge, MA: Harvard UP, 1962.

Murdock, Kenneth B., ed. introduction. <u>Cotton Mather:</u>
    <u>Selections</u>. By Cotton Mather. 1926. New York:
    Hafner, 1965.

Pestana, Carla G. ''The City upon a Hill under Siege:
    The Puritan Perception of the Quaker Threat to
    Massachusetts Bay, 1656-1661,'' <u>The New England</u>
    <u>Quarterly</u> 56 (Sept. 1983): 323-353.

Silverman, Kenneth. <u>The Life and Times of Cotton</u>
    <u>Mather</u>. New York: Harper, 1984.

Starkey, Marion L. <u>The Devil in Massachusetts: A Modern</u>
    <u>Inquiry into the Salem Witch Trials</u>. 1949. New
    York: Anchor, 1969.

Increasing Maximum Life Expectancy: Myth or Reality?

by

Anita Barrone

Contemporary Issues in Science

Section 1F

Professor Alvin Frascall

December 9, 19--

Note: See pp. 123–125 for Anita Barrone's outline.

Increasing Maximum Life Expectancy: Myth or Reality?

Every American schoolchild learns that Juan Ponce
de Leon discovered Florida in 1513 while searching for
the Fountain of Youth, whose water, he believed, would
restore him to youthful manhood. Unfortunately he
never found the Fountain. Instead he found death by an
Indian arrow. Today we smile at the naivete of Ponce de
Leon for believing in a fountain of youth provided by a
beneficent nature. But his dream of extending his life
span was one that many people have had throughout the
ages,[1] and it is a dream that is still very much with us
today.

By now we have pretty much given up hope of
discovering a fountain of youth or a marvelous herb that
can relieve us of the anxieties and debilities
associated with the process of aging. Instead our
hopes are in the hands of scientists. Gerontologists
(scientists who study aging processes) are attempting
to slow down--and perhaps even overcome--nature's
timetable for human aging. Although not all scientists
think that increasing the life span is possible in the
near future, many gerontologists and knowledgeable

Introductory paragraph

Note refers to source offering information for further research, rather than merely citing a source

Thesis statement

commentators are optimistic about our chances because
of the promising results researchers have obtained from
experiments with animals and cell cultures. These
experiments might well lead us to a "fountain" of
extended, healthy life, if not to eternal youth.

Before undertaking a brief survey of some of the
theories behind research into the causes of aging and
of some of the experiments that have inspired
confidence in researchers, we should be clear about
just what gerontologists mean when they speak of
"increasing maximum life expectancy."

To begin with, the question might be asked:
"Aren't people already living longer than they did in
the past?" And the answer is yes and no. If by living
longer we mean that more people are achieving the
biblical three score years and ten, then the answer is
yes. If, on the other hand, by living longer we mean
that people are exceeding the maximum life span that
some human beings have always been able to achieve, then
the answer is no. Rosenfeld (1976) explains this point
in reference to ancient Greece, where "the average
life expectancy was something like twenty-two years.
But individuals did live to ripe old ages in those days
too." True, Rosenfeld continues, not many people in

Indicates organizational approach of the paper

Date of Rosenfeld's work, which can be found in References

Increasing 3

ancient Greece reached seventy, but those who did "had
just as many years to live . . . as does the seventy
year old of today . . ." (p. 9). Diseases, poor
sanitation, deaths related to child birth, and the
generally low state of medical science all played their
part in holding down the average life expectancy of
ancient Greeks. Average life expectancy has improved
as we have become more knowledgeable about how to combat
diseases and as technology has provided better tools
for the medical and health sciences. Despite these
advantages, the utmost limit of life expectancy has
remained the same throughout the ages. More people are
living longer, but no one is living any longer today
than a few of us have lived in previous ages.

In addition, for gerontologists, extending human
life span must also mean extending the number of years
that human beings live useful, healthy, and productive
lives. Walford writes in Maximum Life Span (1983) of a
future in which " 'functional' or 'physiologic' age
will no longer equal 'chronologic' age" (p. 188). If
gerontologists succeed, we will have to change the way
we think about getting old. The years we consider as
old age today will be more like middle age in the
future. As Walford explains: "With life span extended

**Page on which
quotation appears**

to 130 years a person chronologically 75 years old will
have the same vigor and appearance as a 50 year-old
today'' (p. 189).

There is another line of questioning, based on a
concept of the ''good life,'' that has gained a certain
amount of popularity. But this popularity is based upon
misinformation. The line of questioning goes as such:
''Aren't there places in the world, far from the
tensions and pollutions of advanced societies, where
many of the people live to ages of 100 or more? Don't
these people prove that the secret of extended life
consists of living the simple life, which includes hard
work and a simple, healthy diet?''

Alexander Leaf, a professor of medicine, has
investigated areas of the world where, presumably, more
people than average were living lives of extraordinary
longevity. Leaf (1982) examined records and people in a
mountainous region of the Soviet Union known as the
Caucasus. He also visited the mountains of West
Pakistan and the village of Vilcabamba, located in the
Andes Mountains of Ecuador. These investigations led
Leaf to doubt strongly that people in these areas live
any longer on average than people anywhere else in the

world. In Vilcabamba, for example, he found that birth
records were highly inaccurate. In one case Leaf
discovered that a woman reputed to be 106 years old had
been mistakenly assigned the birth certificate of
another woman with the same name who had died thirty or
forty years earlier. Further, Leaf discovered that the
elders of Vilcabamba were prone to exaggerate the ages
of their people and the life-enhancing environment of
their area in hopes of turning Vilcabamba into a
thriving resort area for tourists seeking a few weeks'
exposure to the conditions that might add years to
their lives. In West Pakistan and in the Soviet
Caucasus, Leaf found much the same kind of confusion in
regard to accurate birth records. Wars and political
upheavals have made the validation of reputed old ages
virtually impossible. And because old age is highly
respected in these areas, old people often exaggerate
the length of time they have been alive, especially
since their word is all the proof that exists as to when
they were born. In the end Leaf found no reason to
believe that these areas produced unusually high
percentages of people who lived extraordinarily long
lives. "There has been no extension of the limit of

the lifespan; only the proportion of the population
reaching the apparent biologic limit of about 85+/-
[plus or minus] 10 years is increasing" (pp. 486-487).

Brackets indicate student's explanation of symbols used in source, not part of actual quotation

What we seem to be left with so far is the
proposition that human beings are somehow fated by
nature to live within certain time limits. Some people
die at young ages; a very few reach 100 years or a bit
more; but most of us, if present trends continue, will
die between the ages of 75 and 95. From this
"programmed" point of view there is little we can do to
extend maximum life expectancy, unless scientists can
somehow alter the processes that control aging.

We can gain some insight into serious scientific
attempts to retard the aging process by referring to
the work of Leonard Hayflick and Paul Moorhead, whose
research brought to light a major obstacle to increased
life expectancy. These two scientists carried out
experiments that led them to conclude that there were
built-in limits to the number of times normal human
cells could divide and reproduce themselves, even under
ideal laboratory conditions. According to Hayflick
(1977), normal cells "undergo approximately 50
population doublings . . . before losing proliferative
powers . . ." (p. 161). This finding has come to be

known (in the literature of gerontology) as the
"Hayflick limit," and overcoming this limit is the
task that many scientists have taken on. But before
gerontologists can overcome the Hayflick limit, they
must first come to grips with another observation by
Hayflick, that "the maximum proliferative capacity
. . . is rarely, if ever, reached by cells in vivo
. . ." (p. 168). In other words, human cells undergo
more divisions when they are isolated from the body and
kept alive in chemical solutions under ideal laboratory
conditions (in vitro) than they do when part of a living
human body (in vivo). What this adds up to is the
strong possibility that--even as things now stand--
human beings may be dying prematurely as a result of
cellular malfunctioning or genetic programming that
inhibits our cells from achieving their full
reproductive capacity. Why this should be so, and what
to do about it, are questions that researchers are
attempting to answer.

　　　Scientists have developed a number of theories and
have undertaken many experiments to discover the
cause(s) of biological disintegration. It is not
necessary to discuss all of these theories to
demonstrate the seriousness of gerontological

Increasing 8

research, and, besides, such a survey would be impossible within the scope of this paper. But a sampling of some of the current theories should serve to indicate the general direction researchers are taking in the battle against aging.

In an interview in <u>U.S. News and World Report</u>, July 1983, entitled ''How People Will Live to Be 100 or More,'' Roy Walford mentions a number of theories that scientists are currently following for exploration and experimentation purposes. Those theories are

1. the immunologic theory;
2. the DNA repair theory;
3. the free radical theory;
4. the thymus hormone theory;
5. the brain programming theory.

The Immunologic Theory

The immunologic theory is based upon the concept that as a person grows older his or her immune system does not function as efficiently to protect the body

Only first word of source title capitalized when using APA documentation guide, except when proper name is part of the title

No need for a note—all bibliographic information provided in the text

against diseases as it did when he or she was younger.
In fact one sign of aging is the decreasing ability of
the body to protect itself against such dangers as
infections and cancers. Even worse, there are strong
indications that in its later stages of dysfunction the
immune system operates more and more out of control so
that, as Cromie (1981) explains, the body's defense
system malfunctions and attacks healthy tissue.
Obviously, then, an immune system that destroys
beneficial elements in the body is a system that is
working against extended longevity.

Much research based upon the immunologic theory
is aimed at finding ways to maintain the efficiency of
the immune system so that it does not degenerate into
"autoimmunity"--the condition in which the immune
system goes out of control and attacks beneficial
elements in the body. The problem, Rosenfeld (1976)
tells us, is to decrease autoimmunity without reducing
the aging body's ability to fight against disease.
Scientists working on this problem have had some
success in building up the immune systems of laboratory
animals with the use of various drugs. One method, for
example, consists of injecting mice with thymosin--a
hormone extract from the human thymus gland, but also

obtainable from cows. In summarizing research on
thymosin, a science writer and life-extension
consultant, Kent (1980), sees a good possibility that
thymosin may prove useful in combating diseases
associated with the weakening of the immune system.

In addition to manipulating the immune system with
the use of drugs, some researchers are studying the
relationship between diet and longevity. Success in
extending the life spans of laboratory animals by
maintaining them on low-calorie but adequately
nourishing diets has been the catalyst for much of this
research.[2] Just why stringent, low-calorie diets seem
to have a positive effect on longevity has not been
determined by researchers. Walford (1983) offers the
proposition that ''dietary restriction'' helps the
immune system to ward off autoimmunity by slowing ''the
age-related decline in response to foreign materials''
(p. 106). In this sense, the immune system stays
healthier simply because it is called on less often to
combat the undesirable by-products that enter our
bodies as a result of the food we eat. But whatever the
relationship between diet and aging, one leading
nutrition expert (Watkin, 1983) sees progress in the
fact that evidence is growing to strengthen the link

**Author's name
appears in note—
name not
mentioned in text**

between "appropriate nutrition" and extended
longevity, and he points to studies on laboratory
animals as sustaining "the hope that nutritional
manipulations decelerate the rate of aging by some
mechanism as yet unknown" (p. 19).

The DNA Repair Theory

Because DNA[3] contains the genetic information our
cells need to repair and replicate themselves,
researchers are studying the relationship between DNA
damage and aging. "DNA damage can result in altered
cell growth, division and transcription, and also in
cell death, mutation, and malignant transformation.
All of these phenomena are characteristic of the aging
process" (Schimke & Agniel, 1983, p. 42). Actually,
DNA is always undergoing damage and is always in the
process of repairing itself. Kent (1980) explains that
research shows "an increase in the rate of DNA repair
of about tenfold from the shortest-lived animal to the
longest-lived animal, which indicates that the
increased capacity to repair DNA may be necessary to

achieve a longer life span" (p. 19). Human beings live
longer than most animals because our DNA repair rate is
better than that of most animals. The problem, however,
is that DNA damage takes place at a greater rate than
DNA repair (Walford, 1983). Thus, unless ways can be
found to increase the ability of DNA to repair itself,
the damage rate will continue to outstrip the repair
rate and contribute to the aging process.

    Seeking knowledge about DNA repair capabilities,
Sonneborn (1979) discovered how to boost the repair
rate of the one-celled organisms, Paramecia. She
exposed Paramecia to ultraviolet light, a procedure
that brought on "ultraviolet-induced DNA damage," in
order to study the repair capacity of DNA when the
damaged Paramecia were exposed to "photoreactive"
light. Sonneborn found that "ultraviolet plus PR
[photoreactive] favored a repair process beneficial to
survival" (pp. 1116-1117). It is, of course, a long
way from manipulating the DNA repair system of a
Paramecium to manipulating the same system in a human
being. But optimists like to think that what can be
accomplished with one-cell organisms might one day be
accomplished with human beings. "If," as Sonneborn
puts it, "higher organisms have maintained a DNA

Increasing 13

reserve repair capacity, activation should lead to
reduction in mutagenesis and degenerative diseases in
higher organisms'' (p. 1117).

Another example of experimentation motivated by
the DNA repair theory can be seen in Omnimax, a
scientific research company in Philadelphia. There,
researchers have discovered that the ''packaging'' of
DNA in extremely tight ''supercoils'' in our system
''induces stress in the DNA double helix, which the
helix can relieve by becoming undone, or opening up at
certain spots'' (''DNA Coils,'' 1983, p. 85). Omnimax
researchers are working at finding ways to counteract
this stress-induced damage. According to Phil Lepitz,
the president of Omnimax and a biophysicist, ''Using
supercoiling as a marker for physiological age, we may
have a way to identify potential antiaging drugs in a
relatively short time'' (cited in ''DNA Coils,'' p. 85).

The Free Radical Theory

We know that food exposed to the atmosphere for too
long becomes spoiled, primarily because of oxidation,

Title, in shortened
form, in the note
because source did
not provide author's
name

the same chemical reaction that causes metal to rust.
In oxidation, certain molecules come into being that
attack other molecules, causing cellular damage.
These molecules that inflict damage on other molecules
are known in gerontology as free radicals. Rosenfeld
(1976) tells us that free radicals can do considerable
damage to molecules, accelerate the production of
lipofuscin, and interfere with cellular information.

Denham Harman, a professor of medicine and
biochemistry, theorized as early as 1956 on the
possibility that free radicals were detrimentally
involved in the aging process. Given the fact that free
radicals can also be produced in our bodies through the
effects of ''environmental pollutants such as lead''
(Kurtzman and Gordon, 1977, pp. 168-169), we can
understand that our bodies are continually producing
free radicals that bring on and sustain aging
processes.

To counter free radicals, researchers are
following Harman's opinion that the free radical theory
suggests chemical procedures for extending healthy
life (1956). In other words, if free radicals are at
least partly responsible for our inability to increase
maximum life span, then scientists may be able to

Student chose to put all information in a note rather than in text

Increasing 15

discover chemicals that we can take to combat free
radical damage. For example, Harman, following his own
hunch, was able to show that certain chemicals,
including BHT--commonly used as a food preservative--
"had a beneficial effect on the mortality rate of male
LAF_1 mice when added to the daily diet" (1968, p. 481).
In addition, scientists are following up experiments
which indicate that vitamin E and vitamin C, singularly
and in combination, may prove to be effective anti-free
radical agents.[4] And recently, as reported in Science
Digest, researchers have discovered a "gene cluster"
that produces an enzyme known as "superoxide
dismutase," shortened to "SOD," which combats free
radicals (Supergene, 1982, p. 91). Knowing this,
scientists are seeking ways to stimulate SOD
artificially so as to add to the body's protective
mechanism against free radicals.

The Thymus Hormone Theory

    The thymus hormone theory is related to the
immunologic theory because both theories follow the
premise that aging can be retarded by manipulating the

immune system. Thymus hormone theorists, however, are primarily interested in trying to zero in on a major cause of immune system deterioration. By doing so, they hope to simplify the measures that have to be taken to keep the immune system working efficiently. Thus, rather than work to boost immunology with a number of individual booster strategies, the thymus hormone theory promotes the idea that we may be able to keep the immune system working to our benefit by finding and then learning to control the mechanism that may be the prime regulator of the system. As its name points out, promoters of the thymus hormone theory think that the "thymus gland, once thought to be as useful as the human appendix, may well be the master gland of the immune system" (Marx, 1975, p. 1217).

The thymus gland, which Rosenfeld describes as "the pinkish-gray mass located just behind the breastbone and just below the neck" (1976, p. 82), has become a focus of gerontological research because of the increasing knowledge accumulating over the years about how certain cells function to aid--and also damage--human immunological processes. As Marx (1975) explains, "The thymus is necessary for the normal differentiation and maturation of T (for thymus-

derived) cells'' (p. 1183). If we understand that T
cells, like other white blood cells, protect us against
infections, then we see why a gland that programs such
cells and helps them to mature might well be the center
of investigation by gerontologists.

In general, research into the thymus gland has
focused on trying to discover the hormone(s) that this
gland produces because, as Marx (1975) tells us,
research has shown that T cell growth depends a great
deal upon the secretion of one or more hormones by the
thymus gland. If the thymus secreted its beneficial
hormones at the same rate as we get older as it does
when we are very young, then, the theory implies, we
would probably live longer. But Walford (1983) informs
us that this gland shrinks early in life and becomes
markedly smaller by the time a person reaches puberty.
Hormone secretion becomes less as the thymus shrinks,
and this decline in hormone output continues with age
until its influence probably becomes negligible (Adler,
1975). The attempt to isolate and to study the thymus
hormones, therefore, is being carried on with the hopes
of someday producing a drug or combination of drugs
that we can take to compensate for the decreasing
activity of our shrinking thymus glands.

Thymosin, discussed under the "Immunologic Theory" section of this paper, is one of the first thymus hormones to be identified and extracted. Since then, according to Kent (1980), researchers have reported on "more than two dozen . . . thymus extracts that influence the immune system" (p. 202). These reports would seem to indicate that attempts to manipulate the immune system through externally produced and administered thymus hormones may be extremely complicated, especially if researchers continue to find increasing numbers of hormone possibilities. However, Kent also points out that these thymus hormones may, with further research, turn out to be just a few basic types with a number of variations.

The Brain Programming Theory

As the title of this section indicates, there are scientists who are investigating the possibility that aging may be the result of a programmed mechanism in the brain that dictates just when degenerative aging will begin in a human being. Or, as Moment (1975) stated:

Increasing 19

"For those favoring a more specific program for aging, the brain has become the favorite site for a death clock" (p. 626). As with the thymus hormone theory, interest in the "death clock," or brain programming theory, stems from the attempt to locate the activator, or timing element, of the aging process and to turn it off or divert its effects before widespread disintegration of the immune system takes place.

Specific research into the brain programming concept of aging grew, in part, out of the work of W. D. Denckla, who was one of the first scientists to "suggest that the lifespan of mammals is regulated by a biological clock which, in turn, acts on the endocrines to produce failure of the . . . immune and circulatory systems" (1975, p. 31). Denckla derived this theory from research on dead mammals which indicated that they had all died as a result of diseases related to immune and circulatory failure. This similarity of mammalian death led Denckla and others to speculate on the possibility that there exists a similar process of aging for all mammals and, by extension, a common programmed element for activating this process, located somewhere within mammals. Subsequent research, Walford (1983) informs us, has led some

scientists to conclude ''that the 'clock' of aging
lurks in the hypothalamus, a pea-sized area of
brain a bit posterior to a spot midway between your
ears'' (p. 89).

What has come about as a result of research into
the brain programming theory is an area of
gerontological concern called ''neuroendocrinology.''
This term refers to the relationship between ''the
hypothalamus in the brain and the various endocrine
glands, particularly the pituitary, adrenal, thymus,
and thyroid glands'' (Walford, 1983, p. 170). In
general, neuroendocrinology holds that some change
occurs in the brain, and this change signals the onset
of dysfunction in one or more endocrine glands. As
Finch (1975) explains: ''Changes in a limited, critical
population of cells in the brain (e.g., the
hypothalamus) could have many consequences throughout
the body.'' And because the endocrines are known as
producers of hormones, Finch sees a possible link
between brain cell change and ''multifaceted changes in
aging throughout the body.'' In short, ''in some
neuroendocrine controls, a change of only one hormone
could generate a cascade of events'' (pp. 647-648).

In line with neuroendocrine concepts, Denckla
(1975) suspects that the hormone that starts the

degenerative aging process at the command of the
biological clock is produced by the pituitary, a gland
that rests very close to the brain. He reports ''a
considerable restoration of immune competence in older
rats'' after their pituitaries have been removed
surgically (p. 41). This scientist, however, is also
apparently trying to outwit the death clock through
another approach. Walford informs us that Denckla ''is
presently trying to isolate his theoretical 'death
hormone' and, if successful, to make an antidote or
antiserum to it, thereby avoiding complications
arising from removing the pituitary gland itself''
(1983, p. 179).

Other scientists are experimenting with brain
stimulators, working on the concept that certain brain
cells run down with aging, thereby reducing the
competency of the brain to process the information it
needs to control efficiently the functioning of the
body's control systems. Marshall and Berrios (1979),
for example, were able to improve dramatically the
swimming ability and endurance of aged rats by
stimulating their brains with ''apomorphine or L-
dopa''--drugs that revived brain neurons and, thus, the
''neurotransmission'' ability of the brain. If brain
stimulators can be developed that will help to revive

human brain cells safely and effectively, then we may be
able to "rewind" the death clock that forms the basis
for the brain programming theory.

Whether or not the theories briefly touched upon
in this paper motivate research that will result in
substantial life extension remains to be seen. Perhaps
other theories now being tested, or a theory not yet
formulated will provide the breakthrough sought by
gerontologists in the war against aging. And we must
also consider the possibility that life-extension
believers are involved in a war they may never win.
Some scientists take this point of view. Fries and
Crapo (1981), for example, are not particularly
optimistic about the chances of increasing life span
any time in the near future because they think that
science is still far from having the necessary
knowledge to do so. These doctors see little chance
that the maximum life span will be any longer in the
near future than it has been in the past. Leaf (1982)
is equally unimpressed by the experimental results of
life-extension researchers, seeing in their work no
significant proof that gerontologists will be able to
"stop or retard" the aging process. He concedes,
however, that from time to time, scientists will make
discoveries that will "fire the imagination" of those

**Student introduces
opposing views to
ensure objectivity**

who strive to change the length of our life span. In
like manner, Sir Peter Medawar (1984), while
acknowledging the potential of scientific attempts to
extend human life, especially in regard to the free
radical theory, is not confident that such attempts
will succeed. He doubts that the side effects of aging,
such as infections and cancers, can be controlled, even
if life is extended with the use of drugs to counteract
the damage inflicted by free radicals. But this Nobel
scientist also strongly believes that gerontologists
should continue their attempts to conquer aging,
despite the objections of those who see life-extension
research as some kind of "crime against nature." He
states that his "personal sympathies are with the
daredevils who want to try out these new procedures"
(pp. 19-20).

The scientific world, then, is far from united in
the belief that human life span can be significantly
extended in the near future through research into the
causes of aging. But those who share the age-old dream
of all the Ponce de Leons who have ever lived should
keep their eyes on the gerontological research
laboratories of the world. For it will be through the
efforts of dedicated and daring scientists that the
"secret" of extended life will be discovered--if it is
to be discovered at all.

Conclusion: recalls introduction and restates thesis

Increasing 24

Notes

[1] For a broad historical view of the struggle between those who have championed the cause of life-extension throughout the ages versus those who have accepted the inevitability of aging and death, see Walford, 1983, chap. 2.

[2] See, for example: McCay, C. M., et al. (1939). Retarded growth, life span, ultimate body size and age changes in the albino rat after feeding diets restricted in calories. Journal of Nutrition, 18, 1-13. This is considered a ''classic study'' in the literature of gerontology.

[3] DNA, short for: deoxyribonucleic acid. Described as ''a long, twisted double chain of atoms found in the nucleus of each cell. It controls all the characteristics of living things, including metabolism in cells and body structure'' (Kurtzman & Gordon, 1977, p. 241).

[4] See, for example, Walford's discussion of the possible relationship of Vitamins C and E in retarding the aging process (1983, pp. 145-147).

References

Adler, W. H. (1975). Aging and immunal function.
    BioScience, 25, 652-656.
Cromie, W. J. (1981, January). Genetic trade-offs:
    The hidden cost of survival. SciQuest, pp. 10-14.
Denckla, W. D. (1975, August). A time to die. Life
    Sciences, pp. 31-44.
DNA coils: Link to aging. (1983, April). Science
    Digest, p. 85.
Finch, C. E. (1975). Neuroendocrinology of aging: A
    view of an emerging area. BioScience,
    25, 645-649.
Fries, J. F., & Crapo, L. M. (1981). Vitality and
    aging. San Francisco: W. H. Freeman.
Harman, D. (1956). Aging: A theory based on free
    radical and radiation chemistry. Journal of
    Gerontology, 11, 298-300.
Harman, D. (1968). Free radical theory of aging:
    Effect of free radical reaction inhibitors on the
    mortality rate of male LAF$_1$ mice. Journal of
    Gerontology, 23, 476-481.

Increasing 26

Hayflick, L. (1977). The cellular basis for
    biological aging. In C. E. Finch & L. Hayflick
    (Eds.), Handbook of the biology of aging (pp. 159-
    181). New York: Van Nostrand Reinhold.
Kent, S. (1980). The life extension revolution. New
    York: William Morrow.
Kurtzman, J., & Gordon, P. (1977). No more dying. New
    York: Laurel-Dell.
Leaf, A. (1982). Long-lived populations: Extreme old
    age. Journal of American Geriatrics Society,
    30, 485-487.
Marshall, J. F., & Berrios, N. (1979). Movement
    disorders of aged rats: Reversal by dopamine
    receptor stimulation. Science, 206, 477-479.
Marx, J. L. (1975). Thymic hormones: Inducers of T
    cell maturation. Science, 188, 1183-1217.
Medawar, P. (1984, March). When we are old. Atlantic
    Monthly, pp. 16-21.
Moment, G. B. (1975). The Ponce de Leon trail today.
    BioScience, 25, 623-627.
Rosenfeld, A. (1976). Prolongevity. New York: Knopf.
Schimke, R. T., & Agniel, M. (1983). Biologic
    mechanisms in aging: Summary of conference
    proceedings. Journal of American Geriatrics
    Society, 31, 40-44.

Sonneborn, J. (1979). DNA repair and longevity
    assurance in Paramecium tetraurelia.
    Science, 203, 1115-1117.
Supergene cluster fights aging. (1982, August).
    Science Digest, p. 91.
Walford, R. L. (1983, July). How people will live to be
    100 or more. U.S. News and World Report, pp.
    73-74.
Walford, R. L. (1983). Maximum life span. New York:
    Norton.
Watkin, D. M. (1983). Handbook of nutrition, health,
    and aging. Park Ridge, IL: Noyes.

Index